THE MAKING OF
THE MODERN JEW

The Making of
the Modern Jew

By
MILTON STEINBERG

From the Second Temple
to the State of Israel

BEHRMAN HOUSE · *Publishers*
New York, 1948

TO
EDITH

CONTENTS

CHAPTER   PAGE

   I   THE RIDDLE   19

THE MEDIEVAL BACKGROUND

  II   ITINERARY   31
 III   THE HERITAGE   47
 IV   ISRAEL AND THE NATIONS   63
  V   THE WAY OF THE LAW   80
 VI   THE INNER LIGHT   99
VII   RECAPITULATION AND CARRY-OVER   121

TRANSITION

VIII   THE PROCESS OF EMANCIPATION   141
 IX   DISSOLUTION OF BALANCE   167
  X   SUICIDE   187
 XI   DUSK CHILDREN   207
XII   THE CHARACTER OF THE MODERN JEW   228

THE MODERN SCENE

XIII   FOREWORD TO THE MODERN SCENE   251
XIV   ANTI-SEMITISM   253
 XV   PALESTINE AGAIN   272
XVI   PROGRAMS   295
XVII   EPILOGUE   313

THE MAKING OF
THE MODERN JEW

The Making of the Modern Jew

CHAPTER I

THE RIDDLE

THE Christian world has alternately hated and idealized the Jew; it has never understood him. Consider, for example, that mythical figure, the Wandering Jew. The fact that he is a legendary person must not lead us to dismiss him summarily. For the existence of a myth is always testimony to the presence of a mystery; it is in effect an unscientific explanation of some baffling phenomenon. Now, to medieval Christendom, the Jew was an enigma. His folkways, compounded of strange customs and ceremonies, smacked of black magic and the sorcerer's craft; his books, written in illegible characters, suggested the wizard's charm; his presence everywhere hinted of an alliance with the devil; and his reticence suggested dark secrets. The Jew was strange; he was different; he was ununderstandable; and most bewildering of all, he could not be persuaded to die.

The church, the state, and the mob had conspired against him. They had put a badge of shame on his garment, confined him to a ghetto, refused him the right to till the soil or to acquire membership in the guilds, burned him and his books in public bonfires. By every rule of reason, his very memory should have been obliterated. And yet, stubbornly, uncannily, he persisted and survived. Like truth crushed to earth, he rose again at the first relaxation of pressure. He not only survived, he maintained a culture and made it creative. What could mere reason make of such a spectacle? Wherefore the medieval mind created a legend in which the fantastic immortality of the Wandering Jew mirrored the even more fantastic deathlessness of the Jew of flesh and blood.

The myth is gone; the mystery persists. Israel still runs true to form as a riddle to the nations of the earth, and indeed to itself also. It is a rare Gentile, and almost as rare a Jew, who has any clear notion of how this people contrived to keep going, or what resources sustained it under circumstances in which life should have been intolerable. This then is one mystery we shall seek to explore in this book: Jewish survival.

Still another riddle attends the Jew: the contradictions in his character, which are fully as puzzling as those presented by his history, and of even wider interest and concern. After all, one may readily avoid contact with the Jewish past. It is not so easy to elude modern Jews and their problems.

Now consider, for a moment, some of the paradoxes and conflicts of the contemporary Jewish scene.

Along the streets of some modern city on a Saturday morning, a Jew makes his way from the synagogue. His handkerchief is bound about his wrists, for rabbinic edict prohibits the carrying of even the slightest burden on the Sabbath. Five precepts of the Law of Moses forbid shaving; therefore, no razor has ever touched his face. The weather may be inclement, but he will not ride, even in a public conveyance driven by and for Gentiles. He has recited prescribed Sabbath prayers; soon he will eat food prepared the day before in strictest conformity with traditional rules of diet. Twice more, before the sacred day is finished, he will join in the formal worship of God. At dusk, he will kindle a fire for the first time in twenty-four hours, sending the Sabbath angels away with the sweet savor of spices: for so it was ordained of old. In the eyes of the world, he may be an anachronism, the lingering ghost of a vanishing medieval world. In his own eyes, he is a loyal Jew, obeying God's will as revealed on Mount Sinai and finding the experience graceful and lovely.

Along the same street, in perfect forgetfulness of the Sabbath, another Jew drives his automobile from his place of business to a luncheon engagement. From the point of view of the Jewish tradition, he is sacrilege in motion, a surfeit of sin. He has shaved, he has worked, he is riding, he has not prayed. The food he is to eat is forbidden, and no wine cup will be blessed before he drinks. The game of golf or bridge which will afford his afternoon's entertainment is a travesty on the ancestral conception of a day of rest. If he is at all typical, he has long since ceased to give the matter even a passing thought. At most, he has suffered a twinge of conscience, or momentary longing for an older way of life, and then has dismissed it all as obsolete and fit only for those Jews who are not sufficiently modern to know any better.

Or, consider the following contrast. The Jewish escapist is an interesting figure and deserves a moment of attention. His whole life is concentrated on winning acceptance from the non-Jew. The mark of his triumph is an invitation to a dinner, or membership in some club which excludes other

Jews. To attain his end, he has stripped himself deliberately of every vestige of his Jewishness. He has de-Judaized his name. His home is as conventionally American as he can possibly make it. Because he feels socially insecure, he is driven to ape his neighbors in every detail. Beyond all else he avoids contact with other Jews. He assimilates himself so completely to his environment that he is suspected of furtiveness. His conventionality is so perfect that it proclaims its spuriousness; his patriotic ardor so complete that it betrays deliberation. The Gentile world remains suspicious, cold, and at best, formally polite. It continues to exclude him. He therefore takes refuge in the company of other Jews who also do not want to be what they are, and cannot be anything else.

In direct antithesis stands the Jewish enthusiast, the super-Jew, never oblivious of his Jewish identity, ever eager to call it to the world's attention. This member of the House of Israel may not be conventionally religious; his observance may be more than a little ragged; even his knowledge of the group heritage may be a bit hazy. But he makes up in chauvinistic pride for what he lacks in piety and learning. Were there spiritual, cultural, or moral significance to his allegiance, it might be impressive and meaningful. It is empty, all façade and bravado, devoid of substance. Wherefore it has but little to commend it over the escapism to which it stands so fiercely opposed.

Or, consider that most violent clash of all in contemporary Jewish life, the divergent attitudes of Jews toward Zionism. Most American Jews stood ready, before the proclamation of a Jewish State in Palestine, to make the greatest of sacrifices for its establishment. Against them, to the last moment, were arrayed the Jewish anti-Zionists, approximately ten per cent of American Jewry, as resolute in their denial as the others in their affirmation. To them the whole enterprise of building a Jewish Homeland was a tragic blunder from start to finish, for the nullification of which they would go as far in one direction as their opponents in the other.

This series of sharp antitheses is not confined to conduct and social attitude. It penetrates into the realm of philosophy also. It has divided the theorizers of Jewish life into two major and many minor camps over the most fundamental questions of all: What is Judaism? What is Jewishness? Here, on issues which one would imagine to be the simplest of all and least liable to disagreement, divisions are in actual fact deep and passionately held. There are those who hold that Judaism is basically—some would say exclusively—a religion, and Jewishness a form of membership in a communion. Others contend just as stoutly that the whole business of being a Jew is ultimately something secular, a matter of social identity perhaps, or of membership in the people of Israel, or of nationality or culture. Both camps in turn split into sub-groups: among the religionists, into Orthodox, Conservative, and Reform wings, differing from one another in theology, ritual and ideology; among the secularists, into Zionists and anti-Zionists, Hebraists and Yiddishists.

Out of this chaos of contradictions one truth emerges as beyond challenge: that whatever may have been the case in the past, Jews today are quite without that unity which is ascribed to them in popular imagination. Of all misconceptions concerning them, none is so widespread as the myth that they band together, thinking, acting, and living in an international accord. To be sure, there is some basis for such a notion. Jews have learned by bitter experience that they must pool their individual weaknesses to form a collective strength, that for purely selfish reasons they cannot stand idly by the blood of their fellows. But this mutual protectiveness apart, the Jewish group possesses much less cohesion than is commonly supposed. A folk saying among Jews has it that where there are two Jews there are three opinions.

Snobbery, the common garden variety of it, further compounds Jewish disunity. Thus Jews of Spanish and Portuguese descent, whose ancestors settled in America in colonial days, are likely to condescend to the more recently arrived German Jews. These in turn hold themselves aloof from the East European Jews who were a generation or two behind them in coming to these shores. All alike look down on the newest immigrants of all, Spanish and Portuguese Jews from the Levant, German and Austrian emigres from Hitlerism. So the circle of superciliousness goes full round.

Amid this babble of sects and castes stands many a poor bewildered American Jew who belongs to no particular party or class, but is just an ordinary human being of Jewish descent, trying to get along as best he can in a very complicated and difficult world. This is as near the "typical" Jew as one can find. He is neither an escapist nor a burning survivalist, neither totally observant nor completely indifferent to traditional practice, nor is he altogether clear in mind as to why he maintains some rituals but not others. As to Jewish knowledge, he is neither absolutely ignorant nor adequately informed. He is puzzled and disturbed by anti-Semitism and generally sensitive to the impression he and his fellows make on the Gentiles, yet he will not, if he is aware of it, wheedle or fawn for approval. A Jewish Homeland in Palestine seems to him both necessary and reasonable; necessary as a haven for displaced Jews abroad, and reasonable in that he cannot see why the Jews of all the peoples of the world should be without a land of their own. But if he is pro-Zionist, he is no expert in, and has little patience for, the fine points of Zionist theory and the intricacies of its politics. Such concerns he leaves to experts. All in all, he is a Jew and that, for him, is the end of the matter.

Such are the modern Jews in their conflicts, contradictions, and confusions. Of all the prophecies of Scripture concerning them, one has certainly been fulfilled, even if not in its original connotation: "And ye shall be unto Me a *peculiar* people."

But the whole riddle has not yet been unfolded. There are other characteristics exhibited by Jews, traits typical if not universal among them, which also call for explanation. Thus, almost everywhere in the Western world, the Jews are city-dwellers. They were not such in the Biblical or Talmudic periods. How came they to be urbanized? Again, living in towns, they tend to huddle together in Jewish neighborhoods. Where did they get this habit of gregariousness? How does it happen that whereas in ancient times they were, almost to the man, farmers and artisans, they are these days so preponderantly engaged in commerce and the professions? Where did they pick up their reputation for business acumen and, in some circles, for sharp practices? Or for that matter, their inordinate interest in philanthropy and social justice? Whence did they acquire their bookishness, their ardor for learning, their high concentration in literary and artistic fields? How is one to explain that though, when they were at their peak numerically in 1936, they were still less than one per cent of the world's population, they nevertheless furnished thirteen per cent of the Nobel Prize winners?

Now the Jew may be an unusual person; he is certainly no miracle. For his peculiarities, whatever they may be, some explanation must exist. If he survived the dreadful persecutions which were his lot, something must be responsible, something in him, his way of life or his circumstances. If the Jewish group, which once displayed unity and uniformity to an extraordinary degree, is now torn asunder by differences of opinion, attitude, and practice, there must be some accounting for that too. And if Jews exhibit the differential characteristics which we have just finished enumerating, it must be for some reason or other.

Heredity is the explanation most often offered and most generally accepted for this last phenomenon of typical traits. The Jew, it is contended, is intellectually alert, or philanthropic, or astute in his commercial dealings because he is born with these capacities, because they are in his bloodstream and germ cells, in his genes and chromosomes.

Plausible as this theory may be, it does not hold water. In the first place, it makes assumptions concerning the existence of racial traits and the inheritance of acquired characteristics which are most questionable scientifically. In the second place, it explains too much. Every trait and its opposite is accounted for by the one word, heredity. But a hypothesis which explains anything and its antithesis is fully as worthless as one which explains nothing at all. Most decisive of all, Jewish history proves that it cannot be heredity which accounts for differential Jewish traits. These characteristics, had they been inborn, would have asserted themselves in every generation. Yet, as a study of the Jewish past discloses, they emerged and receded, actually came into being and were wiped away by the stimulus and pressure of events. Clearly then, whatever the role of heredity, the events were decisive.

It is in these events, in sum in the Jewish past, that the clue to our riddle in all three of its phases is to be sought, not only as to the mystery of survival and the conflicts of the contemporary scene, but also as to the special personal endowments of modern Jews.

The history of the Jews, external and internal, explains them. To this history we shall address ourselves in the pages that follow. Yet this is to be no "history book." Of all the historical facts we shall be concerned only with those which are relevant to the questions we are seeking to answer; the others we shall simply disregard. What is more, we shall consistently be less interested in data as ends in themselves, than in their effects on the group life and the individuality of Jews.

Now, if history is to be written at all, a beginning must be made somewhere. We must select some spot in time and say, here we shall commence. Our point of departure will be the destruction of the Second Jewish Commonwealth in the year 70 of the Common Era. Not that there was no Jewish life before then. What were perhaps the most fascinating, and certainly the most momentous episodes in the whole career of Israel, both for itself and the world, had already taken place. That date, however, does mark as sharp a break as is to be found anywhere in the whole sweep of the Jewish past up to its very beginnings. It will serve to get us launched.

As our argument moves forward from that point, we shall come to perceive the unusual yet ultimately understandable forces which made Jewish survival possible. We shall come to comprehend why modern Jewry exhibits such divergent convictions and attitudes. We shall observe too how the chemistries of circumstance made the personality of the Jew into its present guise. Those elements in the Jewish picture which at first seemed to be beyond all accounting will, it is to be hoped, be satisfactorily explained.

Our discussion is intended to make the Jewish present intelligible in the light of the Jewish past. It should not make either appear any the less heroic or worthwhile. An epic grandeur must invest the survival of a people and its tradition despite homelessness, expulsion, massacre, and humiliation—a people and a tradition which have been attended, moreover, by the dignity and humaneness, the courage, faith and vision which have marked the Jews and Judaism all through their long pilgrimage on earth.

THE MEDIEVAL BACKGROUND

CHAPTER II

ITINERARY

ISRAEL has not always been a prodigy among the nations. Time was when its existence was as normal as that of any other people. It occupied its own land, lived its own life and suffered vicissitudes of fortune such as inevitably befall any nation. It was unique only in that it had developed an individual culture and subscribed to an unusual theology and ethic. The crisis in its career, the shift from normality to eccentricity, began in 70 c. e., when, after the fall of Jerusalem, large bodies of Jews were translated to all parts of the Roman Empire.

History has played many a cruel trick on the Jew. It did him only one favor—it allowed him to prepare for his homelessness. By the time the eviction from Palestine was under way, the Jew had already evolved a technique of living as an unwelcome guest in other men's homes. Early in his history, he had become a skilled and inveterate alien. From the sixth century before the common era, Babylonia had a large and influential Jewish settlement, descended from Jews exiled by the Assyrian Sargon and the Babylonian Nebuchadnezzar. In the days of Jeremiah, Egypt had renewed acquaintance with the Jews, a contact that became more intimate when large numbers of Jews settled in the newly established metropolis of Alexandria. The bustling commercial life of the Hellenistic world scattered Jewish settlements far and wide and the closely knit unity of the Roman

Empire encouraged a voluntary dispersion. The origins of most Diaspora communities are lost in obscurity, but it is a safe generalization that by the time of the destruction of Jerusalem, almost every important city in the Empire had its quota of Jews.

About this process of settlement there was nothing peculiar to Jews. It must be remembered that the Hellenistic world was essentially cosmopolitan. National lines had been largely obliterated. Syrians had settled in Rome, Greeks in Palestine, Macedonians in Egypt. The Jewish dispersion was an instance of, not an exception to, a general rule. None the less, these colonies in Babylonia, Egypt, Asia Minor, Italy, Spain and Germany, served as experimental stations against an unborn emergency. Within them the Diaspora built synagogues, evolved forms of communal structure, developed philanthropic institutions, and created schools for the education of youth. Traditional Jewish customs and ceremonies were adjusted to the demands of strange lands. In brief, a pattern of group life was created, adapted to the needs of a minority living amid a hostile or indifferent majority.

This saved the Jewish people when, suddenly, the central homeland was submerged. Broken refugees rarely have the strength to reconstruct an old society *ab initio* or to build a new one. Fortunately for the Jew, deported by Titus or Hadrian, he found a ready-made Jewish world in the land of his exile. He slipped naturally and without serious difficulty into the new scheme of things. Unwittingly, he had built himself a bridge by which he might make safe passage from Palestine to the world. He had never been forewarned; he was accidently forearmed.

Despite all this preliminary preparation, the fall of the Jewish state exacted a terrible toll from the Jews. They paid heavily for their foolhardiness in daring to defy Roman power. The rebellion had been incredibly costly in lives; and of those who survived, thousands were sold as slaves throughout the Empire. The entire Jewish world was impoverished both by the gigantic loss and confiscation of property, and by the necessity for redeeming Jewish captives. Not least of the costs of the war was the damage inflicted on religious and cultural life. The Sanhedrin, the supreme administrative body of the Jewish state, had been dispersed. The Temple, the center of the cultus, was in ruins, and cultural institutions had been wiped out.

The full gravity of the situation seems to have escaped the leaders of the day. They felt, it appears, that the state, the Temple and its ritual would be restored in short order. They were, therefore, concerned essentially with filling a hiatus, bridging a gap, acting as regents during an interregnum. A folk legend of the time had it that on the day the Temple was destroyed, the Messiah, its restorer, was born. Rabbi Ishmael so confidently expected a speedy reconstitution of the national life that he jotted down notes of the sacrifices which he intended to bring once the Temple was rebuilt.

Eventually, they realized that the process of restoring the Temple and the state was to be indefinitely prolonged. Those who had once believed that the Messiah had been born on the day of the destruction now framed new legends of a less sanguine character. These told of a vase which God had placed at the foot of His throne. In this the tears of Israel, wrung by persecution, were treasured. Only on some remotely distant day, when the cup was full to overflowing, would God at last send His redeemer.

Up to this point the Jew had been no exception to Aristotle's sweeping characterization of man as a political animal. He had a natural interest in his own corporate destiny. But now events choked all normal political outlets. The Jew had lost all influence in the direction of the state—his own, or that of others. Without voice or share in the affairs of countries, he made a virtue of his necessity. Those instincts which normally find expression in the pomp and circumstance of office were now diverted into realms moral, legal or intellectual. In schools he found his senates, in religious debate his forums, in the vindication of ideas his sense of mastery. It is significant of the future course of Jewish history that colleges now become the major seats of Jewish authority.

When the state and the Temple were gone, Palestinian Jewry turned its attention to religious and intellectual concerns. For several centuries it remained the cultural center of the whole people in its dispersion. It created the *Mishnah,* the classic code of Jewish law. It edited great collections of folk-lore and moral homilies known as the *Midrashim.* But with the triumph of Christianity, life for the Jew in Palestine became impossible. The intolerance of the church was naturally most intense in a land so drenched with religious association. Bit by bit, the Jews picked up and left. For a time, the schools struggled on against overwhelming odds, then they, too, disintegrated. By the fifth century of the common era, the ancestral soil was virtually denuded of its children. The scepter had departed from Judea, the Jew had gone forth into homeless exile.*

From that time until the present, the movement of Jewish

---

* Even after this period, some cultural life persisted in the Holy Land. For all practical purposes, however, Palestine played a minor part in Jewish creativity thereafter.

history resembles the charting of an insane Cook's tour. The map is crisscrossed abundantly even by the major migrations. When one fills in the retracings of steps, unimportant side-trips and excursions, it comes to resemble a geography book defaced by a childish scrawl.

And yet, for all its appearance of purposelessness, each line represents the logical consequence of definite factors. One tracing is the projection of a forced expulsion, another of economic adversity, a third has been shot out in release from intolerable repression. Each zigzag is a cold symbol of the sufferings and needs of homeless human beings, their hunger, their tears and often their blood.

And the Semitic nomads moved along these threads. At each station they pitched their tents, refreshed their bodies, set up shrines, founded schools, wrote books, produced scholars and saints, learned to love the place of their abode, and then moved on, trailing a new line across the map.

The first important haven for this landless people was Babylonia. Even while the schools of Palestine were at the height of their glory, those of Mesopotamia were a rising power. In them the great Babylonian Talmud was compiled. For five centuries thereafter the academies of Sura and Pumpeditha educated and directed the Jewish world. In their semi-annual convocations they passed on questions of law, ethics, theology and policy, submitted to them from all the lands of the Diaspora. For half a millennium, from the sixth to the eleventh centuries, they provided central and unifying guidance for a scattered people.

And then the same fate which had befallen Palestinian Jewry came to the Babylonian. Persecution and impoverishment led to a mass emigration into more favorable lands. During the eleventh century the great academies declined, their faculties, students and libraries were dispersed. The wandering Jew moved on, turning his face now to the west.

From this time on, the Jewish world was left without a seat of central authority. Before the eleventh century Palestine and Babylonia had successively exercised a unifying directive influence. With the collapse of the Babylonian colleges, Judaism lost its last element of external cohesion. The Jews of each land came to shift for themselves, owing allegiance only to their local leaders. To be sure, the community of one land was often dominated by that of another, as Provence was dominated by Spain in the twelfth century, or Germany by Poland in the seventeenth. But such international influence was the direct result of a voluntary self-subjection to superior intellectual attainments. Lands that produced the greatest Jewish scholars, which possessed schools of larger prestige, inevitably exerted moral pressure. Aside from such influences across borders, Jewry was left without any bonds of formal unity. If the decomposition of the Jewish world remained only a matter of externals; if in its thought and life Judaism persisted homogeneous in all lands, the secret of cohesion is to be sought in the culture behind, rather than in organizations imposed upon, all Jewish groups. That Israel did not collapse into divergent sects, that it remained catholic and not parochial, is due to its unifying tradition.

If it were our purpose to write the history of the Jew, we should be compelled to follow out in detail the record of the Jews of each individual land. That such an effort would be at best doomed to thankless confusion is self-evident. For the historian who deals with Jews is confronted with an uncomfortable choice between continuity and chronological simultaneity. If he takes one land and follows its Jews through to the end, he destroys for the reader the sense of correlation between the events he is describing and those in progress elsewhere at the same time. If, on the other hand, he attempts to preserve temporal unities, he drives his reader mercilessly from land to land, ruining any possibility of clarity.

For us, however, this dilemma loses much of its poignancy. For we are concerned only with that minimal record which is indispensable to the solution of the dual riddle of Jewish survival and contemporary Jewish character. It will suffice for our needs to follow in larger outline the course of two major geographic currents, the Spanish and the Central European.

Like other Diaspora communities, the origins of Spanish Jewry are lost in obscurity. Just enough of its early history is known to render safe the assertion that the Jews of that land lived in peace and security until its Visigothic rulers in the sixth century were converted to Catholic Christianity. Then, for over a century the Jews of Spain were subjected to persecution, the fury of which demonstrates that Torquemada came by his fanaticism legitimately. By the time the Berbers overran the Spanish Peninsula in the eighth century, the Jews had been reduced to actual slavery.

Even under a tolerant Mohammedan rule it took three full centuries for the Spanish Jews to recover from their horrible experiences. And then, suddenly, almost inexplicably, Spanish Jewry flowered into a culture so rich and variegated that the period from the tenth to the fourteenth century has gone down in Jewish history as the Golden Age. Poets and philosophers, grammarians, scientists, Biblical commentators, legalists and physicians—many of the finest talent, and some of genius—followed one another in close succession. Spanish

Jewry of this time is unique in medieval history, not alone for the luxuriance of its cultural productivity, but for its color and tone. No other Jewry was as free or as wealthy and no other Jewry lived with such grace and refinement. Leisure and security invested life with an easy cultured geniality. Unfrightened by the threat of persecution, the Spanish Jew could gratify readily the most diversified intellectual interests. In an atmosphere of free thought and free action, he could afford to be liberal or even radical in his theology, Biblical criticism and Hebrew style. The cultural contribution of the period to the totality of Jewish lore was immense— quantitatively and qualitatively. All in all, the Golden Age was a pleasant interlude in the nightmare of the Jewish Middle Ages.

And then the shadow of Christianity was thrown across the sunlit scene. Nothing in history is quite so ironical as the contrast between the Mohammedan and the Christian treatment of the Jew. By their very religion, Moslems were enjoined to intolerance. None the less, as a general rule, the Mohammedan treated the Jew with liberality, generosity and tolerance. There were exceptions, to be sure, and Mohammedan persecutions of Jews were not unknown, but Moslem practise was much better than its preaching.

In the Christian world, on the other hand, conduct was far inferior to theory. The very heart and essence of Christian doctrine were ostensibly love and tolerance. In practise, no Christian love was wasted on Jews. With each advance in the power of the church went a corresponding repression of Jews. As the Christian kingdoms drove the Mohammedans before them to the southern confines of the Spanish Peninsula, the Spanish Jew, hitherto largely exempt from persecution, now began to feel its full crushing weight. As long as the Moslem was a potent factor in Spanish affairs, and as long as the Jew held a sort of balance of power, Christian rulers exercised a prudent restraint. By the middle of the thirteenth century, Christian power in Spain was secure. During the next century the Inquisition was introduced and the Jew had cause to regret his now vanished Saracenic overlords. In 1391, a climactic wave of massacre passed over Spain. In four months fifty thousand Jews were butchered and hundreds of thousands forcibly converted to Christianity. The decree of final expulsion was to be postponed for one hundred years—but the fate of Spanish Jewry was already sealed. The next century witnessed as cruel a persecution of a minority as history records until our own day.

In such a society, culture became a luxury, refinement an extravagance, and liberalism in thought a dangerous corrosive of internal unity. The rich intellectual life was dissipated by the forces of Christian malevolence. Spanish Jewry was much too intent upon biological and religious survival to concern itself with the cultural amenities. Poetry went by the board as inconsequential in the day of trial; liberal philosophy and theology were interdicted. In a suddenly hostile world, the Spanish Jew was driven in upon himself. He concentrated upon the most essential studies of his culture—law and the tradition. Or else he sought refuge from reality in the phantasies of a theosophic Kabbalah. The culture of a Golden Age yielded inevitably to the rigors of one of blood and steel. Spanish Jewry took on the somber qualities that marked other Jewish communities more typical in their long experience of persecution.

The final expulsion marks a climax in medieval Christian cruelty. Two hundred thousand Jews, confronted by a choice between baptism or exile, left the land on ninety days'

notice. Only Marranos, those who had been formally converted to Christianity but who secretly maintained the Jewish
faith, remained to tinge Spanish blood and thought with a
Jewish tint. From the individual point of view, the expulsion
was a masterpiece of brutality. It tore families from scenes
which had been home for fifteen hundred years. It turned
them loose virtually penniless and completely homeless to
find refuge in lands which did not want them. It exposed
thousands who were defenseless to the rapacity and savagery
of ship captains, brigands and others of like mercy.

From the point of view of all Israel, the Exile was a blow
almost deadly. Spain had been the home of all liberalism
in Jewish thought. There alone had the Jew kept pace with
the progress of the Western mind. The Renaissance was
under way, and only in Spain could the Jew make contact
with it; a new science was in the process of conception, and
only Spanish Jews knew of it. Spain then served world
Jewry in a dual capacity. It was the center of internal enlightenment and the avenue through which the freer air of
the new thought could ventilate all Jewish communities.

And now, just when Christendom was emerging from its
Dark Ages, Spanish Jewry was suddenly dispersed, the sole
source of illumination from without irrevocably shattered.
The Jew was left in the blackness of medievalism while the
rest of mankind turned toward the light. It is the custom
of historians to close the Middle Ages with the fifteenth or
sixteenth centuries. For Jews, the Dark Ages began in 1492,
with the blinding of the eyes of Israel. And all through the
next three hundred years, when the intellect of man moved
as with seven-league boots, the Jew alone was unconscious of
the new vistas of human intelligence. That he emerged
from medievalism only in the nineteenth century, is due to

the violent obliteration of the one Jewish community which stood as his outpost on the way of human progress.

Such were the historical consequences of the expulsion from Spain. The battered refugees were naturally unaware of the wider significance of their fate. As best they could, they sought to pass safely to whatever haven offered itself. Those who escaped the terrors of the way settled in the Levant, in Holland, in Italy, or later in the newly discovered Americas. Their descendants dwell in these lands to this day. There are to-day large bodies of Spanish Jews in the Near East, and smaller groups in the Netherlands, in England, and in the Americas. That the cultural momentum behind them was not at once dissipated, can be attested by the Spanish mystics of sixteenth-century Palestine, and by their career in Holland. But the spirit and the glory were gone from Spanish Jews. The mills of the gods had ground too small. Pride of descent has remained among them, a dignity of manner and carriage, a graciousness and courtesy. But of the intense intellectual life, all that survived was a fading glow. Torquemada had been successful beyond his wildest dreams. He had not only destroyed Spanish Jewry, but, all unawares, the spirit of Jewish liberalism and progress for three hundred years.

About this pilgrimage of Spanish Jewry there hovers an aura of tragedy. Indeed, all the elements of a drama are to be found in the history we have just outlined: a hero displayed at the height of power, an insidious villain plotting to destroy him, and a crashing dénouement bringing ruin and devastation. Even the counter-plots may be discerned in the careers of minor Jewries closely linked to Spain. And if the end of the tale is stark tragedy, at least it possesses an alleviating dignity, such as Aristotle ascribes to all true drama.

But about the Jews of Central Europe, there is no such atmosphere of grandeur. Their story is naked horror, unrelieved by episodes of external magnificence. The origins of French and German Jewries are as obscure as those of the Spanish. It can safely be surmised that Jews inhabited these lands in large numbers as early as the days of the Roman Empire. Relatively little is known of their internal life before the eleventh century. From the Christian world about them, they seem to have suffered no major persecutions. But although the era of wholesale massacre and pillage had not yet dawned, they were subjected, largely at the instigation of the clergy, to a fulness of minor restrictions and petty humiliation. Thus at Beziers, by episcopal decree, it was permitted to all Christians to throw sticks at Jews during the week between Palm Sunday and Easter Monday. The Count of Toulouse had the unique privilege of administering a public beating once a year to the head of the Jewish community of that city. Irritating as such treatment must surely have been, the Jew, troubled for the moment by nothing more serious than this, seems to have made his way with reasonable success and to have enjoyed a moderate security.

The eleventh century produced two sharply contrasting changes. It witnessed the rise of an intense scholarship among the Jews of Central Europe.

Simultaneously, the propaganda of the clergy took bloody effect. For centuries the Catholic clericals had been engaged in poisoning the folk attitude toward Jews. They had protested against such civil and economic liberties as Jews enjoyed, they had objected vehemently to social intercourse between the two groups. Until the eleventh century, they had met with slight success. But in 1095 the first Crusade was

launched and a wave of religious fanaticism swept Christendom. This wave and its successors spent themselves eventually, but in their course they swept to death whole Jewish communities, in their wake they obliterated every right of a normal life by which the Jew had been protected.

To the modern Christian, crusaders are romantic figures. He tends to visualize them as gallant knights, clad in shining armor and imbued with the spirit of a holy quest. There can be no doubt that many, if not most, of the crusaders were fired with a high ideal. That crusading had to be made attractive by indulgences and the remission of debts, does not militate against the sincerity of many who embarked on the great adventure to regain the Sepulcher.

But to the Jew of the Middle Ages, the crusader, or the mob stirred up by his passage, was a curse, a menace and a devouring flame. In 1096, the crusading armies passed through the Rhineland. When they had gone their way, ten thousand Jews who had refused baptism had been butchered in cold blood. As the first Crusade was baptized in Jewish blood, so did it end. When at last Godfrey de Bouillon entered Jerusalem as conqueror, he drove all the Jews of the Holy City into a synagogue and had them burned alive.

Each succeeding Crusade took its toll, now in Germany, now in France, or in England. And when the whole ghastly process was over, the Jew had lost his security entirely. It was understood now that the Jew was fair game. Later generations were not remiss in profiting by experience. The political and economic effects of the Crusades will not detain us now. It will be enough at this point to remark that the crusaders destroyed more than lives and property; they wiped out the last civil rights which Jews possessed.

Only a sensationalist or a sadist would take pleasure in

cataloguing the savagery of the next five centuries; for the misery of 1096 was repeated *ad nauseam* during the next generations. Nor was religion the sole motivating factor. True, Jews were tortured, mutilated and butchered in the name of Christ but the regularity of pillage, of confiscation, and of the burning of certificates of indebtedness, proves that Mammon, too, had his finger in this mess.

On only one of the Central European horrors must we pause for a moment—and then only because of its tremendous consequences. In 1348 and 1349, the bubonic plague, known as the Black Death, swept Europe. Frantic with terror, the Christian sought for a cause and a scapegoat. Like wild-fire, the story passed from mouth to mouth that Jews, in a carefully organized conspiracy, had poisoned the wells. The plague-inducing poison had been compounded from spiders, frogs, lizards, the hearts of Christians, and dough of the wafers of communion. Massacre, pillage and slaughter stalked after this ever-spreading tale. Sober estimates of the number of Jews butchered are so large as to be incredible. What the figures are like can be imagined from the fact that massacres occurred in sixty large cities and one hundred and fifty towns and villages.

Fortunately for the frantic Jews, a way of escape lay open. Poland desperately needed a middle class. For some time, Jews had been trickling eastward to escape the monstrosities of Western Europe. After the Crusades, the movement became a stream; after the Black Death, it grew to a flood. Jews moved into Poland in gigantic numbers. During the succeeding centuries they penetrated ever eastward into Ukrainia, Roumania and Hungary. So large was the migration that up to 1939 almost half of the fifteen or sixteen million Jews of the world lived in Eastern Europe, and the vast majority of American Jews are of East European descent.

Thus it comes to pass that Jews in Magyar Hungary, Latin Roumania and Slavic Russia or Poland, generally carry distinctly Teutonic family names. This is the reason why they speak Yiddish, a dialect of old German corrupted by Hebrew and the idioms of the land of their residence.

The itinerary winds up with four recent movements: the mass migration of the past century to America and other new centers of settlement; the return to Zion; the descent in less than five years of more than five million European Jews into the grave; the scattering of survivors to the ends of the earth.

Such is the chart of Jewish homelessness—in its crude outlines. At best, it is a sketch. We have treated none of the minor movements and omitted many of genuine significance. But even in its baldness it is a strange story, this tale of the continuous movement of the Jew. It is strange enough that a people should have attained physical survival under such conditions. It touches on the miraculous when one considers that through all this movement the Jew maintained, enriched and handed on a great culture.

This perhaps is the ultimate wonder of Jewish history. The Jew, if he would not die, should have become the gipsy of the world, an outlaw in intent as he was in fact. His hand should have been raised against each man, as society's was raised against him. He should have degenerated into a beast concerned only for the food and security which the world sought to withhold. That on the contrary he remained an enlightened human being, that he maintained and transmitted a culture, and against such odds, this is a phenomenon that beggars fiction. The fact of the matter is that the Jew did not become outlaw, gipsy or beast. He was saved from that fate by the heritage he bore with him.

The traditional culture of the Jew is then a matter of prime significance, both in the determination of his survival and of the character he came to assume. It is this tradition to which we must now turn. And since the heart and essence of his civilization were evolved in Palestine, the heritage of the Holy Land is our next theme.

Chapter III

THE HERITAGE

FROM one point of view, the history we have just sketched is the record of a certain number of human beings, and of their material fate. But from another angle, much more is involved. For with the Jew in all his restless movement went not only quantities of tangible objects, but a large body of possessions invisible to the physical eye. Ideas and ideals, as well as things, had their share in the determination of the Jew. The persecutor might torture Jews, might rob and despoil them of every object they called their own, he could not take from them the rich tradition which was theirs by right of inheritance. Through all shifts of time and circumstance, this alone was constant; through incessant confiscations, this remained inexpropriable.

Time recognizes no true beginnings or ends. The cultural heritage of Israel is no exception to this rule. He who would trace it to its ultimate origins must grope backward to those dark eras in which all knowledge fades into ignorance. Our concern, however, is not with origins, but effects. By the year 70, the culture of the Jewish group had attained, if not a final, at least a coherent, recognizable character. Without investigation into its previous history, let us examine it as it was at that point. Let us see what the Jew carried with him from Palestine, as the invisible baggage of the spirit.

The Bible was, of course, the central element in this cultural equipment. To the ancient and medieval Jew, Scripture was more than a book. He regarded it as a literal and complete revelation of the Divine Will. He believed implicitly that its text had emanated, directly or indirectly, from God. As a result, he was convinced that each phrase, each letter, and each punctuation mark, must be significant. God is not man, and when He speaks, there can be no accidental phrasing. No passage of His dictation, no matter how unimportant it might appear, could be inconsequential. Nay, more—every sentence of Scripture must be pregnant with a number of meanings. If the frail mind of man could frame parables and metaphors by which one thought came to imply others, certainly the utterances of Omniscience must possess numberless connotations. Furthermore, by virtue of its divine origin, the Bible must be unimpeachably true. Indeed, it must of necessity contain every verity necessary for man's life. Otherwise a perfect and all-knowing God would have revealed Himself incompletely and imperfectly.

Even when the Jew failed to comprehend the text of Scripture, when it seemed trivial, self-contradictory, or incredible, he was not disturbed. He assured himself that the fault lay in the frailty of his own mind. A text that was a revelation did not have to be intelligible.

From the Bible so regarded, the Jew drew his history, his science, the elements of his theology, the principles of his ethics and the regimen of his ritual. It was to him a complete culture, an encyclopedia of the truth and a guide to conduct—all encompassed in one volume.

Together with Scripture, the Jew carried from Palestine a vast tradition which interpreted the written text—an interpretation which was more significant for his history than the Bible itself. For centuries, before the Exile, he had been busy studying his sacred literature. For generations he had sought to discover the full meaning, the hidden significance of the statements which came from God. Out of his research there had emerged a body of commentary.

In great measure this tradition which clothed the Bible was a matter of law. The Torah, or the Five Books of Moses, in which the ancient and medieval Jew saw the fullest and most direct revelation of God's will, was more than a teacher of cosmology, morality and religion. It was also a code. It laid down rules of conduct concerning crimes and punishment, civil rights, marriage and divorce, ritual, diet and hygiene. It embraced a skeleton system of behavior.

To the Christian after Paul, the Old Testament was a theological text. For the Jew, it was a divinely ordered constitution for his life, both as an individual and as a member of a group.

But when, through the course of centuries, he sought to obey the law which God had ordained for him, he found himself confronted by serious difficulties. He discovered that, for all his fine theories about the Torah, it was not self-sufficient as a standard of action. In the first place, it was often obscure and demanded elucidation. Again, it legislated for a simple pastoral and agricultural society, one far less complex than the Jewish social order at the beginning of the common era. Furthermore, for all its high ethical reach, it reflected occasionally the brutality of a more primitive age. It ordained "an eye for an eye and a tooth for a tooth." It allowed parents to subject recalcitrant children to capital punishment. Such legislation was repugnant to a highly developed moral consciousness.

Man-made constitutions are often faulty and unintelligent but they possess at least the virtue of being open to criticism and amendment. The Jew who sought to obey the Mosaic law was, by his attitude toward it, restrained from altering its text. He felt that only God could modify His own legislation.

Confronted by the dilemma of an immutable code which was practically inadequate, the teachers of Israel adopted the only course open to them. They proceeded to reinterpret Scriptural legislation in conformity with contemporary needs and ideas. When they came upon obscure passages, they deduced explanations for them. When a complex society created situations for which the Law had made no provision, they stretched the text to cover the problem. Those portions of Scripture which they found morally objectionable were explained away. In this way, the Law was for all practical purposes amended, though in theory it remained unchanged. They even read back into the Torah institutions, customs and rules which sprang into being as a spontaneous by-product of Israel's life. By this device they were able to invest socially valuable innovations with a supernatural sanction.

About this process of reinterpretation, there was nothing of conscious casuistry. To the Jewish scholars who engaged in it, it seemed perfectly logical. For them it was inconceivable that there be any situation for which an all-knowing God had not provided in His Law, incredible that He demand any conduct which was not consistent with the highest principles of morality.

For several centuries before and after the collapse of the Jewish state, Jewish scholars were engaged in this process of interpreting, expounding, amending and improving the Law of Moses. Out of their efforts emerged a legal tradition which covered the Bible, especially the Pentateuch. Each generation transmitted to its successor both the Written Law and an Oral Law which clothed and interpreted it. In theory, the commentary merely made explicit the implications of Scripture. Actually, it was an original creation and reflection of the ideals of the interpreters.

By the time of the dispersion, this body of tradition was already in a highly developed form, the Jewish way of life under its influence had taken on definite, authoritative shape. The Jew carried from Palestine not only the Bible, but an interpretation of it which embraced a corpus of civil law, a sharply fixed ritual for synagogue and home, a clearly defined morality, and definitive forms regulating every phase of life. This Oral Law, which was regarded as identical with the Written, was held in equal reverence with it. The Jew obeyed both with the same scrupulousness.

But the tradition which came to clothe the text was not altogether a matter of law. The Bible is more than a code. It includes history, cosmology, ethics, genealogical tables, prophecies, poetry and what-not. These aspects of the sacred literature invited the same treatment as did the legal. Side by side with the juristic tradition which was derived from Biblical legislation, there arose a commentary which was not at all concerned with practise and conduct, which dealt rather with theology and morality, with history and folklore.

As has already been indicated, both the legal and the non-legal traditions were still largely in the making at the time of the Exile. But if neither was a *fait accompli* in the hour of crisis, each was well on its way toward its final form. Early in the third century, Judah the Prince edited a work called the Mishnah, epitomizing and codifying the entire juristic evolution to his day. About 400 c. e., the scholars of Palestine put the totality of their legal tradition into the Palestinian Talmud. A century later, the Jewish teachers of Babylonia edited the Babylonian Talmud. Before the Diaspora had well begun, Israel was equipped with crystallized statements of its traditional law. Simultaneously, the non-legal tradition embodied itself in works called Midrashim, huge, inchoate miscellanies composed of interpretations of Scriptural passages to which were appended legends, historical notes, moral epigrams and theological discussions—in brief, comments on every human interest which was not a matter for regulation.

Such was the provender which the Jew took with him on his itinerary—the Bible, the traditions which had been built upon it, and the literary works in which the traditions found expression. In the Talmud he had a code to direct every detail of his conduct. In the Midrashim, he stored a literature with which to feed his soul.

If the existence of the pre-exilic Diaspora prepared the Jew for his homelessness in one way, the tradition prepared him in another. It gave assurance that Judaism would remain uniform in all the lands of the world. It meant that all Jews everywhere read the same books, studied the same literature, told the same stories, and inherited the same folklore and folk ethic. It meant that from Babylonia to Spain, Jews obeyed a sacred legislation which made them all eat, pray, do business, marry, die and be buried according to universal fixed rules. It guaranteed the homogeneity in thought and action of all Jewry. Therefore, when the lightning struck, it charred but could not consume the prearranged pattern within which all Jews lived.

The ideas and ideals of a people may give it significance, but its group habits give it life. For naked ideas are frail things that often die upon being transplanted to a new climate. The mortality risk of an idea clothed in a habit is much lower. A people in exile fortified only with concepts would have lost both its concepts and its own life. A people bound by a common law, ritual and habitual practises might conceivably save its law, its ideas and even itself. Or, as a modern Jewish thinker once put it, "More than Israel observed its Sabbath, did the Sabbath preserve Israel."

No literature in all the world is quite like the Talmud and Midrashim in which the traditions of ancient Israel are recorded. In quantity it is gigantic. The Babylonian Talmud alone, in its most popular modern edition, embraces eighteen folio volumes. The Palestinian Talmud, though much less extensive, is none the less a huge work. And the Midrashim comprise a small library by themselves.

All these works alike are devoid of any apparent sense of order and coherence. They make no pretensions at literary grace. Even vowels and punctuation are lacking. The editors of these texts employed a cryptic, elliptical style which does not add to the comfort of the student. So intricate is the material, both because of these external difficulties, and those inherent in its subtle complexities, that Jews never speak of *reading* the Talmud, but always of *studying* it.

Like all legalistic works, the Talmud is concerned with court procedure, property, torts, marriage and kindred subjects. But it is a legalism which is unique. Its authors never conceived that law was limited to these issues. They legislated on the assumption that law was coextensive with life, that it covered every human interest, the totality of human conduct.

The legalism of the Talmud is unique in one other and more important respect—in the ethical idealism with which it is shot through. It is a common reproach of most systems of law that they are inferior to morality, that they fall far short of the moral standards of the society which they regulate. This charge can not with justice be leveled against the Talmud, which is throughout afire with humanity and alight with ethical intuitions unexcelled in the history of human aspiration. Here a passionate idealism burns through legal formalism—a passion for justice, for mercy, and for the protection of the socially under-privileged. The Talmud did more than direct the conduct of the Jew. It insisted, both in theory and practise, on the best moral values of which he was capable.

In part, the unusual idealism of Jewish law is due to its association with the Bible. It was derived from a book which was devoted primarily to the good life. It naturally reflects the aspirations of its origin.

But its ethical excellence was also the direct expression of the spiritual genius of the men who evolved it. For the authors of the Talmud were not mere lawyers. They were rabbis and religious teachers as well. The men who made this system of jurisprudence were the same sages who taught of faith and morality, who created the Midrashim, books devoted to the improvement of man and his society. To them, law, religion and ethics were of one piece. Inevitably, these diverse interests influenced one another.

The quotation from the Talmud which follows offers a vivid case in point.

"How," asks the Mishnah in a treatise on court procedure, "shall one impress witnesses in a criminal case with the gravity of their position? One takes them aside and charges them, 'Be certain that your testimony is no guess work, no hearsay, not derived at second-hand, nor by reliance on the observation even of a trustworthy person. Remember, you must face a severe cross examination. Know that a criminal case is by no means like a civil. In the latter, he who has caused an injustice by his testimony can make monetary restitution, but in the former, the blood of the accused and his unborn offspring stain the perjurer forever. Thus, in the case of Cain, Scripture says, "The voice of the bloods of your brother call to Me." Observe that the text reads in the plural, not blood, but bloods. For Abel's blood and that of his unborn seed were alike involved. It is for this reason that God created only one human in the beginning, a token to man that he who destroys one life, it is as though he had destroyed all mankind; whereas he who preserves one life, it is as though he had preserved all men.' Another reason why God created only one primal man is for the sake of peace and democracy, so that no one may say, 'My ancestry is better than yours.' Still another reason might be so that disbelievers may not argue for the existence of many gods. Another possible explanation is that God wished to reveal His great power. For, when a man stamps coins from one die, they are all alike, but the King, the King of Kings, the Holy One, blessed be He, stamped all men with the die of Adam, and yet no man is quite like his fellow. Wherefore, each human has the right to say that he is the end and goal of all creation."

This passage from the tradition is quoted here because it reveals clearly the penetration of the law by moral idealism— a penetration in this case to the point of interruption and intrusion.

For the whole latter portion of this Talmudic text is really irrelevant to the issue at hand. The rabbis, however, were too much concerned with ethics to be able to forget it even in the midst of a legal passage. Time and again in the Talmud, their moral interest expresses itself in parenthetical comments. Everywhere it is implicit, even in the dullest and driest discussion of the formalities of law.

Much has been gained by the progressive secularization of life. But much also has been lost. For, if religion choked its ancillaries, it also spiritualized them. A glory has gone from the esthetic life since it divorced itself from religion—a sense of cosmic significance and purposive devotion. In this fact lies the root of Santayana's complaint against the poets of barbarism, and of Joseph Wood Krutch's regrets over a drama which can no longer be heavy with philosophic connotations.

In law, too, the blessings of secularism are not unmitigated. Jewish law affords a classic case in point. Its ethical standards were, as we have already indicated, largely the echoes of the ideals of its authors. But they were also directly a result of intimate dependence upon a religion. For the rabbis believed literally that man had been created by the infusion of the dust with God's breath. In each human being, then, there was lodged a spark of divine fire. Every person was a sanctuary in miniature, a God incarnate. In each act of violence and oppression, whether perpetrated by an individual or by society, there was implicit sacrilege, an affront to the indwelling Spirit.

Jewish law might have been freer to develop had it not been tied to a theological system; it could never have been as humane.

All through Talmud and Midrash this ideal of the inviolability of the human spirit finds expression. It asserted itself ultimately in opposition to capital punishment. If man be a divine being, even the state should not take life. Perhaps the earliest condemnation of this age-old practise is to be found in the Mishnah.

"A Sanhedrin which imposes capital punishment once in seven years deserves the title of bloodthirsty. Rabbi Elazer ben Azariah says that even if such a conviction takes place once in seventy years, the court is cruel. Rabbi Tarphon and Rabbi Akiba declare, 'Had we lived while the Sanhedrin exercised its powers, no man would ever have been executed.' "

The sanctity of the human personality is a pious ideal widely held. The masters of Israel were not content to allow it to remain an abstraction. They deduced from it a specific corollary. They legislated vigorously against all forms of the exploitation of one person by another.

In an age when slavery was a universal institution, when it had been sanctioned by the noblest in the pagan world, they felt that it was incompatible with their premise of the divinity of man. Even the fact that the Bible authorized it did not deter them. They virtually legislated the practise out of existence. By reinterpretation of the Mosaic Law they so surrounded the rights of the bondsman with protective rules, that the possession of a slave became, as one of them put it, "a millstone around the neck of a master."

Long before the days of trade unions, they recognized the right of collective bargain and strike.

"The laborer has the right to quit in midday. For Scripture saith, 'Unto Me are the children of Israel servants,' which means that no man should be enslaved to any other."

Nor were the teachers above presuming to break the law when it worked hardship on the poor and suppressed.

"Rabba, the son of Bar Chanan, hired porters to transport jugs of wine. The porters, in pure negligence, broke their loads. Whereupon, Rabba seized their garments as compensation. The porters then brought the case before Rav. He ordered that the garments be returned. Rabba objected that his action had been legal. 'Indeed it is,' said Rav, 'but Scripture says, "So that thou mayest go in the way of the kindly."' When the garments were returned, the porters pleaded, 'We are poor men, we have labored a full day, exhausted ourselves, and now we have nothing.' Whereupon, Rav decreed that their wages be paid. Again Rabba objected on grounds of legality. To which Rav replied, 'It is written, "Thou shalt observe the paths of the upright."'"

What is implicit in these legal passages—a hatred of exploitation and violence—is explicit in definite moral injunctions in which sympathy for the persecuted and the ideal of non-resistance flare into dazzling brilliance.

"Be thou of the persecuted rather than of them who persecute, of the reviled not those who revile, of those who hear themselves disgraced and make no reply, who act from love and await life's sufferings cheerfully, concerning whom Scripture saith, 'Those that love Him are like the going forth of the sun in his power.'"

Or again:

"Seest thou a wicked man persecuting a wicked, know thou that God is with the persecuted. If a righteous man persecute a righteous, God is with the persecuted. And even when the righteous persecute the wicked, by the very fact of their persecution, God is still with the persecuted."

Such flights into the ethical empyrean are naturally unusual. Only rare winged spirits could attempt them. Normally, the rabbis were content with a less heroic morality of mercy and kindness, of justice and fair play, and with the embodiment of these in the Law.

In elevating the legal position of woman, they found time to strike off such simple, homely aphorisms as, "If thy wife be short, bend down and whisper in her ear," or, "A mother who has buried a child is not afraid of death."

They preached constantly against dishonesty in business, the lure of profit and absorption in acquisitiveness. But they were not content with mere preachment. The ideal was translated into rigid law. They forbade usury even in remote forms and severely limited margins of profit. In nothing does their practical idealism manifest itself so completely as in their refusal to accept the principle of *caveat emptor,* let the buyer beware. They insisted that the integrity of a sale rests with the seller who is aware of the true worth of his wares. On him, they imposed legal responsibility.

Of the mercy which their legislation exhibited, they never wearied of speaking. Compassion for them extended to all humanity and to animals as well.

"Once it chanced that a calf was being led to slaughter. It escaped and huddled against Rabbi Judah the Prince, and bellowed as though weeping and saying, 'Save me.' Rabbi Judah said, 'Go, for this purpose wast thou created.' Because he had no compassion on a dumb brute, illness overtook him."

*   *   *   *   *

"Once it chanced that a maidservant of Judah's was sweeping the house and she found a nest of young weasels. She was on the point of sweeping them away when Judah stopped her. 'Let them be, for Scripture saith, "His mercies are over all His creatures." ' Since he felt compassion, it was extended to him, and he was healed."

Homely as the morality of the tradition often was, un-pretentious as was its application in the codes, it rarely stooped to the expedient. The rabbis never recommended honesty as the best policy nor the good life as a means to an end. And if much of the tradition, legal, theological or moral, is often prosaic, there are leaps of genius that raise the whole heavenward.

"How shall a man die; let him cleave to life. How shall a man live; let him cleave to death."

* * * * *

"How shall a man be like God? As He is merciful, so be thou merciful. As He is gracious, so be thou gracious."

* * * * *

"What is hateful to thee, do not to thy neighbor. This is the whole law, the rest is commentary."

Through all the tradition, legal and moral, there is heard constantly one affirmation: that life is good. Neither the law nor the ethic was ascetic. They did not despise the flesh nor ask the mortification of the body. They advocated marriage, and at an early age; not because it is better to marry than to burn, but because only in marriage does man find fulfilment. The body is not to be crushed; it must be disciplined. The passions shall not be suppressed; they must be enjoyed, though sanctified and turned to ideal ends. Or, as they put it, the man who refuses a legitimate pleasure is an ingrate against God who made it possible.

But in the tradition, pleasure—even sanctified pleasure—was neither the goal nor the purpose. The good life consisted in two things: knowledge and righteousness. To be noble, one must be both a scholar and a saint. For a man must *know,* if he is to be virtuous.

Knowledge, from their view-point, was naturally confined to the Law and its tradition. In these, God had revealed the fulness of truth, and no other text was necessary.
The rabbis often concerned themselves with extraneous intellectual interests, but only as these threw additional light on
the heritage, or as they diverted and intrigued the mind.
They were "side dishes to wisdom." But if their conception
of the nature of knowledge was sharply limited, they approached their sacred study with fervor and intensity. In
it they found a fulness of satisfaction. Proficiency in it was
the greatest of all virtues. It was life's purpose. "If thou
hast learned much Torah, ascribe not merit to thyself, for to
this end wast thou created."

But for all their insistence on scholarship, they were
acutely aware of the fact that learning is not always associated with virtue. When they were compelled to choose
between the two, they recognized that righteousness is of
infinitely greater significance. Learning was then both an
end it itself, and the means to a higher end. The ultimate
purpose of all the tradition was the way of justice, mercy
and truth; or, as they would have put it, to be like God.
From the divine the entire system proceeded; in approxi-
mation to the divine, it found its end.

This entire discussion may at first glance seem unrelated
to the dual problem of Jewish survival and character posed
in the beginning. The irrelevance, however, is only super-
ficial. The tradition was a determining factor both in
keeping the Jew alive and in making him what he now is.

Thus it came to pass that the Jew took with him as provision for his pilgrimage the Bible and a commentary. These
nourished him with a multitude of spiritual foods. They
afforded him a huge literature with which to occupy himself.

They regulated his external life. They channelized his conduct in accordance with high ethical standards. They equipped him with a body of knowledge and a set of ideals. They took the place of the land which he had lost and the political life which was denied. In them he found a field for activity, an interest for his mentality, a teacher of morality and theology.

Among the heirlooms which Karl Marx has bequeathed to the twentieth century, not the least is the stranglehold of the theory of economic determinism on sociology. Modern historians are prone to assume blandly that all historical evolution is only an epiphenomenon of economic activity. It has become the fashion to treat contemptuously the influence of ideas on the careers of human groups. In Jewish history, we shall find one vindication of the importance of culture. The heritage of the Jew, for all its imponderability, was a real factor in the making of his destiny. No interpretation of him can hope for competence if it does not reckon with those immaterial possessions which the Jew took with him as he set forth.

Chapter IV

ISRAEL AND THE NATIONS

The typical history of medieval Europe is generally oblivious of the existence of Jews. It will describe with patient detail the political and social development of some land, but at best a few scanty passing references are accorded to its Jewish residents. The notorious "man from Mars," reading a serious historical account, might never dream of the presence on the scene of that peculiar group. Sensitive Jews tend to suspect a conspiracy of silence on the part of historians. They will not hesitate to accuse them of anti-Semitism, and a malicious attempt to withhold recognition where it is due.

And yet, the historian's reticence is easily understandable. In self-defense, he can argue that Jews have lived in many lands, but, until recently, were never part of them. They constituted an undigested mass in each body politic, occupying a disproportionately small place in their religious, political, cultural and economic milieu. In brief, they were isolated from their environment. To live in a country and to participate in its life are two radically different things. Witness the gipsy; witness, as we shall soon see, the Jew.

As the human organism walls off an infected area, as a city quarantines a pest-hole, so did medieval society isolate the Jew. For Israel was to the Christian mind a focal center of moral and religious disease. The Jew clung to his theological perversities; he was steeped in blind error. That contact with him might be dangerous was readily apparent. The devil was an ingenious person; he was not above exploiting the Jew in his conspiracy of damnation. From the viewpoint of the Catholic church, the segregation of the Jew was pointedly sane. The clergy knew that heresies, such as the Albigensian, were inevitable wherever free intercourse was encouraged. Each conversion to Judaism—and they were not unknown—gave confirmation of the need for prophylactic sanitation if the Christian soul was to be saved.

But it did not suffice to separate Jewish disease from Gentile health. An example must be made of the infidel. It must be shown to the believer that the way of the transgressor was hard. Otherwise, wherein lay the reward of faith? In consequence, a program of humiliation and degradation was pursued with noble zeal. With each suppression of the representatives of the Antichrist, the Christian cause was so much the more desirable.

Why, then, did not the church obliterate the Jew? Why did it not wipe out his very memory? A churchman answering this perplexing question would naturally have advanced a theological reason. He would have pointed to prophecies in Scripture concerning the ultimate conversion of Israel; he might argue that God had preserved some Jews, albeit in degradation, as a horrible example for Gentiles. Actually, the Jew was spared not for theological but for economic reasons. At each successive stage in medieval life, he fulfilled some useful function. It was always to somebody's interest that Israel be preserved. At times the economic value of the Jew was forgotten and a program of extermination adopted. But never for long. The howl of the injured purse soon drowned out the strident insistence of the pulpit. Economic interest has never been truly pious. Even the piety of the Middle Ages could not keep Christian kings from protecting Jews against the church.

But if the Jew served the interests of one class, he must
retard those of another; a sponge for rulers, he must be a
leech for the ruled. Those whom he hurt demanded his
death, organized massacres and planned raids—always, however, under the guise of religious devotion. When certificates of indebtedness were burned, it was to the greater
glory of God. When financial records were destroyed, it
was for the sake of the Savior. So long as the exploiter prevailed, the Jew had a breathing spell of tranquillity. With
the dominance of the exploited, he bowed his head and held
his breath until the storm should pass.

One idiosyncrasy of the medieval scene should be indicated. The Jew was protected often for theological reasons—
more often for economic—but rarely on the grounds of mercy
and humanity.

Much as the Christian world desired the degradation and
isolation of the Jew, it effected them only slowly. Under
the Roman Empire, the Jews of Europe had possessed full
rights of citizenship along with all other provincials. The
Christianization of the West had almost no immediate effects.
Jews continued to enjoy a wide tolerance and broad
opportunities.

Only as the church rose to a position of power did circumstances change. The clergy resented the peace of the
Jew. It was not right that those who had crucified, and, in
their denial of Him, daily recrucified the Christ, should live
in security. Nay more, Gentiles and Jews ate together;
Hebrews employed Christian domestics, and friendly religious discussions were as dangerous as they were frequent.
To the scandal of Christendom, many Christian rulers employed Jews in official capacities and entrusted their bodily

health to the diabolic skill of unbelieving physicians. Worst
of all, peasants sometimes preferred Jews to clericals in blessing fields and cattle for fertility. That such amity was
intolerable, unbecoming and dangerous to the true doctrine,
was self-evident. The church set about to correct this great
wrong.

The first Crusade at the end of the eleventh century was
the logical consequence of the policy of the church. Then
the propaganda yielded its horrible harvest. The masses
tasted of Jewish blood with impunity; the last bonds of social
cordiality were brutally severed. Politically, as well as
socially, the year 1096 marks a turning-point in Jewish-
Gentile relationships. Not only did the Jew lose at last the
friendship of the Christian, he lost also his own political
status and his right of citizenship.

For, as the crusaders moved through Europe, whole Jewish
communities in terror sacrificed their freedom for security.
They gave themselves as possessions to the rulers of Christian
states. Their object was to gain the protection of sovereigns.
They hoped that as property they might win a forbearance
which was denied to them as citizens. The emperor, king,
duke, or bishop, accepted the Jew on this new basis. The
protection, of course, was not forthcoming. The damage,
however, was done. When the crusaders had gone their way,
the Jews had ceased to be citizens. They had become the
personal property of rulers, *servi cameræ,* slaves of the royal
chamber.

Toward this change of status, the whole theory of feudal
society made its contribution. The logic of the feudal system
demanded that each person find some place for himself in
the succession of overlords and vassals. Only when the Jew
took on his new status, or lack of status, did he fit into the

structure of medieval society. In addition, with each expulsion, the Jew lost caste. For though he might be a citizen of the country from which he was expelled, he entered a land of refuge only by giving himself to his new ruler. Thus, when Philip Augustus allowed Jews to return to France, he permitted them to choose their overlords, but once their choice was made, there was no change or escape.

Whatever the causes, by the thirteenth century the Jew was nowhere a citizen, and everywhere a chattel. In each land he sojourned by tolerance and not by right.

Rulers everywhere availed themselves of the new status. Jewish communities became to them so much property to be given away, exchanged or exterminated at the caprice of the master. Jews were given away as dowries to royal sons-in-law, in payment of debts to creditors, as tokens of esteem to favorites, as harlots' hire to mistresses.

But if the person of the Jew was a chattel, his property belonged to his overlord. To this extent, the rulers of Europe were logical; they regarded the property of Jewish communities as their own. They taxed, extorted and confiscated with a free conscience and perfect legality. Obviously, the richer the Jew, the more valuable he was as an object of possession. The Christian sovereign then encouraged the Jew to attach himself to his realm as a leech, knowing full well that a decree could squeeze from the Jew all the blood which had been sucked from the Christian. The ruler who would not, or dared not, overtax his subjects, was now not without recourse. Let the Jew bleed the Christian for a while, and then confiscation of Jewish property and the exchequer was well supplied.

When Henry II of England wished to finance the Third Crusade, he confiscated one-fourth of the movable property of his Jews. To ransom Richard the Lion-Hearted, for whom Jews had little reason to feel affection, the small Jewish community of England contributed three times as much as the entire city of London. When the King of France found his treasury empty in 1306, he expelled all Jews, pre-empting their entire property, including the debts owed to them by Christians. In the Golden Bull of 1356, Jews are listed between mines and taxation as a source of revenue.

The Jew, then, as property of the ruler, had a definite economic value. No sane person, unless the priests had undue influence over him, would allow his possessions to walk away. Sovereigns sensibly denied to Jews freedom of movement in much the same spirit as one locks a barn door upon domestic animals. No Jew could change his residence without permission or monetary compensation. Bishops and dukes accused each other of the theft of Jews, and Louis IX found it necessary to enjoin barons to return the runaway or stolen Jews of other nobles.

But if Jews lost their citizenship, control over their own property and the right of movement, they were often rewarded by some compensating protection. Even feudal nobles knew that it was not wise to kill the goose which laid the golden eggs. A technique of extortion was evolved. It was discovered that Jews yielded more if confiscations were so spaced as to allow for a recuperative breathing space. To permit the mob to kill Jews was simply wanton indulgence and extravagance. Even the church must not interfere. The clergy was subtly dangerous. They were always trying to baptize Jews. They promised them stipends upon conversion, they made Christianity socially and politically attractive to the convert. That feudal nobles were often pious Christians is indisputable. But they rarely approved of the baptism of Jews. For, once the Jew became a Christian, he was no longer the property of his overlord, but a free Christian subject. On many occasions, nobles felt constrained to administer severe rebukes to the churchmen. Many an over-zealous prelate was shocked and hurt to have his prospective proselyte snatched from his grasp.

It was then generally the part of wisdom for the feudal lord to protect his Jews against theft, violence, over-extortion and even conversion. But there were times when Jews ceased to justify themselves economically, when popular resentment against them flared into dangerous violence, or when the church put its foot down. Then they might be expelled, or turned over to the mob, exactly as any sane business man washes his hands of an unprofitable or dangerous investment.

Such was the political status of the Jew from the eleventh to the eighteenth century. Minor changes were not unknown during this period. When medieval cities emancipated themselves from their feudal overlords, title in their Jewish residents was transferred to town councils. When centralized monarchies rose above feudal nobilities, Jews became the property of kings rather than dukes. But such modifications of position were purely formal and trivial. All through the seven hundred years prior to the French Revolution, the Jew was a chattel, without rights or substantial privileges. He was something to be exploited, a person to be protected only when it suited the economic interests of those who owned him, to be abandoned if prudence dictated.

The Jew, however, was not a passive pawn. What the world would not give him, he attempted to create for himself. Within his own group, he built a stable society. Each Jewish community possessed a full communal structure, presided over by rabbis and elected elders. It organized councils, educational and philanthropic institutions. Since the Jew had no standing in a Christian court; since, in any event, it was dangerous to air internal Jewish quarrels, he provided for himself a complete system of courts. Before Christian judges, a Jew's oath was valueless. The Jew found it safer to bring his disputes before rabbinic bars of justice and to have them adjudged according to the traditional law which he knew and revered.

The Law had been finally fixed and crystallized with the close of the Talmud. Ever-recurring emergencies made it imperative that new legislation be instituted. For this, too, Jewish communal life provided. In the hour of crisis, synods of rabbis convened and issued *Takonoth,* or ordinances, for the direction of communal life.

In the presence of the hostility of the world without, the Jew adopted a policy of secrecy. He felt correctly that the less the Gentile knew of his internal affairs, the better for him. Only a rare and traitorous Jew ever had recourse to Christian justice in preference to his own. No one in all Jewry was so despised, feared and hated as the *moser,* the informer, the man who revealed dangerous information. Such a man was an active menace. One never knew what such tale-bearing might bring in its trail.

Without police, jails and armies, the Jewish community contrived to enforce its will, and that despite the fact that any rebellious Jew could escape by appeal to the Gentile world. Taxes were paid, penalties imposed, and life regulated despite the absence of instruments of coercion. One whip alone the Jewish court possessed, but one that could be used with terrible effect—the *Herem,* or ban of excommunication. If a Jew defied Jewish authority, the penalty was swift and crushing. He was ostracized fully and completely. No Jew would speak to him, do business with him, even pass near him. The use of this lash was, however, generally unnecessary. Jews obeyed as a matter of self-discipline. They recognized that only by voluntary subjection to the group will could they withstand the pressure of the outer world.

Until the French Revolution, then, the Jews constituted an *imperium in imperio,* a self-contained, vacuum-sealed world in, but not of, the larger whole. In the tumultuous flow of European history, Jewish communities were rock-bound islets, buffeted, but unmoved.

Step by step with the progressive political degradation of the Jew went a parallel economic tragedy. In the tenth century, Jews were either farmers, artisans or merchants. By the fourteenth, they were universally notorious as usurers. No greater catastrophe ever befell the Jew than this shift in economic position. It confined him to the unwanted scraps of the world's economy or to those branches of it which were stigmatized by social disapproval. It exposed him to the hatred of exploited masses. It opened him to the charge of parasitism, so loudly echoed in Germany of late. It distorted and unbalanced his life. To cap the climax, the whole evolution was none of his making. He resisted it desperately and yielded to it only when his strength failed. But if he did not make himself what he was, he was compelled, none the less, to assume full responsibility.

The economic story of the medieval Jew is like his political history, the record of a succession of expulsions from one realm to another. Feudal society drove the Jew out of agriculture, by making it impossible for him to live as a farmer. In the first place, the law often explicitly forbade his own·

ing land. Even where no such restriction existed, the feudal system demanded a Christian oath to the overlord. The church refused the Jew the right to employ Gentiles. Last of all, intermittent riots and massacres made life on an exposed farm most undesirable. There was much less chance of being butchered in cities where Jews were more numerous. For centuries Jews attempted to evade and circumvent the law. They gave their farms to churches, monasteries or friendly Gentiles, and got them back for a nominal rental. But neither the church nor the friend could always be trusted, once the land had formally changed hands. At last the Jew capitulated in despair and turned to other methods of making a livelihood.

The same tale can be repeated with reference to the handicrafts. As medieval society took on fixed and definite form, the guilds came to hold a monopoly on the manufacture and sale of virtually all objects of manufacture. Unfortunately for the Jew, guilds were definitely Christian organizations. Jews engaged for a time in bootleg production. Ultimately they were compelled to confine themselves to such craft work as was too petty for Christian effort. For all practical purposes, by the fourteenth century, the Jew was out of manufacturing as he had been driven from agriculture.

Despite the popular impression of the Jew as a natural business man, the Hebrews of Biblical days showed little inclination toward commerce. That branch of human activity was left to other peoples. In fact, in the language of Scripture, the word *K'na-ani* means alternately Canaanite or merchant. And yet, in the early Middle Ages, the Jew so completely dominated the commercial life of Europe that the words *Judaei* and *Mercatores* were used interchangeably. Jewish monopolization of trade was the result not of inher-

ent instinct, but of definite social advantages which Jewish
society possessed.

In the chaos of the Dark Ages, only Jews had a universal
language. At a time when justice stopped at the borders
of a principality, and when no subject of one prince could
expect a fair trial in the domain of another, the Jews alone
possessed an international court system. A Christian of
Provence was at a distinct disadvantage in bringing suit for
collection against a Moslem of Andalusia, or even against a
fellow-Christian of Burgundy. A Jew, on the other hand,
had full rights in any Jewish court anywhere. There existed
then only for Jews a machinery for validating commercial
agreements. In an age when roads were overrun by brigands, when hostelries were dens of robbers, the Jewish merchant and his wares were invariably safe with another Jew.
He could always trust the information of his co-religionist,
he could count on him for intercession and ransom if he were
waylaid.

With such advantages, the Jew needed no special flair for
commerce in order to monopolize international trade. But
with the Crusades, the situation changed radically. As men,
money and ships were transported to and from the Orient,
the Christian learned something about trade routes; he
caught a glimpse of possible profits. At once, commercial
houses sprang up throughout Christendom; branch offices
under royal patent were opened everywhere. With superior
resources, and with governmental favor behind him, the
Christian easily drove the Jew off the trade routes. Jews
continued in commerce, but on a secondary and relatively
unimportant scale.

It is a curiosity of Jewish history that all three movements
of displacement should have come to a head at about the

same time. In the two centuries following the Crusades, the Jew was forced from agriculture, excluded from industry and driven from commerce. Since he had to live somehow or other, the Jew went into money-lending. That the conscience of the Jew rebelled was natural. A hungry stomach, however, has a compelling logic of its own. And if the Gentile would not permit the Jew to make an honorable living, then the Jew would make one dishonorably.

Like all disreputable professions, that of the usurer was of ancient lineage. As it happened, the position was unfilled in Europe just as the Jew was displaced from his older occupations. For until the early eleventh century, churches and monasteries served as the usurers of Europe. When popes and public opinion at last put a stop to this unecclesiastical condition, Europe was left without banking facilities. With all other doors closed against him, the Jew was pushed into the usurious trap.

There can be no question but that Jewish money-lenders performed a useful service for the medieval economy. A new commercial life was awakening in Europe. The Jew was its involuntary financier. In addition, as we have seen, kings and nobles had slight objection to Jewish usury. It was much less odious to bleed a tolerated Jew than to tax a people. That the Jew made a success of his new venture can not be doubted. Necessity is notorious as a mother of invention.

But even usury and money-lending were not to remain long in Jewish hands. The great commercial magnates of Italy who had driven the Jew from trade now began to compete with him in money-lending. Backed often by the church, equipped with vastly greater wealth and protected by patents, the Lombard bankers soon had the best part of money-lending in their own hands. As they had left to Jews only the rags and shreds of trade, so they left of usury only cheap, small and petty transactions. By the time the fourteenth century dawned, Jews lived on the crumbs of artisanry, and on the droppings of the commercial and financial splendor of the Italian cities.

It is a common belief that Jews by nature make shrewd business men, that they are acquisitive, that they are acutely interested in money for its own sake. If all this be true— and like all popular impressions, it is radically doubtful—the Jew has acquired his peculiar aptitude for business because of the Gentile. Other groups, during the Middle Ages, might find wealth desirable. It was not a condition for their being. Only with Jews was money indispensable for survival, only to them was ready cash as necessary as food or air. For, when the monarch called, there must be gold forthcoming. If the noble threatened, there must be a handsome gift. Even when the mob growled, without silver there would be no way of bribing public officials to extend protection. Money, then, was a prime prerequisite in Jewish life. Without it, the Jew was defenseless. If, then, there has crept into the Jewish mind a disproportionate interest in it—shall the Jew not say with Shylock, "The villainy you teach me I will execute"?

How the intelligent Jew felt about usury and its value to him can be seen from a letter written in the thirteenth century:

"And how shall a man gather up gold and silver, if not through usury? To be sure, the Jews of the East support themselves by manual labor. But then, if the Mohammedan kings are evil and sinful, they at least have enough sense and understanding to take a definite tax annually and from each according to his wealth. But such is not the case among us; our kings and princes think of nothing but to fall upon us and take away our gold and silver. . . . Indeed, blessed be our God, and the God of our Salvation, who multiplied our wealth by means of which we can defend our lives and the lives of our sons and daughters, and also frustrate the designs of our enemies and spoil the plots of our opponents. So why should you complain against us?"*

Society, unfortunately, was not yet done with the Jew. It was not satisfied with depriving him of all political status and forcing him into a most disreputable economic interest. It still held in reserve two other devices to make his life next to intolerable.

In 1215, the Fourth Lateran Council prescribed for Jews, male and female, the compulsory wearing of a badge of shame. The ostensible reason for this legislation was the fear of churchmen that if Jews and Christians dressed alike, sexual relationships between the two groups might be possible. In actuality, this move represents only the logical climax of the whole movement of the church toward the social ostracism of the Jew.

Jews knew full well what this new ordinance meant. They foresaw that the wearing of a distinctive sign would expose them to the insults of the mob, that it would be a provocation to violence. They lobbied at the Lateran Council, they pleaded, petitioned and bribed. For a time in some communities, they succeeded in postponing the inevitable. Eventually, they yielded to necessity. They sewed on their Jew badges and furtively slunk through the street hoping to remain unnoticed.

---

* Quoted from *The Church and the Jews in the XIIIth Century*, by Solomon Grayzel, Dropsie College, Philadelphia, 1933.

One thing more was needed to complete the program of political outlawry, economic degradation and social ostracism—compulsory segregation. It was not long in coming. By this time, the Jew was as eager to be segregated as the Gentile was to segregate. Long before ghettos were formally instituted, all the Jews of one community tended to live in one neighborhood. It was natural, in so cold and angry a social climate, for Jews to huddle together for warmth. They found it more comfortable, more congenial and more secure. This inclination the Gentile encouraged, violently in his rioting, peacefully by making it clear that he did not want a Jew as his next door neighbor. The institution of the Ghetto of Venice in 1516 merely recognized and gave sanction to a fact, merely made a voluntary self-isolation of Jews a matter of legal compulsion.

At first Jews greeted the establishment of ghettos with mingled feelings. If the last bits of their liberty had been pared down a bit more, at least a greater measure of security had been made possible. Surrounded by walls and gates, Jews breathed more easily.

Only as time went on did the Jew discover how savagely he had been trapped. If ghetto walls protected him on some occasions, his close confinement made wholesale massacre all the simpler. The quarters assigned for ghettos were rarely desirable. They were likely to be the slums, bottom-lands along rivers, or districts exposed to military attack. To make ghetto life the less pleasant, Christian authorities developed the ingenious idea of locating legalized houses of prostitution in Jewish quarters.

The great curse of the ghetto was overcrowding. Though the Jewish population grew, civic authorities would give no space for expansion. In Frankfort, four thousand people lived in less than two hundred houses. Rental space was at a premium. Even marriages in some communities had to be postponed until some one died and room for a new family became available. The dead themselves did not escape Christian persecution. In the very grave there was no rest. For, like living quarters, cemeteries, too, became full. Then it became necessary to bury the dead one above another. Of sewage systems and public sanitation, medieval cities were innocent. Great plagues were an inevitable consequence. That the Jew, for all his close confinement, seems to have suffered less than the Gentile, is due in large measure to the hygienic code prescribed by the tradition.

The ghetto was not kind to the Jew. It shortened the days of his life, it bent his body, it infected his lungs, it cramped his height. He came in time to be accustomed to squalor and filth, to corruption and decay. In such surroundings, styles and clothes ceased to matter, poise and carriage became matters of no consequence, good manners and delicacy of taste appeared irrelevant. Life settled down to elemental tasks, that of keeping body and soul together, that of preserving the Jewish people, and of nurturing the tradition. In the presence of such painful concerns, esthetics, refinement and the graces died of slow suffocation.

From the eleventh to the fourteenth century, the outer world had been at work. It had, during that time, reduced the Jew politically to a tolerated outlaw, it had degraded him into an economic pariah, it had stamped him socially as an outcast, it had confined his life to a noisome ghetto. By the fourteenth century, the task had been completed. The Jew was no longer a part of European life.

By that time a balance had been struck between the Jewish and Gentile worlds. The Christian, having attained his objective, was satisfied with his work. The Jew had reconciled himself to his unpleasant fate and ceased to hope for better. For five hundred years this equilibrium persisted. For half a millennium, from the fourteenth to the nineteenth century, Europe had no Jewish problem. Politically, socially and economically, the Jew had ceased to matter. During these centuries, there were, of course, changes. Pogroms and expulsions came and went. But nothing disturbed the *status quo*. The more circumstances changed, the more the system of isolation remained unchanged. An external paralysis had seized the body of Israel. But if its outer organs no longer moved visibly, its heart still beat, its brain still thought, and its soul still aspired.

Chapter V

THE WAY OF THE LAW

EVEN a Jew does not enjoy misery. If, following Shylock's advice, you tickle or prick him, he will recoil from the feather or the pin. Why, then, did the medieval Jew not flee his Jewishness as a plague; why did he not escape his miseries by the simple device of baptism? He was not stupid; he could have contrived an exit. The astounding fact is that, for all the cruel ingenuity of the world, for all his homelessness and suffering, the Jew enjoyed his Judaism. Compelled to make a virtue of necessity, he found it a pleasant activity. That he distilled peace from pain and extracted sweetness from gall is due to the intensity of his inner life. It was this which compensated him abundantly in satisfactions, intellectual, social and esthetic. For this he might count the world well lost.

Granted imagination and will, even a prison, for all its confining walls, can become, by a mental *tour de force,* a palace. The external horror of the Jewish scene has passed before our eyes. The medieval Jew, however, never saw it in its naked brutality. He viewed it through the rosy spectacles of his own spiritual and intellectual life. So regarded, the drabness took on color, the horror ceased to be intolerably horrible. For example, the Jew believed literally and vividly that he was a member of a Chosen People. In the dim days of the earth's beginning, the Creator of the Universe had elected his ancestors, the Patriarchs. On them He had conferred

His blessings to be transmitted to their children to the end of all time. Each Jew shared in the merits of his fathers, inheriting a divine benediction as naturally as he received his bodily traits.

And then, at a certain moment in history, God had revealed His will to the people of Israel. Standing at the foot of Mount Sinai, the Jews' forefathers had received the Law of Moses, the eternal inheritance of the congregation of Jacob. In that Law there was embraced a divinely ordained scheme of life. Through that Law, the Jew became the sole possessor of absolute truth.

To the medieval Jewish mind, Israel was not merely one of many peoples. It was the one nation which had been selected by Providence as its peculiar treasure. As one Jewish theologian of the twelfth century put it: in the cosmic organism, Israel was the heart. It alone knew God's will and exemplified it. Only through Israel could salvation come to humanity.

For God had intended His world to be perfect. Unfortunately, the sins of the first generation of mankind alienated the Creator. The nations, in their stubborn perversity, were still plunged in the iniquities of their ancestors. Only because Israel, through its keeping of the Law, manifested obedience to the divine will, did the world find moral justification and God's grace. Eventually, the Jew believed, the Gentiles would come to see the truth. They, too, would obey the Law. Then, at last, the kingdoms of this world would pass away into the Kingdom of God. But the Utopian time was not yet at hand. In the interim, the Jew had a unique mission to perform. He must serve as faithful guardian of the Law until the day came when all men alike would revere it.

For all his claims to exclusive possession of the saving doctrine, the Jew was not unconscious of the merits of Christianity and Mohammedanism. While both these religions were to him imperfect and incomplete in their neglect of the Law, they were definitely better than pagan idolatry. In this partial tolerance, the Jew was vastly superior to his Christian contemporary, to whom Judaism was *perfidia,* a *superstitio* and a blindness. The Jew recognized appreciatively that both alien religions were opposed to polytheism, to idolatry, that they taught moralities akin to his own. As such, even if they were inferior to his own faith, they were at least a preparation of the world for it. Thus Judah Halevi, twelfth century poet-philosopher, says explicitly: "These faiths are a preparation and preliminary for the Messiah who is awaited."

The finest and most sympathetic insight into the inner integrity of Christian and Moslem, though with no mitigation of the Jewish claim, is to be found in the "Royal Crown" of Solomon Ibn Gabirol, a Spanish Jew of the eleventh century.

"Thou art God, and all things formed are Thy servants
        and worshippers.
Yet is not Thy glory diminished by reason of those that
        worship aught beside Thee,
For the yearning of them all is to draw nigh to Thee.
But they are like the blind,
Setting their faces forward on the King's highway,
Yet still wandering from the path,
One sinketh into the well of a pit
And another falleth into a snare,
But all imagine they have reached their desire,
Albeit they have suffered in vain."*

---

* From *Selected Religious Poems of Solomon Ibn Gabirol,* Jewish Publication Society of America, Philadelphia.

To moderns who have grown skeptical of monopolies in truth, there may be a touch of arrogance in Ibn Gabirol's condescension to the non-Jew. Nevertheless, such an attitude bespeaks an unusual tolerance. And if, during the later Middle Ages, the Jew lost his initial respect for Christianity, he can scarcely be blamed in view of the lack of self-respect displayed by the Christian.

But if Israel was the heart, the protagonist, the instrument for the achievement of God's plan—why did He abandon it so completely to the malice of the world? Was the medieval Jew so blinded by this theory of his mission that he could no longer perceive the realities of his position? How, indeed, could he claim special election, God's unique favor, exclusive possession of the truth and a dominant rôle in the cosmic theater when in actuality he exhibited none of the qualities of importance? Had the Jew been rich, powerful, secure and respected, he might well have argued that his status reflected his significance. But he was poor, hated, hunted and despised. What, then, became of his claims?

Of this contradiction between his poetic theory and an ugly reality, the Jew was acutely aware. Even had he been tempted to ignore it, Christian and Moslem alike took special glee in flaunting it before him. And yet, he felt that he knew the answer, that he could resolve the paradox. Despite persecutions and expulsions, Jew badges and ghettos, he was still the chosen servant. And for the challenge of unpleasant realities, he had his answers prepared.

After all, the facts of his life, far from refuting his claims to election, confirmed them. The very suffering to which the Gentile pointed as a denial of the Jewish scheme was really its demonstration. The Jew suffered, in the first place, because he deserved to suffer. He had never been truly loyal to the God who had chosen him. At the very foot of Sinai, his ancestors had built a golden calf. On the peak of Carmel, they had hesitated between Jehovah and Baal. Reluctantly, unwillingly, God had punished again and again. He had, for the sins of Israel, destroyed the two houses where His glory dwelt. And still this stiff-necked people refused to obey the Law, and to exemplify the nobility of a kingdom of priests. When, then, the medieval Jew read Scripture, he knew why he was persecuted. It was not that God had abandoned him as the nations claimed, but that He was chastising him into obedience. Israel suffered because it was not equal to its moral purpose. Not that the Gentiles were better than Israel. They were, if anything, much greater sinners. But their conduct did not matter to God. They were not the instruments of His will. Thus, the very fact of Israel's exile and persecution, by a strange logic, proved God's love. After all, it is the beloved child who is most carefully disciplined by an anxious parent.

But there was another reason for Jewish suffering—a reason implicit in the very nature of service. In the book of Isaiah, the Jew read the prophet's description of Israel as the suffering servant of God. There he learned that all moral grandeur, each devotion to an ideal, is somehow inexplicably linked with pain. On the mind of medieval Jewry, this doctrine made a vivid impression. The Jew suffered because suffering is an indispensable prerequisite to salvation.

Among the Kabbalists and mystics, this intuition became vocal. Even God, they asserted, would not be truly God unless He suffered. Certainly Israel could never serve its purpose unless first it had been purified by walking in the valley of the shadow.

With the truth of medieval Jewish theology, we are not

concerned. What is of interest is its effects on the morale of the Jew, and these were incalculable. The theory of election and mission invested him with a sense of dignity and importance that more than atoned for his social insecurity and insignificance. It told him that without his aid God and His universe could not find fulfilment. In the drama of mankind, the Jew felt himself a protagonist. Without his cooperation, the whole universe was meaningless. To desert the Jewish people, to abandon the Law, was treason to God; it was also tantamount to a final defeat of the divine purpose for man. Nay, more, what goal in life was so worthy as the service of the Almighty, and participation in His program? Let those who so chose enjoy the power and pleasure of the world, let them minister to chambermaids and hostlers; the Jew served the King.

Not least of the values of this philosophy was the reaction it induced in the Jew to his trials. Under its influence, persecution ceased to be a sign of God's displeasure. It became instead an expiation for an inveterate stubborn rebellion and a discipline for a high cause.

"In this suffering," said a medieval Judeo-Spanish philosopher, "lies our greatest glory. For any of us could, if he so chose, spare himself shame and bondage and be allied to our persecutors by simply uttering a word. That we will not do."

Pain knows no triumph where it is gladly received. The Jew could not prevent the damage done to his body. But by his attitude to his sufferings, and by his cheerful acceptance of them as contributory to higher ends, he saved the health and sanity of his soul.

The way of the Law, for all the sacrifices it entailed, was not without its compensations. The medieval Jew felt assured of his rewards. For he believed that his God would

repay him for his martyrdom in this world with the glory
of blissful immortality. The tradition taught that, while one
must not serve God in the hope of reward, the reward was
there none the less. After the sleep of death, the soul awoke
to a world in which injustice was no more. As it had sowed,
so would it reap. He who had served God and mankind
would find eternal blessedness; he who had rebelled would
receive his deserts.

It is curious to note that while the Jew claimed a monopoly
of God's revelation, he did not claim exclusive possession of
its reward. He never asserted that the non-Jew could not
attain to it. As a matter of fact, he insisted that "the righteous
of all peoples have their share in the world to come." Indeed,
to attain immortality, less was required of the non-Jew than
from him. His reward demanded unswerving loyalty to a
difficult and persecuted Law. If he deviated from it, or
deserted it, he had thrown away his opportunity.

The assurance of reward gave to the medieval Jew patience
with a painful present. Let the nations rage against Israel
because it obeyed its divine revelation, let massacre and persecution engulf it. What significance could be ascribed to a
few brief decades of humiliation and pain when one considered the eternities of happiness treasured up for the righteous? Loyalty became easy with such a prospect. Even
a death of torture lost its terror.

In 1096, the Jews of Xanten were presented by crusaders
with a choice between baptism and death. The small Jewish
community was assembled at a Sabbath table when the moment of decision arrived. The subtle efficacy of the doctrine
of immortality in encouraging loyalty is transparent in the
following extract from a medieval Jewish chronicle which
describes the event.

"Whereupon the saintly man of faith, the priest elevated above his brethren, began to speak unto the community assembled at the table. 'Let us recite grace over our meal unto the living God, unto our Father in Heaven—for as an altar of sacrifice is this table spread before us. Then, let us arise and ascend to the House of God, yea, let us do His will speedily. Though it be the Sabbath, let each man slaughter his son, his daughter, and his brother, that blessing may come upon us this day. Let none spare himself nor any other. He who remains last, let him slay himself, so that the impure defile us not, nor the hands of wickedness with their abominations. We shall offer ourselves as a sacrifice to God, as a whole offering coming upon God's altar.

" 'Then shall we enter upon that other world which is all good, in Eden, where one sees as through a clear glass, where we shall behold eye to eye His glory and majesty. To each of us will be given a golden crown for the head, set with precious stones and pearls. There we shall sit amidst the Pillars of the World; we shall dine in the company of the Righteous; we shall be associated with the martyred Rabbi Akiba and his fellows. And as we sit on our golden thrones in the shade of the tree of life eternal, we shall behold Him, and say, "Lo, this is our God; we have waited for Him that He might save us. This is the Lord; let us be glad and rejoice in His salvation." Then shall we be free to observe the Sabbath, for in this world of darkness, it is impossible to keep it as is fitting.'

"Then, all answered together and in unity—'Amen, so let it be, and so let it be His will!' "

More potent than the sense of election and the confidence of reward was the Jew's assurance of ultimate vindication. He knew that his cause was a true one, and must ultimately prevail. The tradition told him that his discipline of pain would reap its reward of triumph. At the end of days, when history had run its course, when the sin of Israel had been expiated, the true Judge of nations would give a true verdict. On that day, and no man knew when it would arrive, God would interfere catastrophically in the affairs of men. He would send His Messiah, the son of David. Israel would be restored to its ancient land, to live in peace and security. The peoples of the earth would recognize the truth of the Law, and as penitents, they would come to Zion to learn it. All the evil of exile would pass away like a bad dream under that new heaven and on that new earth which was to be illuminated by the sun of righteousness with healing on its wings. Then the peoples who had mocked and persecuted the Jew would behold and be ashamed. For it would be made clear that through the weary centuries the Jew had been the loyal servant of God.

The hope of final vindication is an incalculable power in encouraging persistence. It is often detected as the consolation of disappointed idealism, the solace of misunderstood and unrecognized genius. It is also the courage of martyrs.

In this faith, the Jew found his patience. As an individual he bore his suffering cheerfully because he knew that it was worth while and that it would be repaid with personal immortality. As a member of a persecuted people, he carried his burden joyfully because he awaited a triumphant issue. He settled down and hoped. As storms rose about him, he constantly reminded himself of the salvation to come.

But if the Messianic expectation gave to the Jew the spirit of patient perseverance, it often drove him to an irritable impatience. The end was so far deferred that it was difficult to wait quietly. Especially in times of crisis when the cup of suffering filled to overflowing, when it seemed that Israel could not longer endure, at such times the Messianic hope leaped into anxious prominence. All through the Middle Ages, Jews searched Scripture and the tradition for some hint of the time of deliverance. So dangerous became this attempt to force the future, that one of the rabbis of the Talmud put an interdict upon it.

"Blasted be those who calculate the end. For when the time they predict arrives, and the Messiah still has not come, people grow weary and say, 'He will never come.' Wiser it is simply to wait. Even as it is written in Scripture, 'Though He tarry, wait thou for Him.'"

Neither interdict nor sensible counsels of patience could keep the Jew from abusing his hope. Whenever his lot became intolerable and his patience exhausted, he turned from passive hope to active anticipation. Now, he would tell himself, the Messiah must come, else it will be too late, for our strength is failing. As his desire for deliverance approached the breaking point, the wish became father to the thought. A false Messiah appeared.

No chapter in the saga of the Jewish soul is quite so fantastically romantic as the lives and works of these false Messiahs. Some of them were unquestionably charlatans who deliberately exploited the hopes of an agonized people. Most of them, however, were as earnest and sincere as the people they misled. From long brooding over the misery of Israel, from yearning for a deliverer, it was a simple step to the conclusion, "Perhaps I am that deliverer." With the advent of believers and followers, it was another short step to the elimination of the "perhaps."

Through the eighth century a succession of Messiahs appeared in Persia. Late in the tenth century, an adventurer named Eldad, of the tribe of Dan, brought to the Jews of North Africa fabulous reports of the lost Ten Tribes, of which he claimed to be a member. But only in the sixteenth and seventeenth centuries do these bizarre characters assume wide importance. By that time Spanish Jewry had been crushed, the régime of persecution had taken its effect and Jewish despair had become intolerable. Thus, in February of 1524, there appeared in Venice one David Reubeni, claiming to be ambassador to Christian lands of the lost Ten Tribes. His advent stirred the depression of the ghettos and stimulated Messianic speculation.

In 1523, under his influence, a young Marrano of Portugal, Solomon Malko by name, reverted to Judaism, steeped himself in the Kabbalah, announced himself as a forerunner of the Messiah, and came to a tragic end at the stake of the Inquisition.

But these lesser prophets were only a rumble of thunder before the storm of the greatest of the false Messiahs— Shabbetai Zevi. In 1665, in the city of Smyrna, this Turkish pretender proclaimed himself the Redeemer. A wave of hysterical release swept the ghettos of Europe. Believers and skeptics fought over the claim in every *Judengasse*. Jews, in the immediate expectation of triumph, prepared for the return to Palestine. The bubble burst suddenly, the mirage faded away, and the ghetto returned to its darkness—to wait for a deliverer who never came, to hope for salvation, and by the very process of hoping, to attain survival instead.

Thus did the tradition equip the Jew with a weltanschauung which colored an ugly scene, which veiled from him the unpleasant reality of his lot. Thus did it furnish him with an ideology that gave him dignity, a sense of importance, a hope of reward and an assurance of victory. The Marxian will dismiss it all on the ground that it can be reduced to economic motifs. The psychologist will see in these concepts only a series of compensatory mechanisms. All of which may be perfectly true and yet irrelevant. The thing that counts is that, regardless of source, these doctrines participated in the conspiracy to keep the Jew alive.

The way of the Law, then, mitigated the conditions of Jewish living by a set of alleviating concepts. But it went further; it helped make life bearable by a round of customs and ceremonies. The tradition, as we have seen, embraced an elaborate ritual and observance. The Jew observed numberless rites; feast days and fast days followed one another in close succession.

Let us follow a medieval Jew through a typical day. He rose and bathed his hands in accordance with an ancient ordinance. He slipped on a fringed garment prescribed by the Law of Moses. He bound his phylacteries on his arm and forehead, and recited a long morning prayer. Before he touched food, he washed his hands again, and uttered a benediction; and after he had eaten he intoned a grace. He was then free to go about his business; but should any unusual incident occur, there was always a prescribed blessing to be uttered. A flash of lightning, a clap of thunder, the smell of spices, the sight of a scholar, a dwarf, a learned Gentile, a king and his court, great mountains, the sea, the donning of new clothes, the tasting of a fruit first in season, the receipt of good news or bad—each of these was the occasion for a benediction. During the early afternoon, he recited one religious service, at sunset another, before he retired to his bed, a third. This was the minimum observance prescribed by the tradition. If he had any pretensions to learning, he would attend some class during the day in which some part of the tradition was interpreted. He might perhaps engage in individual study. Should his piety be greater than the Law required, there were untold rubrics of special worship for his use. At the stroke of midnight, he arose, seated himself on the floor of his chamber, put ashes on his head, and bewailed the Temple destroyed some fifteen centuries ago, and prayed for the speedy coming of the Messiah.

No aspect, no phase, no detail of his life escaped regulation by the tradition. Diet, hygiene, clothes, even the physical functions of his body must conform to ancient norms.

Such was the normal week-day of the medieval Jew. On festivals, the routine was interrupted by unusual rites. On the Sabbath, he refrained from work, indulged in fine foods and rest. On the Feast of Tabernacles, he lived in a booth that recalled Israel's habitation in the wilderness. The Passover table, the Hanukah lights, and the Purim gaiety, awoke memories of ancient deliverance. On the Black Fast, he bewailed the fall of Jerusalem; on the great White Fast of Yom Kippur, he atoned for his sins. This ritual penetrated constantly into the home. Candles were lighted, dishes separated, spice-boxes sniffed and leaven cast forth, in an atmosphere compounded of ritual dignity, pontifical pomp, and family festivity.

Much of this routine was purely mechanical. Long habitation had hypnotized the Jew. But just because it was all so familiar, it was very dear to him. It was an integral part of himself; he would have been lost without it. Through all the routinization, traditional rites affected him profoundly. They never allowed him to forget his past, his God, his culture, his moral ideals and his hopes for the future. Above all, he took delight in his complicated ceremonialism. By religious decree he was told that he must enjoy his rites and customs and he succeeded surprisingly. His attitude marked an almost unique instance of genuine pleasure by edict. On the Sabbath he rested with vigorous enthusiasm, on Passover he celebrated the Exodus from Egypt with elaborate conviviality, and at Purim he rejoiced riotously in the fall of Haman. He even mourned and fasted with zest. In addition, all this afforded the Jew esthetic satisfaction. It was the one element of poetry and beauty in his life. It was romantic with huge cloudy symbolism.

The ghetto, moreover, was rich not only in an ideology that transformed reality and in a ritual which made it romantic. It possessed also an intimate and friendly social life. Huddled together as Jews were, there was naturally little of personal privacy. Facing together the constant threat of the outer world, they sought for none. In the face of the terror that walked in darkness, it was much pleasanter to hold hands in comradeship.

The joys and sorrows of each individual were to medieval Jews the joys and sorrows of all. An entire community drank its good wishes at a ceremony of circumcision, extended its congratulations in the synagogue on the naming of a newborn girl. Invitations to weddings were taken for granted. All who chose were free to attend, feast and dance. In like fashion, sorrow was widely shared, and a death involved the whole ghetto.

Above all, Jewish communities exhibited toward the Gentile world unbroken solidarity. Whatever differences might exist within, whatever factions might bicker and quarrel, Jews stood together whenever a Christian appeared. About this compactness for common interest, there is almost an animal quality. It suggests the crowding together of a herd under attack. Especially when one member of the community was threatened did this fellowship assert itself. It was considered a religious virtue of the highest order to contribute toward the ransom of a captive Jew. Almost without exception, all Jewry rose to extend aid to a persecuted community. And each Monday and Thursday morning, when the Torah was read in the synagogue, congregations recited special prayers for fellow-Jews who faced disaster.

"Our brethren, the whole House of Israel, who are given over to distress and captivity, whether on sea or on land, may the Omnipresent God have compassion upon them and bring them forth from their straits to enlargement, from darkness to light, from bondage to deliverance, now, speedily, and at a near time, and let us say, Amen."

Such was the comradeship of those who walked the way of the Law. Because joy was shared among many, it proved to be all the sweeter. Because sorrow was distributed, it was the easier for each to bear. Only by such communal participation in calamity and happiness was life for the Jew made bearable.

The Jew was, as we have seen, almost totally isolated from his environment. None the less, he was acutely aware of sharp differences between his own life, as regimented by the tradition, and that of the Gentile. Of two distinctions in particular he was vividly conscious—one of a theological nature, the other ethical. Both put his own society into favorable contrast from the Christian.

The medieval Jew had no theology in the sense of an official creed, body of dogma, or statement of doctrine which, as a Jew, he was compelled to accept. There was nothing in Judaism to correspond to a Nicene Creed, an Apostles'

Creed, an Augsburg or a Westminster Confession. In this respect, Judaism was the direct antithesis of Christianity. In the latter, right faith tended to be a matter of prime concern; conduct and observance only secondary. In the former, action and morality were carefully regulated; but within certain broad lines, the individual was free to think as he chose. The Jew, then, was religiously, but not theologically, minded. The bond of his unity lay in a social pattern, an ethical code and a historic loyalty. He enjoyed consciously a liberty and freedom of thought which was denied to the Christian. Jews took advantage of this latitude, and Jewish religious speculation reveals an amazing diversity of fundamental position. When, then, the Jew considered Christianity, he congratulated himself that he was free in a nebulous "climate of belief" rather than confined by a fixed, exacting and imperious system of dogma.

And the more he considered Christian doctrine, the more he was repelled by it, not so much because of its restraining authoritarianism as because of its content and nature. He remained Jewish because to him the Christian system was incredible, because being anything else than a Jew involved a radical impossibility. Nurtured on intellectual liberty, he could not bring himself to say, *Credo quia absurdum est.* The trinity, the sacraments, the mysteries, the virgin birth, the incarnation, the divinity of Christ and the authority of the church—all these were too much for him to swallow. Had the Jew known Latin, he might have revised the taunt of Horace and flung it back as *Credat Christianus Apella.* The Jew may often have had difficulty in putting his hands on his own amorphous theology, but he knew that it did not choke him with its authority; that it was relatively credible; it was minimal and made few unnecessary demands on his capacity for faith. It was, by comparison, simplicity itself. The Christian and Moslem themselves encouraged the Jew in his fidelity by granting the truth of the principles of his faith. They merely insisted on adorning them further. These decorations the Jew found repugnant. Considering the Gothic façade or baroque interior of the church, he turned with relief to the white-washed simplicity of the synagogue. What else could the Jew be save loyal to his tradition? What alternative way of faith could possibly attract him? Reared on a simple diet of doctrine, he knew that, like his stomach, his mind would revolt at assimilating those elaborate concoctions on which the Gentiles feasted.

Even as a comparison between religions tended to confirm the Jew in his Judaism, so a contrast between ethical standards reenforced his sense of superiority. The tradition as contained in the Bible, the Talmud and Midrashim, in the heritage which he brought to Europe from Palestine, was heavy in ethical connotations. A respect for life, a sense of the rights of others, an ideal of family purity, high standards of decency and honor, a strong sympathy for the exploited and persecuted—all these were explicit in the Book and implicit in Law and custom. When the Jew compared his morality with that of the world, he felt that the contrast favored him immensely. For all his political, economic and social inferiority, he felt superior to the Gentile. He entertained a healthy contempt for the violent militarism of a feudal society. The armed chivalry of the Middle Ages was to him barbaric. The Christian world was bloodthirsty; it laid none of his emphasis on learning; it was less temperate than his; it did not have his standards of family life.

In condemning hunting as cruelty, Rabbi Meir of Rothenburg, in the thirteenth century, characterizes that sport as typically Christian.

Wife-beating, says Rabbi Tam, in the twelfth century, with perhaps an oblique reference at Gentiles, is something which is simply "not done in Israel." In the same spirit of invidious contrast, Rabbi Meir of Rothenburg insists "Jews are not addicted to the prevalent habit of ill-treating wives."

Drunkenness especially was regarded as a typical Christian vice. As late as the last century a Jewish folk-song which emanated from Eastern Europe, had it that, when the Jew would divert himself, he entered a synagogue for prayer; the Gentile resorted to a tavern. The refrain alternated between:

> Oh, drunk is a Gentile;
> He must be drunk; he must drink
> Because he is a Gentile.

And, on the other hand:

> Oh, sober is a Jew;
> He must be sober; he must pray
> Because he is a Jew.

There is about all of this contrast in morality a self-righteousness, almost an arrogance, which is both uncharitable and distasteful. How far facts justified the Jewish sense of contrast is an open question. The medieval Jew felt that a real difference existed, and derived a sense of superiority from that conviction. This attitude received occasional, though forceful, confirmation through a pogrom or massacre. It was easy to develop contempt for the man who, for no reason other than superior strength, played the bully and

wielded the cudgel. Had there been no other restraining influence, the sensitive Jew would have found passage into
the Gentile world difficult. It seemed to involve the painful
exchange of a moral good for its ethical inferior.

Such was the way of the Law and such its contribution to
Jewish life—a weltanschauung that preserved Jewish self-
respect and hope, a routine of observance that enlisted Jewish loyalty, a solidarity in the face of the world, and a feeling
that Judaism was superior to Christianity as a religion, that
Jews were better than Christians as human beings. And
because of all this, when the world cast him out, the Jew
had the strength to repudiate the world in return.

Thus it came to pass that, amid poverty and persecution, he
could still recite with paradoxical enthusiasm in his daily
prayers, "Happy are we; how goodly is our portion and how
fair is our lot."

CHAPTER VI

THE INNER LIGHT

JEWS, surveying their own past, often express astonishment at
the breadth and depth of the civilization which they have inherited. It seems unreasonable that such exquisite and
variegated flowers should have blossomed on a sterile soil
and in an uncongenial atmosphere. Amazement disappears
when one considers the urgency which impelled Jewish
cultural life. For, since the Jew would not die, he had his
choice of only two alternatives. He must either cultivate a
compensating culture or go stark mad. This accounts for
the passionate devotion of the Jew to ideas, for his intense absorption in books, for his reverence for scholarship. With
other peoples, culture was an afterthought, a by-product of
normal living, an amusement for leisure hours. With the
Jew it was a condition for sanity.

Out of rigid necessity the Jew concerned himself with
study and instruction. In no other society was education
taken so seriously as in the ghetto. Mothers in their lullabies
assured their infants that Torah was the best of all wares.
Jewish parents held always before themselves the example of
the mother of Rabbi Joshua ben Chananyah who "used to take
her child to the door of the academy in his crib so that his
ears might early become accustomed to the sound of learning."

The quaintest of folk ceremonies revolved about the child's
education. The day on which he made his formal entrance

into a school was a family holiday. Drops of honey were sprinkled into a Hebrew book, and the child was told to bend and lick the pages. In this way he was to learn how sweet were the words of wisdom. As he bowed his head, a shower of small coins was dropped onto the open book. Angels, he was assured, had presented him with a gift to show that scholarship had its rewards. Wrapped in a prayer shawl, he was carried to the school and his formal education launched.

The primary schools of the ghetto conformed to few modern standards of pedagogy. They were noisy, dirty and undisciplined. Instructors never spoiled the child by sparing the rod, nor was any attempt made to enlist spontaneous interest. Hours of study were unconscionably long. But for all their failings, ghetto schools were effective. The child learned the rudiments of the Hebrew language, the translation of the Law of Moses and its major commentaries. He picked up, incidentally, all the external forms of Jewish learning. He imitated his teacher who swayed back and forth as he studied. He learned to recite his lessons aloud in a plaintive singsong and to be undisturbed by the chanting of his fellows.

When he had mastered the translation of the Torah, he was hurried into the intricacies of the Talmud, into the labyrinthian discussion of civil law, ritual practise, or even marriage and divorce. The materials of study were grotesquely ill adapted to a childish mind. The ghetto, however, was conservative. Like its customs, its educational procedure was made sacred by a hoary antiquity.

Medieval primary schools had no graduations. The time came when the pupil no longer needed his teacher, when he could decipher a normal passage of the Talmud without aid. Then his parents simply transferred him to the Yeshivah, or college.

The Yeshivah was often only a room adjoining the synagogue, or else a barnlike study hall. Of furnishings it was almost totally bare. Jewish poverty allowed only for the simplest equipment—long benches lining the walls, an oven for winter, tall reading desks mottled by the drippings of innumerable candles; in one corner a barrel of water for drinking and ritual ablutions, against the east wall an ark with Scrolls of the Law; huge dilapidated bookcases lined with equally huge and dilapidated tomes.

As an institution of learning, the Yeshivah was a masterpiece of disorganization. It had no regular hours of attendance. Students came and went as they chose. Curricula were vague and uncertain, examinations sporadic. Each student pursued his own studies with a minimum of supervision. About the academy there was always a touch of bedlam. Scholars ate, drank, conversed, prayed, jested and slept in the study hall. They intoned their lessons aloud in a dolorous chant which filled the air with a discordant tumult. Terms of residence were entirely elastic. Some students remained only so long as caprice held them; others until marriage or business took them away; still others until a rabbinic ordination was conferred. But there were those who, once having entered, never left; who lived out their entire lives over tall tallow-dropped desks, who pursued the knowledge of the sacred tradition until death graduated them into a celestial academy on high.

The Jewish student expected the way of learning to be difficult. Long before the ghetto awoke to its daily routine, he was already before his desk chanting his lesson. Long after the ghetto slept, his candle still flickered before him.

Many a night was for him a "watch night" when he studied until the sky grew light with dawn. His food depended on petty stipends and on the uncertain generosity of pious householders. He hungered and thirsted and went barefooted. The bare bench was often his bed, his ragged coat his pillow. He never complained. In the Mishnah itself he read that such was the inevitable sacrificial discipline of scholarship.

> "This is the way of instruction. A morsel with salt shalt thou eat, and water in limited measure shalt thou drink; on the ground shalt thou sleep, and a life of hardship shalt thou live as in the Torah thou toilest. But if so thou doest, happy shalt thou be, and it shall be well with thee. Aye, happy in this world, and well with thee in the world to come."

The Bible and the Midrash were, of course, parts of the curriculum. But chiefly the student concentrated upon the huge complications of the Talmud. To know this was knowledge; to master this, a life-purpose.

Fortunately for the student, this literature was vast in scope. One could spend a dozen lifetimes in it without exhausting it. Besides, it was widely varied and diversified in content. Absorption in it did not induce an exhausting boredom. On the same page of the Talmud, one passed from law to folklore, from history to ethics, from mathematics to morality. A refreshing variety imbued the whole. But most of all, the student was bewitched by its subtlety. It intrigued him as it edified, it challenged as it instructed. Each page presented its complexities, each passage was a riddle to be solved. As he learned, the scholar was inspired by a sense of mastery and conquest. Long hours lost their terror in the close concentration which the Talmud required. No student could allow his attention to waver. The whole mind was demanded as the price of achievement. In return, the Talmud gave freedom from the world. In the stormy sea of discussion, reality was swallowed up, consciousness submerged. As a modern might find escape from the pain of life in a detective story or jigsaw puzzle, the medieval Jew attained it in the study of tradition. "Is a man afflicted with a headache," says the Talmud itself, "he can lose it by studying the tradition."

For the medieval Jew the Talmud was more than the life of reason, it was also a religious devotion. In his tradition the Jewish student saw God's will manifest. Study, then, was also communion and learning was an act of worship. Scholarship in the sacred literature was regarded as a means of serving God. A religious passion underlay Jewish learning, endowing it with intimations of the divine. Only in the creative arts and in scientific research is there to be detected an analogue of the fervor and intensity of the Jewish student. But even these offer at best a mild parallel. For neither sculptor nor scientist feels so certainly that his wisdom is sacred, that it is unimpeachable, that it leads directly to deathlessness. These assurances the Jew had. That is why, even in the night watches, he was inspired by an enthusiasm that was almost a fanaticism.

Such intensity could not be confined within the frozen text of the Talmud. It must inevitably overflow into creativity. The tradition gave room for originality in only one direction—in writing of commentaries. Of making these, there was in the Middle Ages no end. There were commentaries on the Torah and commentaries on the Talmud, commentaries on the Mishnah, and commentaries on the Midrash, commentaries on legal tractates, and commentaries on ethical passages, grammatical commentaries, exegetical commentaries, commentaries for reference and commentaries for reading. There were commentaries on the basic text and commentaries on commentaries. From a long procession of expositors, these issued unceasingly until even the vast outlines of the Talmud were submerged and the Yeshivah itself was transformed into one huge commentary.

As numerous as were commentaries, so numerous were codes. For all the finality of the Talmud, it possessed one curious characteristic. It rarely stated its decision, it supplied rather the debates of ancient rabbis, the raw material from which definite law must be carved. With the same enthusiasm with which the Jewish mind turned expositor of the tradition, it turned codifier. It produced codes civil, codes criminal, codes ritual and codes marital. Nor were these codes a matter only for academic study, they were intended to regulate life. When the whole process was over, the academy had regimented conduct down to its finest detail.

About the Yeshivah hovered an air of unreality. Into it a group of men had withdrawn, poring over code and commentary, in serene indifference to the actualities of the world. As though this divorcement from life were not sufficiently fantastic, the student tended to be concerned with matters remote and irrelevant to conduct. In the first place, a large part of the tradition had become obsolete. The Talmud, for example, contained regulations for a Temple that had been destroyed, a corpus of constitutional law for a state which had ceased to exist and a criminal law which could not be enforced in an alien land. All the better for the Yeshivah. In these fields it was untroubled by practical exigencies. Besides, as the unending succession of code and commentary continued, the time came when every obvious thing had already been said, when only the clever, the unusual and the brilliant could win a respectful hearing.

Into study there crept an echo of the ascetic unreality of the life of the student. Confined by no practical restraints, he allowed his imagination to run riot. Toward the end of the medieval period, Jewish learning tended to become more and more a matter of ingenuity for its own sake, subtlety became an end in itself. Scholars searched all the tradition to find two passages which could be made to appear mutually contradictory and then, having created an artificial problem, they proceeded to resolve it. And no simple resolution would do. No scholar with self-respect would stoop to the transparent. Only in such a mental milieu could a story become current of a student who had an astoundingly clever solution but who could not find a question equal to it.

From one point of view this later development of the tradition was an intellectual tragedy. It turned the best spirits of Israel into a community of impractical *luft- menschen;* it diverted fine minds from the solution of real problems to the sterility of code and commentary. It confounded intelligence with cleverness and casuistry. But it was not without its compensations. It trained the Jew to think and think hard. It disciplined the mentality of an entire people.

Even when the Yeshivah was most hopelessly barren in its specious cleverness, it still taught a high morality. The saintliness of its most skilful casuists and logic-choppers argues much for its ethical instruction. Above all, the tradition gave to the Jew an interest, an escape from life. In the midst of some casuistic argument, the ugliness of the ghetto was obscured by a fictive structure of glittering logic. Nor must we forget that this intellectualism provided the Jew with purposefulness. There were no objectives for him among men, no worlds for him to conquer. He found them instead in the realm of books and ideas.

More than the synagogue, the academy was the temple of the Jewish spirit. Day and night, its devotees worshiped at its shrine. Students in their perpetual vigil were its ministering priests, the acrid smoke of tallow candles was its incense, the plaintive chant of the Talmud was its melancholy litany, devotion and earnestness in scholarship were its religion.

The intellectual life of medieval Jewry centered about the academy, it was by no means confined to it. Everywhere in the ghetto the language of learning was heard, the aura of scholarship perceptible. Education was the great purpose of medieval Jewish society. No parents were so envied as those of a precocious child. The rich merchant could find no better mate for his well-dowered daughter than a promising student.

Long before the advent of modern pedagogy the Jew engaged in adult education. The hours between the afternoon and evening prayers, the freedom of the Sabbath were especially devoted to class work or individual study. It was a rare Jew who did not participate in some fashion in this universal thought life, an unusual home from which books were entirely absent. In many a ghetto family, the housewife engaged in business so that her husband, freed from worldly care, might devote himself entirely to scholarship.

In his last testament, an obscure Jew of the fourteenth century leaves the following instruction—a passage which reveals the medieval attitude toward study:

"Each of my children shall always have in his house a chair on which a volume or two of the Talmud or its commentaries shall rest; so that he can always open a book when he comes home. Let him read what he can, making it a duty to read in any book he likes, at least four lines before taking his meals. Again he shall not omit to read each week the prescribed passage from the Torah, twice in the Hebrew text and once in the Aramaic translation."*

Even those who were mentally incapable of study had their place in the system. They might furnish meals for students, or contribute toward their support. And if this was beyond their means, they could always supply fire-wood or carry water for the academy and thus participate in Israel's devotion to its Law.

Thus did the study of the tradition penetrate medieval Jewry. None escaped its drag-net. The saint studied because of his piety, the intellectual to exercise his sharp wits. Even the worldling pursued scholarship, if only for the respect and acclaim it brought with it. In such a society, the Utopian dream of Plato found a refracted fulfilment. The philosophers of the ghetto were its kings; scholars sat in the seats of authority.

This system of education was the irreducible minimum of Jewish intellectual life. Every Jewish community, without exception, exhibited it at all times. But the tradition, absorbing as it was, did not exhaust the mental career of Jewry. Wherever freedom allowed for expansiveness, additional interests appeared. As soon as the Jew was exempt from persecution and need, other intellectual currents joined the river of Talmudic research.

---

* From *Ethical Wills*, by Israel Abrahams, Jewish Publication Society of America.

Of such broader pursuits the Jew of Central Europe was almost totally innocent. At no time did his circumstances allow for them. Bowed by the weight of persecution, it was enough that he studied the tradition. He did produce some poetry. But it scarcely deserves mention: it is poor in form, trite in spirit and, worst of all, largely elegaic. Its purpose generally was to bewail the fate of some massacred ghetto. Of philosophy, the German or French Jew had only what trickled to him from the reservoirs of Spain. Life in most lands was too exacting to allow for the dissipation of mental energy on any pursuits other than the traditional.

Only in Spain were freer interests manifested. There, an all too brief period of tolerance and prosperity permitted the Jewish spirit to expand. Not that the Spanish Jew did not study the tradition closely. In that respect he was typical of all Jewry. But even in his approach to the Bible and the Talmud, his broader vision expressed itself. When Abraham Ibn Ezra wrote commentaries on Scripture, they were strangely unlike those of the French or German Jew. His exposition was objective and critical; it did not hesitate to suggest interpretations which ran straight into the teeth of tradition. When Moses Maimonides codified the totality of Jewish Law, his code was such as no Jew of Central Europe would have written. It opened logically with a statement of first principles; it was systematic and lucid rather than confused and disorderly. Most typically it was not entirely orthodox. In its very attitude toward the heritage Spanish Jewry reflected its liberalism and its scientific approach.

But it was in his poetry and philosophy that the Jew of Spain revealed himself most completely. In these he displayed his atypical divergence from tradition, his catholicity of interest, his graceful humanism.

One passes lingeringly over the poets of the Spanish Golden Age. They possess a charm which still enchants, a message that even now strikes responsive chords. In the pessimism of Solomon Ibn Gabirol, the totality of man's frustration finds echo.

"The days of youth like clouds of smoke will pass.
Ere evening falls thou shalt be withered grass
Though morning saw thee like a lily blow." *

The ultimate tragedy of death is there in his lines:

"And when his hour is come, he passeth from the courts
of his house to the courts of Death,
And from the shadow of his chambers to the shadow of
Death,
And he shall strip off his embroidery and his scarlet
And shall put on corruption and the worm." †

One passes with the poet from the ephemerality of this world which is but "a shut-in dream" to its interpretation in a God of Light. With him one seeks the Infinite.

"I will flee from Thee to Thyself.
And I will shelter myself from Thy
wrath in Thy shadow,
And to the skirts of Thy mercies will
I lay hold until
Thou hast had mercy upon me." ‡

It is a far cry from this religious passion to the satirical lines of Abraham Ibn Ezra on his bad luck in business, on

---

* From *Selected Religious Poems of Solomon Ibn Gabirol*, Jewish Publication Society of America.
† *Ibid*.
‡ *Ibid*.

the flies that annoy him, on the watered wine which his host serves at a banquet, or on the fact that he is not placed in a seat of honor at the head of the banquet board.

It is another long leap from this poetry of sarcasm to the blasted romance of Moses Ibn Ezra, and to his gentle, melancholy hedonism.

"Suspect Fate—its gifts are the venom of asps sweetened
   with a dash of honey.
When it beguiles you at dawn, await its caprice at night.
Drink then by day—ere the day turn and the sun's silver
   turn gold—
And by night—ere it flee darkly with the morning star
   trailing in its wake."

The whole of man's life is but a slow progress to death.

"Let man remember while he lives
   That he is moving to death
Each day one easy stage
   Though he seems at rest,
Like one asleep aboard a ship
   That rushes on the wind's wings."

And the end of man is blind oblivion in the grave.

"Where are the graves of men dead upon the earth from
   yore?
Grave hewn over grave, sleeper prone upon sleeper.
In holes they huddle together—fragments of potsherd
   and broken rubies."

Among all these poets Judah Halevi stands preeminent by right of poetic genius, of personal charm and of diversity of gifts. In him are united all the varied breadths of Spanish Jewish life. A physician who was yet rabbi and poet, a philosopher who condemned metaphysics as "having flowers but no fruit," the whole wealth of his ill-fated age is distilled in his verse. No Central European Jew would have written as Judah Halevi wrote:

"Ophra washeth her garments in the waters
Of my tears, and spreadeth them out in the sunshine
   of her radiance.
She demandeth no water of the fountains, having my
   two eyes,
And no other sunshine than her beauty." *

No rabbi of medieval Germany would unbend to say of his beloved:

"The warmth of her cheeks, the veil of her hair
Golden like a topaz, covering
A brow of smoothest crystal—
She was like the sun making red in her rising
The clouds of dawn with the flame of her light." †

The ghettos of the Rhineland did not know the urbanity of a message to an absent friend which read:

"I lift my greetings on the wings of the wind
To my friend, when the heat of the day beginneth to
   cool
I ask him naught but to remember the day of our
   parting
When we made a covenant of love by an apple tree." ‡

---

* From *Selected Poems of Jehudah Halevi*, Jewish Publication Society of America.
   † *Ibid.*
   ‡ *Ibid.*

Only a Spanish Jew who had opportunity to observe nature, could write of a sunset:

"And the night, when the sun hath come down the steps
Of the starry host, captained now by the moon,
Is like an Ethiopian woman in raiment of gold
And of blue inset with crystals.
And the stars have lost their way into the heart of the
    sea
Like exiles banished from their homes. . . ." *

It is significant of this entire literary movement and revelatory of its latitude that its greatest spokesman should have written on a wide variety of themes. His richest creations, however, were concerned neither with the emotions nor with the praise of God, but with Palestine, the land of his fathers. When he spoke of Zion, he could say, in all earnestness:

"I am a harp to thy songs."

In all the range of Hebrew literature, no poetry is so rich, so authentic, so heavily brocaded with bold metaphor as are these hymns to a land. Expressive of a true emotion of the Jewish people, his odes to Zion became literary classics in every ghetto. And long after the brief hour of Spanish sunlight had faded, long after the Jew, under persecution, had forgotten the variegated literature which his genius had created in one favored land, even then the ghetto remembered and recited these poems of mourning and exaltation over an ancient homeland.

Nor did poetry exhaust the creativity of Spanish Jewry. It expressed itself also in the evolution of a scientific Hebrew grammar and rhetoric, in systematic Biblical criticism,

* From *Selected Poems of Jehudah Halevi*, Jewish Publication Society of America.

in research in the natural sciences and in treatises on ethics.

Side by side with this literary activity went the growth of a distinguished philosophy. The Saracens were master metaphysicians, and while there was no schematic philosophy in the Jewish tradition, the Jew learned quickly from his neighbors.

All of medieval Jewish philosophy came to a brilliant climax in the work of Moses Maimonides. Born at Cordova in 1135, serving in Egypt as physician to Saladin, this master was one of the encyclopedic minds of the Middle Ages. He was the author of a classic commentary of the Mishnah, of a huge code of Jewish Law, but above all, he created the *Guide to the Perplexed,* a synthesis of the Jewish religious tradition with Aristotelian philosophy.

In this physician, legalist, mathematician, logician and philosopher, there was no blind enslavement to traditional concepts. He did not hesitate to reduce the vivid, personal God of the Bible and Talmud to a metaphysical abstraction, to make the tradition teach Aristotelian cosmology, to deny for all practical purposes the immortality of all souls except that of the philosopher, and to make the acquisition of abstract truth the goal of the Law. In sharp contrast to the flexibility of the Jewish religion, he attempted to reduce to fixed form the principles of Judaism. Such radicalism was too much even for Spanish liberalism. So long as Maimonides lived, his critics dared not bait him. But once the lion was dead, chaos broke loose. The *Guide to the Perplexed* was attacked, excommunicated, burned and even denounced to Gentile authorities. It is a curious irony of Jewish history that this work, at first the scandal of the orthodox, came during the later Middle Ages to be the second bible of orthodoxy.

How this whole controversy might have ended is hard to say. Destiny cut it short. Within a century after the death of Maimonides, the weight of Christian oppression in Spain led to a crumbling of Jewish life. Poetry died in an uncongenial atmosphere. Philosophic quarrels were forgotten in the face of a major peril. Philosophy itself was discarded as disruptive of Jewish unity. The light faded from the Spanish Jewry world as the peace which had made possible a brief expansiveness was no more. The Jewish mind withdrew into its last citadel of sanity—the Talmud. By 1400, Spain was but slightly different from other lands. In it, too, the life of the intellect had become limited to the tradition.

The end of the fifteenth century marks a turning-point in the intellectual career of the medieval Jew. Spanish Jewry ceased to exist, its mental life was dissipated. It could no longer serve as a center for the diffusion of a liberalism which quickened less favored ghettos and which kept them alive to the progress of general thought. Until this time, the learning of the Jewries of Central Europe had been narrow but intense and, within limits, creative. Exhausted by long resistance to persecution and deprived of the stimulation which once came from Spain, the intellectual life of the Jew everywhere entered upon a period of rapid degeneration.

With the universal beclouding of the Jewish scene, with the cumulative misery of life, those Jewish minds which could not be content with the tradition alone found release in a strange universe of discourse—the Kabbalah. For long centuries a tradition of mystic doctrine had run parallel to that of the Law. In that stream of thought speculation had centered on the relation of God to the world. God, it was held, in His infinity, had overflowed first into intermediary emanations and then into the physical world. The soul of man was a fallen spark from the divine and must revert to its source through ascetic mortification, a knowledge of the Kabbalistic tradition and meditation.

As long as life was tolerable, this theosophy attracted only minds naturally given to mysticism. But when the lot of the Jew suddenly became hopeless, the Kabbalah spread like an infectious disease.

Lost in weird speculation in the Reality behind Appearance, the Kabbalist took refuge from a world of darkness. The Torah and Talmud were searched for hints of the mystic doctrine. Letters and numbers acquired new significances. A delirium swept the Jewish mind.

Most dangerous of all was the so-called "practical Kabbalah." Knowledge to the mystic was power. If only one knew the true doctrine, if one had the right combination of letters, numbers and words, the very physical world could be made to yield obedience. Out of this insane dream, came intense preoccupation with charms, formulæ and amulets, with secret significances and superstitious rites.

The Kabbalist was always a bit suspect to the ghetto. A sound mental hygiene repelled him and his esoteric teaching. But choked and tortured, the Jew breathed in particles of the system. In time, while actual Kabbalists were few, almost every Jewish mind had been infected in greater or less degree by these doctrines.

Much in the Kabbalist stream was noble and pure. It contained a subtle metaphysics, a mystic's path to God, and a morality that is often of unparalleled majesty. In the mystical schools of Safed in the sixteenth century, a delicate ethics of mercy was carefully taught. No system that could produce the saintliness of an Isaac Luria or Joseph Karo could be without virtues. That the Kabbalah became a fungus on the Jewish mind, a plague of superstition and magic, is due not alone to its inherent weaknesses. Some part of the responsibility must be laid upon Christian machinery of suppression which ultimately succeeded in degrading the Jewish mind as it crushed the body.

By 1500, the job had been done. For the next two hundred and fifty years, the ghetto was insulated against all stimulating alien currents. All through these two and a half centuries the world moved on and the Jew stood still. He clung to a Ptolemaic astronomy though Galileo, Copernicus and Newton had overturned the world. Of Bruno, Descartes and Leibnitz, of the new weltanschauung which they had constructed, he was completely unaware. He still concerned himself with doctrines and concepts which time had outmoded. Even news of the discovery of America penetrated into the ghetto belatedly. In the very generation of Spinoza and Locke, Jewry could still go frenzied over the claims of a false Messiah in Turkey.

No intellectual life could long endure in such a vacuum. Like plants, cultures require blasts of the fresh air that blows from free climates. They live only if pollenized by the life seeds of different breeds. Ventilation and cross-fertilization were denied to the Jewish intellect. It turned listless and withered.

The tragedy of the culture of Israel lies in this, that it lost both the opportunity and the ability to assimilate just at the time when the world had most to offer. Until the time of the Renaissance, Jewish thought had been alert and vigorous; it was ahead of its time. During this period, however, the Christian mind had little to contribute to it. By the time the civilization of the West became productive, the Jewish mind had been stunted. It no longer had access to the new civilization which had grown up so recently about it; it could not have absorbed it had the opportunity presented itself. Until the French Revolution, Jewry continued to live mentally under a medieval régime, to breathe the atmosphere of the fourteenth century though the eighteenth had already dawned.

For a time, while philosophy, poetry and the sciences died in the ghetto, the river of tradition flowed on in full strength. Eventually that, too, began to run dry. The study of the Law lapsed into casuistry and lost itself in empty intellectualism. By the time of the scientific revolution of the seventeenth century, the entire ghetto festered with stagnation.

No people that had lived as hardy an intellectual life as did the Jewish allows itself passively to degenerate. Twice during the eighteenth century Jewry quivered with life; twice, from its failing reserves, it drew the strength to resist its own decay. Half-consciously the Jew seemed to sense the perils which threatened him. He knew instinctively that his horizons were narrowing dangerously and that his thought life was being emptied of all reality. Two waves of reform swept East European Jewry—one in the schools, the other in the religious life.

In 1720, Polish Jewry produced Elijah of Vilna, one of the great masters in the tradition.

From the point of view of pure learning, Elijah was one of the greatest Talmudists in Jewish history. But most significant was his attempt to reform the schools. He insisted on the importance of an education in science and mathematics. In this way he attempted to resist the progressive limitation of the Jewish mind. He protested against the spirit of casuistry and aridity whch had come to dominate the Yeshivah. He demanded a critical, useful scholarship in the tradition. For all his withdrawal into an ivory tower, he saw keenly in which direction danger lay.

Israel, the Master of the Name, the second reformer of the ghetto, was born some twenty years before Rabbi Elijah of Vilna. Elijah was the scholar par excellence; Israel, by ghetto standards, almost completely unlearned. Elijah's entire life was spent in schools; Israel's, on the wooded hills of the Carpathians and among men.

After a youth spent in resisting attempts to educate him, Israel withdrew as a recluse to the mountains. There, apart from humanity, he meditated on God, the Law and its fulfilment. When he returned to the valley, he brought with him a new doctrine.

The teachings of the Master of the Name have been transmitted only through his disciples, each of whom gave to them his own personal coloration. But what his message was in itself can be stated with reasonable assurance.

First of all, Israel insisted on the immanence, the indwelling presence of God. But if the divine infuses all things, all things must be good. And if everything is good, man must be continuously happy. Melancholy and despondency are equivalent to a denial of the goodness of the God inherent in the world. The Law, to be sure, is a revelation of God, but its major purpose is to enable man to serve his Creator with joy.

In such a system, learning and especially a cold scholasticism had no place. From this view-point, even observance was meaningless unless it led to the exaltation that sprang from a consciousness of God's presence. More than anything else, religious joy was the gospel of the Master of the Name.

Nothing could be more pathetic than the eagerness with

which the Jewish masses seized upon the new doctrine. Its teachings became the core of a pietist movement in the ghetto known as Hasidism. To it literally millions of Jews subscribed. Not the novel theology of the Master, not even his humane ethics won their allegiance. The Jew snatched at Hasidism largely because he saw in it a remote chance for a taste of happiness. Here was a people poor and afflicted, suffering and outcast. The Jew could not change his hostile environment; Hasidism told him that he could modify his inner life to the point where even the pain of living might become cause for exaltation. Wherefore, he sang, and feasted and danced as the Master had prescribed; he prayed ecstatically, hoping to hypnotize himself into a happiness for which there was no material cause.

But if ghetto masses plunged into Hasidism for an escape from the unbearability of reality, they contributed much to the doctrine. Into this movement, they poured their starved yearnings, their moral judgments and their broken hopes. And if the message soon degenerated into a superstition, it left behind it a folk-lore and a folk ethics which accurately reflect the soul of the common Jew. He who would know the heart of the eighteenth-century Jew must turn not to scholars and not to schools but to the tradition of legend and morality which common people built about the Hasidic doctrine.

The world was too strong. The educational reforms of Rabbi Elijah created a stir and then were lost. Hasidism ran itself into blind channels of superstition where its soul died. Fundamental reforms in the ghetto were no longer possible. The world without was too cold; the spirit within, too weak. After these last quivers of life, the ghetto returned, as though hypnotized, to its old routine. Ceremonies were observed, but the vitality had gone out of group patterns. In the academies, the voice of learning was loud—but, despite the Rabbi of Vilna, instruction was still a matter of sterile brilliance.   Persecution and isolation had at last succeeded in killing the soul of Israel.   The ghetto remained in its stagnation.   It sat, like a crone, still mumbling ancient formulæ, now without meaning; still repeating gestures from which grace had fled; still dreaming vaguely of the glories of a vigorous life lost beyond hope of recalling.

And then, just at this time, when the Jewish body was broken, when spirit and soul had shriveled; just at this time when the vitality of Judaism was at its lowest ebb, when its powers of resistance and adaptation were gone, the storm of the Emancipation broke over Israel.

Chapter VII

RECAPITULATION AND CARRY-OVER

Non palma sine pulvere, said the ancient Romans. There is no attainment without the dust of struggle. The reader has been led a chase. He has been dragged over the whole restless itinerary of the Jew, has been compelled to examine the baggage of the spirit which Israel took with it from Palestine, has been harrowed by the grim record of medieval suppression and persecution. He has been introduced intimately to the religious, moral and intellectual life of the ghetto. It is a long way which he has been asked to travel, almost as long as that of the Jew himself, and perhaps as wearisome.

And yet, our discussion has not lost sight of the problems posed at the outset. The argument has been pointed toward the dual question of Jewish survival and contemporary Jewish character. We shall now attempt to disentangle from the text of the preceding chapters the relevant threads and weave them together into an explanation.

These are the factors which enabled Israel to survive despite its homelessness, its suffering and its humiliation:

A. *The Factors of Preliminary Preparation.*

Unconsciously, undeliberately, the Jew, while still in Palestine, had been preparing for his Exile. He had evolved institutions and a tradition which made it possible for him

121

to pass from the normal existence of a people in its own land to the abnormality of a long exile.

1. *The Preparation of the Diaspora.* The Jew found ready for himself in the Diaspora a chain of Jewish communities. In these, Judaism had adapted itself to an alien world. Into these he could slip without undue jolting of his loyalty.

2. *Unifying Central Authorities.* When the Temple, the Sanhedrin and the state had been destroyed, the Jew, as we have already seen, was not left without central regulating bodies. Until the fifth century, Palestine served in a directive capacity. From the sixth to the tenth centuries, the academies of Babylonia united the Jewish world. These two administrative bodies made possible concerted and uniform adjustment by the Jew to his new status. After the tenth century, each Jewry had made its own adjustment and was able to stand on its own feet.

3. *The Heritage of Palestine.* With him in his wanderings the Jew carried a tradition. He possessed a vast literature with which to occupy himself. His life conformed to pre-established patterns of conduct which assured the uniformity of Jewish practise throughout the world and threw a protective wall of habit around the intellectual and moral content of Judaism.

Such were the elements of preliminary preparation. Had they not been present when the hour of transition arrived, had there been no Diaspora refuge, no regulatory centers to ease the passage, no heritage of a literature and folk-ways, the career of the Jew might perhaps have ended in the year 70.

B. *The Factor of External Pressure.*

At no time during the period we have described did the world cease to exercise pressure upon the Jewish world. Political persecution, economic degradation and social exclusion combined to drive the Jew to ever stronger internal cohesion. The church, true enough, welcomed conversion, but the machinery of Christendom as a whole went to discourage centrifugal tendencies in Jewry. There was almost something mechanical about the relation of the two worlds. The more force Gentile society applied, the more Jews cohered.

It is interesting to speculate upon what might have happened had the Christian been not endlessly hostile, but sympathetic. Would the Jew then have wrapped the cloak of his identity stubbornly about him, or would he, like the man in the fable, gradually have opened it and, when the sun became pleasingly warm, have discarded it entirely? But such speculations are idle. The fact remains that the world put its full weight behind the effort to suppress the Jew. It evoked in response the united front which all Jewry presented.

C. *The Ideological Factor.*

"The world is my idea," said Schopenhauer, in opening his great philosophical treatise. "My ideas have helped preserve my world," the Jew might well have said.

1. *Religious Concepts with Survival Value.* Israel was equipped for its ordeal by a set of concepts and ideas which mitigated the horror of Jewish life, and which compensated the Jew for his sufferings.

The belief in the doctrine of a Chosen People enabled the Jew to maintain his pride in the face of constant humiliation. The notion of a mission, a central rôle in the cosmic drama, gave him a sense of dignity and importance. Faith in the divinity of the Law made loyalty to it a matter of allegiance to God. The confidence that his trials would be rewarded by immortality equipped the Jew with patience. The hope of a final vindication enabled him to endure his present for the sake of a future justification.

2. *The Contrast between Judaism and Christianity.* In addition, the Jew was acutely aware of sharp contrasts between his own world and that beyond the ghetto walls. He felt that his religion was simpler, more readily credible. He knew that Christian and Moslem alike granted its truth. Had he wished for escape, he would have had difficulty in bringing himself to accept the complicated and, to him, unreasonable dogmas of the church.

3. *The Contrast in Morality.* Morally, too, he believed in his own superiority. Trained and disciplined in an ethical code, he found that Christian society fell far short of his standards. The abandonment of Judaism seemed to involve the exchange of a moral excellence for an inferior way of life.

D. *The Factor of a Compensating Culture.*

In the pleasures and glories of the world the Jew had no share. He consoled himself with the satisfaction derived from his own intellectual life.

1. *Culture as an Escape.* Into the study of his sacred literature and tradition he threw himself. It gave free play to his restless mind, it intrigued him with its subtle difficulties. And all the while he felt that his research was more than an intellectual pastime, that it was the truest service of God. As such, it evoked a tense enthusiasm and a fanatical devotion.

In books and ideas the Jew found an escape from actuality. They afforded an outlet for his pent-up energies. In the mastery of them he won compensation for the sacrifices he was compelled to make.

2. *Mass Education as a Discipline.* Nor must we lose sight of the social effects of the ghetto's system of mass education. Every Jew participated in the process to some extent. Each Jew in consequence was indoctrinated with Jewish ideas, ideals and attitudes. When the literary giants of a people become its folk heroes, when scholars and authors are household names, when the concepts of a tradition are common property, even the masses are won to group loyalty. For, from knowledge of a rich culture, comes pride in it. And pride leads inevitably to devotion.

The medieval Jew knew nothing about modern publicity and propaganda. In his own unconscious fashion, he exploited an educational system to create a public opinion, to infuse each Jew with pride of identity and with loyalty.

E. *The Factor of Segregation.*

The total effect of the entire medieval scheme was to segregate the Jew completely from his environment. Politically, socially, intellectually, he was cut off from all contact with the larger scene of man's activities. Ostracism is never a pleasure to an individual; it is the very bread of life to a minority group. The Jew might languish in his confinement but Jewish group life thrived. The leaders of Israel were acutely aware of that fact. They exploited it consciously and deliberately.

1. *The Deliberate Use of Isolation for Survival.* In Jewish Law there is to be found a juristic phrase, *hukkath goyim,* "statutes of the Gentiles." The term has an ancient and honorable history. It is borrowed from the eighteenth chapter of Leviticus which reads, "Ye shall not walk in their statutes." When the danger of assimilation became a real

one, the rabbis of the Talmudic age took hold of this pro-
hibition and expanded it into a general rule. Under their
reinterpretation, the Biblical phrase came to mean that the
Jew must avoid any imitation of the Gentile, that he must
strive to be different from his neighbor.

All through the Middle Ages, the Talmudic rule was
calculatingly exploited. The very fact that an institution
was Gentile was sufficient to make it taboo for Jews. Every
mark of distinction between Jew and Gentile was stressed,
every tendency to obliterate such marks was enjoined as a
violation of the Biblical ordinance. This conscious accentuation of difference went so far that Jews would not adopt
even wise and reasonable practises if they were prevalent
among non-Jews. Even so cultured a Jew as Maimonides,
in his code of Jewish Law, quotes the tradition on this issue
approvingly. "Jews do not walk in the statutes of Gentiles.
They must not resemble them in garb, in hair-dress, nor in
anything of like nature. Even as Scripture saith, 'Ye shall
not walk in their statutes'; or again, 'Lest ye be ensnared
after them.'"

The existence of such legal principle may be deprecated
but it is valid testimony to the deliberate use of segregation
for survival. The wider the gap between the two groups,
the more difficult it would be for the individual to pass from
one to the other. How keenly the Jew appreciated the
value of his isolation for survival can be seen from the fact
that in the Napoleonic age Jewish leaders in Holland objected to release from restriction and to emancipation from
confinement. Not that they loved freedom less, but that they
feared its effects on group life and solidarity.

From the view-point of group survival, this attitude was
pointedly sane. Isolation, enforced and self-imposed, guar-

anteed the continuity of the tradition. Consider its effects.
It protected Jewish culture from alien, disturbing influences.
Civilizations may crumble from inner decay, they fall also
because new styles of thought and novel modes of conduct
disturb their inertia. Greek slaves undermined Roman
society. The Saracens and Byzantines, through their systems
of thought, delivered the *coup de grace* to the Christian
system of feudal Europe. From experiences analogous to
these, the Jewish organism was spared. The ghetto had so
little knowledge of Gentile belief and practise that it never
considered seriously the value of other social patterns. In
complete oblivion of Christian universities, the Jew never
questioned the unique worth of the Yeshivah. No reading
of the newly-born science and philosophy of the outer world
disturbed the Jewish weltanschauung. No intimate contact
with the Gentile ever led the Jews to question the unique
wisdom and virtue of his scheme of life. Within an air-tight
compartment, no alien mode of thought could ruffle his
intellectual peace, no contrasts could crack his assurance,
no novel patterns of living could move his inveterate
habits.

2. *Segregation and Social Unity.* Further, segregation
guaranteed the continuity and potency of Jewish social pressure. Every society tends to force the individual into conformity with its norms. Only when enough individuals rebel
does a social order undergo revolutionary transformation.
On the Jewish "island within" social pressure was un-
opposed. Every Jew observed all of Jewish practise and,
within narrow limits, followed the prescribed intellectual
paths. Each minute divergence in conduct or belief was immediately apparent and instantaneously suppressed. Many
an irreligious Jew must at times have grown weary of inces-

sant synagogue-going. But to synagogue he went, none the less. Otherwise the whole ghetto would have noticed his absence. Many a silent heretic must have set rebelliously over the Talmud, not daring to speak his mind in the face of the united will of Jewry. Conformity was much the easier way. Heresies and heretical movements were surprisingly rare in medieval Jewry. Even a headstrong dissenter must have thought twice before airing some heterodox opinion which would disrupt the unanimity of the ghetto. No Jew ever forgot that unity against the Gentile was to be valued beyond all else. And if neither group pressure nor the need for solidarity restrained the potential heretic, there was always the dreadful ban of excommunication. Most Jews obviously had no desire for rebellion, but against those who were so inclined, the ghetto exerted its full powers. Not even in ancient Sparta had the weight of society's will been so dominating as it was on the Judengasse.

3. *Economics and Survival.* Even economic factors conspired, under this scheme of isolation, to support survival. For, although business relations often brought the Jew out of his shell, within the ghetto, trade and commerce operated to maintain the *status quo.* To this extent, at least, economic persecution defeated itself. In its very forcing of the Jew into a few crafts and trades, it enabled tradition to tame these poor monopolies. Had the Jew participated in the more general economy, he must of necessity have sacrificed some part of ancestral practise to it. But, because Jewish business was largely confined to Jews, it was free to respect traditional sanctities and to regulate itself in rabbinical courts. In this way a conflict between economic interest and group welfare was avoided.

As a result, industry and trade enforced tradition. When Jews dealt with Jews, it was natural to suspend business for religious festivals. It was easy to observe the Sabbath and Holy Days when there was nothing afoot in any event. There was no difficulty involved in reciting prescribed afternoon prayers if customer and shopkeeper interrupted their negotiations automatically for that purpose. In a world where a culture dominates an economy, the economy will in return unwittingly support the culture.

4. *Segregation and Attrition.* Last of all, segregation obviated attrition; it guaranteed that there would be no gradual wearing away of Jewish loyalties, habits and ideas. No person breaks suddenly with his environment and background. A period of preparation, however unconscious, is a prerequisite. Had the Jew had intimate contact with the outer world, such preparation would have been possible. He might have learned to prefer Gentile ways, might gradually have abandoned his own for their sake. His ideas might slowly have been transformed, his loyalties imperceptibly transferred. When he had come to feel himself more closely identified with interests and attitudes other than Jewish, he could then have slipped easily into assimilation with another world. But the Jew had no such contact; he had no opportunities, had he wished for them, for a period of preparation. He could leave the ghetto if he desired. But it was for a world that was frighteningly strange and unknown, in which he would find no familiar landmark. He could desert at any time. The church waited with eager arms and the baptismal font was always ready. But he had to do it in one wild leap from the accustomed to the unfamiliar. He must pass from within to without in only one step.

Some few Jews there were in the Middle Ages who made the jump. But as a rule the Jew had no desire for flight. The change involved was too violent to be attractive. It was more comfortable to stay put.

Such, then, are the factors of Jewish survival: a preliminary preparation, an external pressure, an ideological equipment, a compensating culture and a preservative isolation. The wheels of the mechanism are now apart. Or, more aptly, the body has been dissected. For, the life of a group resembles less an inanimate machine than a living organism. Its disparate aspects fuse and melt into each other in a unity which defies clean intellectual discrimination. But when the lesson in anatomy is over, a haunting suspicion still remains. The brain, the skin, the muscles and the heart are revealed.

But is there not in the body perhaps some vital force, some Bergsonian élan which eludes the finest probe? And in the organism that was Israel, might there not have been present some analogous power of persistence that no scalpel can uncover? Did the Jewish people perhaps possess a group will-to-live, a collective determination, a resolution to persist? Is it not possible that some such influence, part psychological, part metaphysical, part even supernatural, must be postulated even after the most careful anatomical investigation?

There are times when the observer inclines toward such an assumption. There are moments when even the factors we have enumerated seem not quite adequately to account for the miracle of Jewish survival under such incredible conditions. Like the disciplined biologist who at times toys with the idea of a life force or vital principle, the historian of Jewish life is tempted to postulate some element not entirely susceptible of reasoned analysis. But ours is a rationalistic age; we have all been trained to make liberal use of Occam's razor. We will not make avoidable assumptions; we will not multiply entities beyond necessity.

The same discussion which throws light on the first of our two riddles, that of survival, illuminates in part the second, that of contemporary Jewish character. There are in the Jew to-day qualities, attitudes and peculiarities of personality which are the direct results of his medieval experiences.

The gregariousness of Jews is one trait which asserts itself constantly. Jews, if they are poor, huddle together in East Sides and Whitechapels. Even if they are prosperous, they tend to occupy gilded ghettos. The average Jew likes to live with and among Jews. As a result, every city with a considerable population has its distinctly Jewish quarters at all levels of economic position. At least in part, the explanation of this phenomenon lies in the group habit established over long centuries. After generations of living together, the process has become next to instinctive. Long after ghettos have ceased to be compulsory, Jewish children are born and reared in Jewish neighborhoods. They tend naturally to seek them when as adults they establish their own households.

In his economic life as well, the modern Jew reflects his medieval background. For centuries the Jew has been excluded from agriculture and the handicrafts. He has been forced to become a petty trader, a shopkeeper or a merchant. Even the emancipation could not dissipate an inclination developed over long periods of time. To this day the Jew earns his living largely through trade. While notable exceptions have appeared with changes of circumstances, he is still essentially the middleman of each economy in which he participates.

It has become the fashion for the anti-Semite to condemn the Jew as a parasite, who derives his livelihood from handling the products of the labor of others. The question of the productivity or parasitism of the merchant and trader must be left to economic theorists. But if Jews find themselves largely a people of shopkeepers and merchants, they have been made what they are by the spiritual forebears of their modern critics.

Whether the Jew is an unusually dishonest business man, whether he is less scrupulous in his dealings than is the Gentile, is an open question. There is no way of taking a census of the relative number of Jews and non-Jews who engage in sharp practises. Most sweeping generalizations about whole peoples are more often the result of quick prejudice than of deliberate investigation. The belief that Jews are unethical business men is of a kind with the statement that all Frenchmen are philanderers, and that all Englishmen are without a sense of humor. There are, to be sure, amorous Frenchmen, dull Britons and dishonest Jews; but these qualities are never confined to, nor exceptionally exhibited by, any special group. It is a safe presumption that, common prejudice notwithstanding, the Jew is as scrupulous a business man as is his neighbor.

Only this grain of truth is there in the common libel. It seems roughly true that the Jew is shrewd, energetic and ambitious in his business. Even this statement must be qualified. The Jews of North Africa and Arabia show none of the aggressiveness which the Western world associates with Jews. But if this trait be truly Jewish, then it is the product of medieval treatment of the Jew. Medieval bishops, dukes and church councils have no slight share in the fact that a twentieth-century Jew proves to be successful in his management of a department store. In the world which we described, the Jew had to be shrewd and aggressive if he was to live at all. Life had been made so difficult for him that it called for intense preoccupation with economic matters. Even to-day a Jew, to attain position, must work much harder than a Gentile. If any special aptitude for business exists among Jews, it is not a matter of blood, but of circumstance. The Jewish child in the Middle Ages grew up in a home in which the question of a livelihood was one that taxed all energies. He watched his father's thrift, industry and resourcefulness. He learned to imitate them.

The Middle Ages, moreover, have left their mark on the Jew's psychology. Thus, Jews have never quite lost their attitude of suspicion toward the Gentile world. In the midst of perfect security, they fear constantly a change of heart. They never quite trust the friendship of the non-Jew. In their experience, such kindliness has been so rare as to be suspect. They are likely to look for ulterior motives in the Christian, especially when he comes to them bearing gifts.

Nor have Jews ever quite stripped themselves of their protective secretiveness. They will not reveal their internal quarrels. They are frank and open among themselves; in the presence of non-Jews they become reserved. They still tend to feel that the less the Gentile knows about them, the better.

And, subconsciously, most Jews have acquired from their medieval background a sense of superiority. Even the Jew who is a social climber condescends the least bit to the very Gentile whose friendship he is trying to win.

Such psychological quirks are distasteful and unfortunate. Jews, when they are conscious of them, deplore them sincerely. But they represent a carry-over from a grimmer day when secretiveness was a real protection and a sense of superiority an indispensable compensation.

The influence of the medieval ghetto on the contemporary Jew reveals itself perhaps most powerfully in the strong sense of loyalty to the group which most Jews feel. The modern world has done much to transform the individual Jew and his collective life. It has not yet succeeded in dissipating an intense allegiance developed under pressure. Long after the Jew has ceased to be conscious of any reasonable grounds for his sentimental attachments, long after he has discarded his traditional theology, has departed from every ancestral practise and forgotten his inherited culture, he still has the sense of *belonging*. Every misfortune to Jews pains him, every liberation is a cause for personal joy. Without quite knowing why, he is deeply pained at the persecution of Jews in Europe, intimately humiliated when a fellow-Jew has disgraced himself, elevated when a Nobel Prize falls to one of his number.

A strange negative unity has also survived from the ghetto. Modern Jews possess no internal cohesion. They are divided on every issue which normally separates men and on some issues peculiar to themselves. But in one respect they are entirely in harmony: they stand together under attack. The German Jew has long despised his Russian brother, but after the Kishinef massacres, he rallied to his defense. The Polish Jew has long resented the condescension of the German, but he has derived little satisfaction from the rise of Hitler. Even the most rabid anti-Zionist, the most thoroughgoing assimilationist, found himself strangely and profoundly shaken by all that has gone on in Palestine of late.

The Jews of the Western world have been generous in coming to the relief of less fortunate Jewries. Millions of dollars poured into Eastern Europe after both World Wars. Much of this was due to a strong sense of philanthropy, much the result of high-pressure campaigns, but fully as much of the lavishness was due to the fact that Jews remember a bitter lesson taught to them in feudal Europe—the lesson that they either hang together or hang separately.

Besides, the Jew has inherited a strong impulse toward charity. In the ghetto, philanthropy was a prime virtue. Its special place was due in part to the tradition, in part to the fact that poverty among medieval Jews was so widespread that sharing was a condition of life. The tradition has been largely discarded; the rigors of medieval life have been ameliorated, but this predilection for charity has survived in the modern Jew.

The moral values of the ghetto generally have shown a surprising hardiness. They have outlived the ghetto itself, its religious faith, custom and ceremony, even loyalty to the Jewish group. Many a de-Judaized Jew exhibits a strong sense of the sanctity of life, a bitter resentment against all forms of exploitation. To him these ethical judgments may appear as universal human ideals. He would scoff at the notion that these standards are part of a Jewish heritage. None the less, the moral ideas of the ghetto have been subtly communicated from generation to generation. Not all modern Jews are idealists, and of those who are, not all have derived their idealism from their past. But ghetto morality still lives among the Jews of our day in a transfigured immortality.

One trait of modern Jewish character is a direct product of medieval experience—the intellectualism of the Jew. From the Yeshivah have come a reverence for brilliance and acumen, a respect for books and ideas, and an insistence upon education. The ghetto Jew had all of these traits. He transmitted them to his posterity. As he was a *luft-mensch,* a student and a debater, so are his descendants. In the eagerness of the Jewish intellect, the whole history of Israel reveals itself. And if a Jew is a successful author or a gifted scientist, the cause is to be sought not in his heredity, nor in superior mental capacities, but in the fact that during the Middle Ages, learning and scholarship by necessity became folk ideals. The afterglow of a world that has died still illuminates contemporary Jews in laboratories and libraries.

It must be remembered that we have carried the history of the Jew only through the Middle Ages. Our explanation of his survival and of the making of his character is limited to the same period.

The divisions of history into ancient, medieval and modern are, in great measure, entirely arbitrary. They represent only a convenient device of the scribe. But, in so far as they reflect actual distinctions, the Middle Ages for the Jew were of much longer duration than for the rest of mankind. With other peoples, medievalism ended with the Renaissance, the Reformation and the scientific revolution. For the Jew, the modern era began only with the dissolution of the system of suppression; in other words, with the French Revolution of 1789.

To our record of the Jew a long sequel must now be appended. This will relate how, during the eighteenth century, he was suddenly emancipated. It will tell how ghetto walls collapsed, corroded by the acids of modern rationalism, undermined by the slogans of the French Revolution, and bombarded by a new economic order. One by one, we shall watch the old factors of survival cease to be effectively operative.

We shall see the suddenly emancipated Jew, blinded by the light that streams in on him, step forth into a larger world.

We shall watch him stagger and grope bewilderedly as he strives to find his way, dazzled by the unwonted illumination and confused by the absence of ancient landmarks. We shall notice, too, how strange and novel influences began to play upon him, how they transform and remake his character until he becomes the person we know to-day. In brief, we shall hear the last testimony on how the Jew survived and what made his present personality. And, throughout, we shall see him standing in the Valley of Decision, asking himself why he lived, trying to make up his mind upon the ultimate issue: Shall the Jew continue to exist, or shall he turn to the world and cry, *"Plaudite cives,* the tragic comedy of Jewish existence is ended."

TRANSITION

Chapter VIII

THE PROCESS OF EMANCIPATION

Western Phase

More than the Bastille fell on July 14, 1789; in its capitulation feudalism gave up the ghost. Through the thunder of falling beams could be heard the tolling of a death knell. An old order had changed, yielding place to new. Yet for the nations of Western Europe the French Revolution was a spectacular rather than a decisive event. It introduced no violent changes in the tenor of mass life; the medieval economy and polity had been for all practical intents long since dead. The events of the last decades of the eighteenth century were little more than the elaborate rites of a decent burial.

But here, too, the Jew ran true to form as an anomaly among the nations of the world. For him alone the French Revolution inaugurated a real revolution. Only his world experienced radical transformation. When the smoke and dust of struggle subsided, his seclusion was at an end; he had been transformed from a passive and indifferent spectator into an active and interested participant; his personality and character had been remade; his very existence had been challenged by the change.

The Jew then did not slip unconsciously from medievalism into modernity; he was catapulted into it headlong. Just as

141

he passed from Palestine to the Diaspora in one decisive step, so he moved dizzily from the Middle Ages into the modern world within a few fateful decades. The ghetto of 1750 may be assigned chronologically to the eighteenth century; in spirit it lived in the fourteenth. For five hundred years the withdrawal of the Jew had become more and more complete. The Renaissance had come and gone, the Protestant Reformation had been born, an industrial economy had been created, a new science and a new philosophy had been conceived: but, except in isolated instances, none of these had penetrated into the Judengasse. There time had stopped. For the half-millennium prior to the French Revolution, the Jew was a living anachronism, a chronological absurdity. And then time remembered that it had forgotten him. It seized him by the forelock and dragged him in fifty years over a span of five hundred. The general history of Europe closes the Middle Ages with the fourteenth or fifteenth centuries; it allows three to four hundred years for the transition to modern society. The Jewish historian turns one page—dated July 14, 1789.

Sudden and catastrophic as was the passage of the Jew into the world, it was not without prognostic symptoms. On review prophetic signs of what was to occur can be discovered as early as the seventeenth century. It has already been indicated that for some time before the formal dissolution of the ghetto a lethargy had fallen upon it. Its vitality ebbed, its intellectual life stagnated. The virile powers of resistance which had once characterized it were dissipated. Like some debilitated organism, it lay helpless, a potential prey to any disruptive disease which might attack it. In its weakness, it was ready for the dissolving events of the late eighteenth century.

The first actual breach in the wall was made by the new commercial economy. Even in the days of most complete segregation, Jew and Gentile had done business with each other. Economic interest constituted as a result a persistent threat to the stability of the ghetto.

In many a European court in the seventeenth century, a prodigy appeared: the Jewish business agent of a Christian sovereign. The rulers of Austria and of the German states discovered that the Jew had other uses besides that of a sponge. He was often an astute business man, he had connections throughout the ghettos which gave him control of large sums of money. He was especially valuable as a purchasing agent, as a financier for an extravagant royal ménage or a costly military campaign. And if he was an infidel, after all, business was business. The restrictions, so long in effect against the whole despised group, were lifted so that these useful individuals might be free to come and go, buy and sell, and have cash ready when the exchequer was low.

One of the first of these *Hofjuden,* or Court Jews, was Jacob Bassevi, who served Ferdinand II of Austria during the Thirty Years' War. As a reward for his services as a banker, he was given a title of nobility, together with a patent which is eloquent of the restrictions suffered by more typical Jews. By royal decree, Jacob Bassevi was free "to engage in any business whatever, in any part of the empire, whether cities, towns or market-places, in Prague and Vienna, and other places where Jews are allowed to reside or are not; to acquire property and to reside anywhere he pleases."

The existence of such Hofjuden was, of course, a distinct advantage to Jewish communities. It gave them an advocate at the court. Thus, Samson Wertheimer, also financial agent

to the Hapsburgs, used his influence to secure the suppression
of an especially vicious anti-Semitic treatise which appeared
at Frankfort in 1700.

Thus it came to pass that for a century and a half before
the French Revolution a few Jews made contact with the
world. It was, they discovered, a remarkable place. It was
broad and spacious, cultured, elegant and rich in opportunity. They brought back glowing accounts of strange
wonders, they sowed the seed of restlessness and discontent.
The young man heard and his ambition was fired; the page
of Jewish learning appeared tedious at the thought of new
worlds waiting for conquest.

Together with bills of exchange and large fortunes, these
favorites of fate brought back shadowy invoices of European
culture. These told of a science that had shattered ancient
theologies, of the decline of authoritarianism in religion, of
a cult called Deism, of a new faith in Reason. They hinted
of a literature easily as rich as that of the tradition, of majestic
music and captivating arts such as the Jew had never experienced. They reported most significantly that there were
some in that unknown world which lay beyond the walls
who believed in human equality—even for Jews—and who
planned a new order based on liberty for all.

For a new spirit was abroad in the world, a new dream
and a new hope. The old Christian dogmatism was dissolving before the onslaughts of the Newtonian physics; men
were talking of a universal religion of reason, of natural
rights which all men share merely by virtue of the fact that
they are men. In such an intellectual atmosphere, religious
tolerance was rapidly becoming an accepted ideal. At first,
attempts were made to limit the application of these new
concepts. Pierre Bayle and John Locke, for example, both

felt that religious forbearance should not be extended to Catholics—it was as yet superfluous to talk of Jews. But words are potent things; they are possessed of a peculiar dynamism. There was really no way of keeping concepts like tolerance, liberty and equality from finding some application even to Jews.

The extension of eighteenth-century ideals was by no means a steady process. Some of the most enlightened minds of Europe, for all their liberalism, opposed measures of emancipation. Frederick the Great of Prussia may have been, by the standards of his time, a most progressive monarch, but he was not above reviving old restrictive legislation against the Jews. Even Voltaire, great champion of human rights, knight errant of the Enlightenment, hated Jews as bitterly as any benighted bishop. Goethe, who can scarcely be accused of Christian orthodoxy, opposed solidly any move to alleviate the conditions of Jewish existence. Fichte had this interesting suggestion to make with reference to Jews:

> "The only way I see by which civil rights can be conceded to them is to cut off all their heads in one night and to set new ones on their shoulders, which should contain not a single Jewish idea. The only means of protecting ourselves against them is to conquer their promised land and send them thither."

On the other hand, there were not wanting those who recognized the implications for Jews of the new ideology. Lessing, beyond all others, strove to present to the world the cause of a persecuted people. In a day when the Jew was despised as an inferior moral being, he dared to make a Jew the hero of his drama, *Nathan the Wise,* and to portray him

as an ideal personality.   In the thin chorus of protest, Mon
tesquieu joined.

> "You Christians complain that the Emperor of China
> roasts all Christians in his dominions over a slow fire;
> you behave much worse toward Jews, because they do
> not believe as you do.   If any of our descendants should
> ever venture to say that the nations of Europe were cul-
> tured, your example will be adduced to prove that they
> were barbarians.   The picture that they will draw of
> you will certainly stain your age, and spread abroad
> hatred of all your contemporaries."

Two years before the Revolution, Mirabeau published a
tribute to the Jewish philosopher, Moses Mendelssohn.   In
the course of it, he turned to the problem of the status of
the Jew.

> "If you wish the Jews to become better men and useful
> citizens, then banish every humiliating distinction, open
> to them every avenue of gaining a livelihood; instead of
> forbidding them agriculture, handicrafts and the
> mechanical arts, encourage them to devote themselves to
> these occupations."

The status of the Jew became a pet subject for debate.
Shortly before the Revolution, the Royal Society of Science
and Arts in Metz offered a prize for the best essay on the
subject, "Are there means to make the Jews happier and
more useful in France?"   But all this discussion touching
the emancipation of the Jew, all the argument pro and con,
was confined largely to literati and philosophers.   In their
ivory tower they debated the problem, while life wagged
on in its old way undeflected by their discussion.   The whole
issue might have remained entirely academic, even after the

Revolution, had it not been weighted by economics. With
the coming of the industrial revolution came also the rise
of the bourgeoisie and the deification of business. The man
of commerce has always been an anarchist. When law and
convention choke the channels of trade, he rebels, always.
By the middle of the eighteenth century, the middle classes
of Europe were in smoldering revolt against all those remnants of the feudal order which restrained the free movement of trade. The restrictions imposed upon Jews were,
to bourgeois eyes, part and parcel of the whole outmoded
system. When the physiocrat, Quesnay, insisted that "the
most useful work any legislative body can do is to abolish
useless laws," he was attacking incidentally the machinery
of the economic suppression of the Jew.

For profit is no respecter of persons: a Jew and a Christian are alike so far as the "economic man" is concerned. As
a corollary to the protest against feudal paternalism, went a
protest, with less enthusiasm, against the restraints which
made difficult profitable dealings with Jews.

The Jew, especially the economically favored Jew, was
aware of what was happening in the world. He knew that
an intellectual tide had set in in his favor, that contemporary
economic tendencies were freighted with promise for him.
A schism appeared in Jewish life. The masses continued as
always, controlled by hypnotic momentum of two thousand
years. But the materially and socially elect were now of
divided soul. Their loyalties to the ghetto wavered in the
presence of a new hope. They imported teachers of French
and German to prepare their children against the day of
liberation. The Talmud and tradition were neglected in
favor of books alien to Judaism. With each step upward on
the ladder of wealth, they filled their homes more and more

with a foreign art and music. Long before Germany and France told them that they were French and German citizens, they identified themselves in their own minds with the larger life of the lands of their residence. And because they felt that they had no justified part in the society they desired, they out-Teutoned Teutons and out-Frenched the Franks. They even, in imitation of the Gentiles, held salons where the half-citizen of the ghetto could discuss the anti-Semitism of Voltaire and the critical philosophy of Kant. And when, miracle of miracles, some Christian, either unusually broadminded, like Lessing and Schlegel, or else too shabby to be concerned about his social position, attended their gatherings, the cup of happiness was filled to overflowing. But not the most sanguine in the upper stratum of ghetto society really expected the tempest which was brewing.

From the Jewish angle, the Revolution in France opened most inauspiciously. With the fall of the old régime came a period of disorder during which Jews, especially in Alsace, were vigorously attacked. Public opinion, however, had so advanced that in the Rights of Man, adopted on August 23, 1789, a clause could be inserted which read, "No one shall be molested on account of his religious opinions, in so far as their outward expression does not disturb public order as established by law."

When, however, liberals sought to implement this statement of principle, to carry it over into actual legislation in relief of the Jewish lot, ancient prejudices proved too strong. Not even a world-shaking revolution could shatter so quickly an inveterate bias. For all the eloquence of Mirabeau and the Abbé Grégoire, the Jewish issue was referred by the National Assembly to committees where it regularly died. Ultimately, however, the issue was forced. After all, it was uncomfortably inconsistent for the revolutionary to mouth the three slogans of the Revolution—liberty, fraternity and equality—always with the reservation, except for Jews. When in September of 1791 the final draft of the Constitution was presented to the Assembly without any statement concerning Jews, a Jacobin deputy rose to protest. "I believe that freedom of thought does not permit any distinction in political rights on account of a man's creed. The recognition of this equality is always being postponed. . . . I demand that the motion for adjournment be withdrawn and a decree passed that the Jews in France enjoy the privileges of active citizenship." The motion, despite some opposition, was adopted and the next day a law was passed abrogating all discriminatory legislation directed against Jews. Thus in two years the age-old machinery of suppression was scrapped by French liberalism.

To the upper levels of Jewish society, those touched by the world, all this seemed the miraculous fulfilment of a dream. Cerf Berr, an Alsatian Jew, wrote rhapsodically to his fellows throughout France:

"At length the day has arrived on which the veil is torn asunder which covered us with humiliation! We have at last again obtained the rights of which we have been deprived for eighteen centuries. How deeply at this moment should we recognize the wonderful grace of the God of our forefathers! On the 27th of September we were the only inhabitants of this great realm who seemed doomed to eternal humiliation and slavery, and on the very next day, a memorable day which we shall always commemorate, didst Thou inspire these immortal legislators of France to utter one word which caused sixty thousand unhappy beings, who had hitherto lamented their hard lot, to be plunged suddenly into the intoxicating joys of the purest delight. God chose the noble

French nation to reinstate us in our due privileges, and to bring us to a new birth, just as in former days He selected Antiochus and Pompey to degrade and oppress us. . . ."

Even to ghetto masses, to whom such eloquence was unin‧telligible, all this was a bewildering and refreshing experience. They generally greeted their change of status enthusiastically; they availed themselves of their new rights and privileges; they learned, in an incredibly short time, to take them for granted. Breathlessly, they watched the extension of equality throughout Western Europe.

The solvents of the Revolution were too pervasive to be confined to France alone. The new ideals seeped into surrounding countries. They were exported deliberately, first by the Armies of the Republic, and then by those of Napoleon. As Alexander once had planted Greek culture throughout the Orient in the track of his phalanxes, so the Little Corporal dropped the seeds of revolutionary ideas wherever his foot struck. The entire feudal order collapsed like a house of cards, carrying to ruin the ghetto.

Within twenty-five years from the Fall of the Bastille, the Jew in every land in Western Europe had attained at least partial emancipation. In 1796, over the opposition of Jewish leaders, emancipation came to the Jews of Holland. In 1808, the Jews of the Napoleonic Kingdom of Westphalia were declared full citizens, subject to no special restrictions. In 1811, the Duke of Frankfort sold to his Jewish community a body of rights such as were current elsewhere. In 1812, Prussia accorded the Jew equality, with the single reservation that he might not hold office. Only in Bavaria, Austria and Saxony were concessions confined to a minimum or allowed under the threat of French arms.

During the hectic generation of Napoleonic conquest it seemed that the emancipatory process would run its full course. Tenaciously Jews clung to these newly acquired rights; eagerly they hoped and reached for more. Their knuckles were rapped for their greed. In 1815 came the violent counter revolution. The survivors of the feudal order, in solemn session at the Congress of Vienna, voted to move back the clock. They resolved that every trace of the nightmare of the Revolution must be obliterated. Europe must return to "normalcy," to the glory of ante-bellum days. And if the ancient régime was to be restored, the Jew must be put into his old place.

The world, however, had changed much; time could not be completely reversed. It was no longer possible for the Congress to ignore the Jew completely. A statement was included in the Act of Federation for German States:

"The Congress of the allies will consider how the civil improvement of those professing the Jewish faith in Germany is to be effected in the most harmonious manner, and how, in particular, the enjoyment of civil rights and participation in civil duties may be secure to them. The rights already conceded them in the several federated states will be continued."

The first sentence of this article was obviously a hypocritical platitude. The second, however, was a much more serious matter. It bound German states to guarantee Jewish equality. A storm of controversy raged over this sentence. Finally, the deputy for Bremen offered an ingenious compromise which made the entire clause innocuous. For "in" read "by"; no more than this was necessary. Now the sentence read, "The rights already conceded the professors of the Jewish faith *by* the several federated states will be continued." The joker was just this: The rights conceded to Jews had been granted not *by* the federated states, but by the French. And if the states had themselves conceded no rights, they were under no obligation to continue them. By this lawyer's quibble, it was possible to wipe away all Jewish rights won over a quarter of a century.

But the evasion on paper at Vienna was trivial compared to the reaction which swept Europe. The Napoleonic era was followed by a period of religious bigotry and of intense nationalism. Jews, who for a generation had been free citizens, were now once more subjected to the old repressions. In Frankfort and Hanover, in Brunswick and Hesse, all concessions allowed were withdrawn. In Lübeck and Bremen, a movement was launched to expel Jews altogether. Fredrick Ruhs, professor of history at the University of Berlin, laid the responsibility for Germany's political prostration directly upon the Jews. The Teutonic state of the future, he insisted, must be a Christian state in which Jews were to have no active part. A professor of science at Heidelberg issued a work significantly entitled *Danger to the Welfare and Character of the Germans through the Jews.* During the summer of 1818, pogroms took place sporadically throughout Germany, while students raised the cry so faithfully echoed a hundred years later by the Nazis, *"Jude, verreck."* In Italy, in Spain, in Austria, in virtually every land except France and England, the same story was repeated. Five years sufficed to wipe out the gains of a generation.

The Jew was shocked and sobered. Once again he heard the order: "Dog, to your kennel." Once more he timidly doffed his hat whenever a Gentile called, *Jude, mach Mores.* The great masses of Jews, schooled in disappointment, obeyed with a shrug of the shoulder. In their age-old suspicion of Gentile kindness, they had never quite trusted the permanence of the new order; they had felt that it was too good to be true. Patiently they left their new homes to return to the ghettos they had abandoned; stoically they withdrew their children from schools and universities, and asked them to forget their dreams of careers in the professions.

But there were some who had pinned their hopes on the emancipation, and for long years had watched its approach, who found it incredible that the cup be dashed from their lips just as they were beginning to sip. There were some who loved the world more than Judaism. To them a return to the ghetto meant spiritual suffocation. Like trapped animals, they sought for a way of escape. They found it in the wild leap to conversion. Perhaps if they changed their religion, they might still avoid interment in reconstituted ghetto graves. And so the early nineteenth century witnessed a strange travesty—a parade of hypocrites to the baptismal font. The convert had little faith in sanctified waters, but he knew that the church registry might win him admission into a university and a chance at a career. The Jewish renegade was rarely sincere. Baptism for him was a matter of expediency, not of faith. By it one might become a Christian, not in religion, but in social advantage.

The convert, however, underestimated the intelligence of the Gentile. He did not realize how transparent his motives were. For all his faith, the Christian did not attribute to holy water the power to change Jewish spots. He believed in baptism for Christians. He agreed with the attitude of one clergyman who, when asked by a middle-aged Jew about the right costume for a baptism, replied laconically, "Diapers!" In the eyes of the law, a converted Jew was a

Christian, entitled to certain rights and privileges. What the law demanded, the Christian allowed, but no more. And the Christianizing Jew discovered too late that he had made a hypocrite of himself, had sold his self-respect, only for the privilege of leaping from the frying-pan into the fire.

The history of the Jew in the nineteenth century is thus a recurrent succession of concessions and their denial. In 1848 the game entered upon a more successful inning. The powers which had evoked the French Revolution had been checked, but they were not dead. From 1815 on, movements for national freedom stirred among Italians, Hungarians and Poles. Liberal ideas and ideals were propagated vigorously, though often, by necessity, under cover. The increasing influence of the bourgeoisie gave weight to the cause of liberalism. In fact, to that generation, all three movements were so intertwined in unified opposition to the *status quo* that they were confused with one another. The purposes of one became the purposes of all.

During the twenty-three years of reaction, the Jew had not been quiet. He had tasted too freely of liberty to accept its denial passively. He had little reason to love the world as it was. He joined naturally in such movements as promised to correct its wrongs, either general, or specific to him. He propagandized and agitated for a new order. Heine's *French Conditions* and Borne's *Letters from Paris* pointed a finger of criticism at German reaction. When the Revolution finally broke, Jews played a conspicuous rôle. It was left to a Jew, Johann Jacoby, to reply to Frederick William IV, when he refused to listen to revolutionary deputies: "It is a great misfortune of kings that they will not listen to the truth." The Jewish sympathy with the revolutionary cause is easily understandable. In part, it lay in a selfish desire to liberate the world so that the Jew, too, might have his place. In part, it was an expression of the democratic idealism which dominated all liberal thought of the day. But much more it was motivated by a hatred of the whole feudal structure with its stupid restrictions on human activity, a hatred more intense in the Jew because he had had more complete experience. As Ludwig Borne put it, "I, a slave from my birth, love liberty more than you; yea, because I was trained in servitude, I understand liberty better than you."

The revolution of 1848 brought with it extensive gains. Such freedom as the Jew in Germany possessed until Hitler was a direct product of that liberal outburst. Elsewhere, the gains were swallowed up by a speedy counter-revolution. From then on the Jews acquired liberty piecemeal and only after long agitation. Not until 1867 were the Jews of Austria declared legal equals of the Christians. Only in 1895 was the process duplicated in Hungary. Italy removed its last bars against Jews in 1870, Switzerland in 1873. England, long the home of tolerance, admitted a Jew to the House of Commons in 1858, and to degrees at Oxford and Cambridge in 1871.

By the turn of the twentieth century, the mad game was apparently over for all time. The Jew had won much. He was a full citizen in every land in Western Europe. He enjoyed legal equality and unrestrained economic and intellectual opportunity. His hands were full, but it was of the odds and ends of freedom, of the semblance of emancipation, not its essential integrity.

For in no land and at no time has the Jew enjoyed full freedom. The law protects his rights but it can not guarantee their execution. He may vote and run for office but his Jewish origin is a definite handicap in the way of his political career. He has free choice of his occupation, but he knows of long columns in the newspapers which specify, "Christians only." He is free to live where he chooses, but there are neighborhoods in which he is distinctly unwelcome. No college avowedly closes it doors to Jews, but many have adopted quotas and percentages. The process of legal emancipation since the French Revolution has run its full course in Western Europe and America. It has conferred political, social and economic equality on the Jew. It can not complete the process of liberation, it can not remove the barriers which still exist, not by law, but by prejudice. That is why we have described the liberty of the Jew as a semblance. It exists *de jure* but not *de facto*.

Even his political status is not overly secure. Laws are, in the last analysis, only a crystallization of public opinion. With a change of heart, the statute can be repealed or annulled. All the paper guarantees of equality can not still in the Jew the dread that this pleasant state, too, will pass away. He remembers that 1815 followed 1789, that 1848 was succeeded by 1849. He feels that he has slight assurance that a similar reaction may not overtake him in France, England or America. And if he seems overly morbid, let the reader recall the Ku Klux Klan and the Christian Front in the United States, Oswald Mosley's League of Ex-Service Men and Women in England; let him consider Nazi Germany, Fascist Italy and Vichy France. Only Jews ignorant of history and blind to circumstance can take either their freedom or security for granted.

Eastern Phase

ALL of this is the record of the process of liberation in Western Europe. It is by no means the whole story. It does not account for the history of the vast Jewish communities of Slavonic lands. For the movement of emancipation was not simultaneous in all countries, nor did it run a parallel course everywhere. The Jews of Poland, Lithuania and Roumania, long after their Western kin had been freed, continued in bondage. The democratic revolution reached these lands only belatedly, asserting itself feebly and winning at best a doubtful triumph. Our narrative now concerns itself with slow and faltering attempts at emancipation in Eastern Europe, predestined alas to a tragic end.

And yet it is a story which must be told if our account of the modern Jew is to be complete. It concerns what used to be, before Hitler, the world's largest Jewry and the one most rich in cultural achievements. Out of these countries has come the vast number of the Jews of America. The very fact that the Jewries of the East were exposed so slightly to a dissolving liberation makes them doubly significant. While the Jew of Germany or France was being de-Judaized and assimilated, his brothers to the East continued largely under the ancient régime. There the old pattern was still maintained. These, then, were Jews in the raw, unworked by the new order, still exhibiting the traditional way of life. They served in modern, pre-Hitler days as Israel's backlog of human materials, its reserve of traditional lore and loyalty.

Jews came into Poland in large numbers during the period of violent persecutions in Germany from the eleventh to the fifteenth centuries. There they found refuge from the horrors of the West. There they were welcomed by Polish kings and lords. For Poland, until its Partition, was a feudal society. It has its nobility and peasantry, but no middle class. In the Jews, its rulers saw an economic opportunity, an occasion to acquire ready-made shopkeepers and peddlers, tax farmers and traders, innkeepers, money-lenders and stewards. In return for the advantages to be derived from Jews, the ruling houses conferred protection, religious liberty and, for some time, even a considerable measure of administrative autonomy.

Nevertheless, life was no fool's paradise for the Polish Jew. Violent persecutions were not unknown. In 1648, a Cossack uprising precipitated one the bloodiest massacres of Jews in all history. The church in Poland ran true to form. Nor was the economic position of the Jew an unadulterated blessing. As the factor of the nobleman, he served as catspaw for the exploitation of the peasantry. He collected the taxes and gathered unto himself the hatred of the serf. He kept the inns where the Gentile drank up his meager funds, the shops whither the farmer's pennies flowed. As in Western Europe, his economic fate laid him open to the charge of parasitism. As in Western Europe, he derived slight returns from his risks.

For all his disrepute, the Jew of Poland had two advantages. By the process of settlement, he was scattered over the countryside. As a result, he was never confined to an urban ghetto. In addition, he successfully nurtured an intense, though narrow, cultural life. The Academies of Poland became very early the chief centers of the study of the Talmud. Even Germany imported Polish rabbis and teachers. When medieval Jewish culture stagnated into death, only Polish Jewry had the spiritual strength to resist the process of decay. Both the attempt of Rabbi Elijah of Vilna to reform Jewish scholarship and the Hasidic pietist revival emanated from the East of Europe.

The French Revolution and the final Partition of Poland by Russia, Austria and Prussia, took place within six years of each other. Both events were fraught with tremendous consequences for the Jews. The first, in 1789, opened that long struggle in Western Europe which culminated in a final emancipation. The second, in 1795, subjected the largest Jewish community in the world to a government which, to its very end, resisted liberalism generally and tolerance for the Jew specifically.

Until the first Partition of Poland in 1772, Jews were legally excluded from the sacred soil of Russia. The Holy Mother acknowledged no legitimate Jewish children. It goes without saying that some few Jews evaded the law. Their numbers, however, were so slight, their tenure of residence so insecure that Russia was really until that time without a Jewish problem.

Only when the czars seized the lion's share of Polish spoils, did they acquire as an unpleasant consequence a vast Jewish population sprawled over a huge territory. Unfortunately for the Romanoffs, Poland could not be taken without its Jews. Russia is then the only country which fought for the privilege of having a Jewish problem which it did not want.

The czars never exhibited overmuch kindness to their legitimate subjects. It was not to be expected that they should be generous to unwanted stepchildren. As early as 1791, Catherine the Great set the fashion for Russian repression. She quarantined all Jews against close contact with the Muscovite Empire. Alarmed by her new Jewish population, anticipating that it would soon be augmented by the final division of Poland, she established the Pale, a sort of *cordon sanitaire,* along the Russian frontier. Jewish residence and commerce were confined to specific provinces in the west of the enlarged Russian Empire. This created a ghetto of a unique type. It segregated Jews not within a quarter of a city but in a definite portion of a realm. Even within the Pale, residence was not free. Cities and districts of special commercial or strategic importance were deliberately closed to Jews. To this residential restriction was added an elaborate system of unequal taxation, cultural exclusion and civic degradation.

This pattern Russia followed closely until the entire czarist régime collapsed under the weight of its own sin in 1917. Variations from it in detail came and went but one thing was fixed: a policy which insisted that the Jew was not to participate even in those limited privileges which the Russian Government allowed its subjects. When statesmen in St. Petersburg felt that it was wiser to have Jews settled in the countryside, Jews were expelled from the towns. When they changed their minds, Jews were moved again. When, in 1824, military strategists insisted that the presence of Jews in frontier districts weakened Russia's defenses, twenty thousand families were ordered, in the dead of winter, to find other abodes for themselves.

The climax of cruelty was reached under Nicholas I. In 1827, the system of military conscription was extended to Jews in a vicious form. Thousands of Jewish children, often mere babes, were drafted for military service and farmed out with Christian peasants. Every device was employed to force these infant soldiers to accept Christianity. The duration of military service was set at twenty-five years. The inhumanity of this régime was accentuated when the heads of Jewish communities were made responsible for the procurement of recruits. Jews were compelled to serve as executioners against their fellow-Jews.

For one brief interval, after the death of Nicholas I, the ideals of Western Europe seemed to touch one Russian ruler. Alexander II, who came to the throne in 1855, was a person of liberal tendencies. The same impulse which led him to free forty million serfs impelled him to a new policy toward Jews. The system of military conscription was abolished, schools and universities were opened to Jewish youths, forbidden cities and districts were reduced in numbers.

The Jews of Russia were well aware of what had been happening in the West. Impatiently they had waited for the liberal ideology to infect the Russian régime, for a parallel evolution in their own lives. The very fact that their hope had been so long deferred made the attitude of Alexander II so much the more a Messianic fulfilment. The great day of liberation it seemed had dawned. They took full advantage of their rights and privileges. They flocked to schools and universities; they threw themselves whole-heartedly into Russian life, especially into liberal movements. Among Jewish intellectuals, great attention was given to the procedure for best preparing the Jewish masses for the day when emancipation would finally come. They debated vehemently the question of the advisability of full assimilation. A new sun was rising; it would be a violation of natural law if day did not follow.

Then, to their profound disappointment, the false dawn faded. Alexander was, at best, a timid liberal. He grew frightened when he caught glimpses of the revolutionary horrors which his policy might evoke. Toward the end of his reign, he reverted to reactionary type. With this general reversion went an about-face in his Jewish policy. The participation of Jews in liberal movements made a return to repression the more logical. Yeshivahs were closed, rights recently granted recalled, the whole machinery of anti-Semitism again put into motion.

The intellectual Jew was filled with bitter despair. As in Germany during the first quarter of the eighteenth century, so in Russia during the third, the parade to the baptismal font began. History repeated itself. Baptism proved no escape. The Russian Jew was left dissatisfied with the old Jewish life, unable to participate whole-heartedly in it, yet denied entrance into the world which he now desired.

By 1881, when Alexander II was assassinated, Russia had slipped back to its old routine, leaving bitterness, resentment and broken hopes as the only results of its brief excursion into liberalism. Under Alexander III, a wave of romantic reaction swept Russia. A new doctrine was enunciated. Russia must turn its back on the Western world and return to its medieval form. Liberalism became a detested doctrine, tolerance toward the Jew a betrayal of the true soul of the Slav. Typical of the reborn Russia was the statement of Pobiedonostzev, Procurator of the Holy Synod, "One-third of Russia's Jews must be converted, one-third driven to emigrate and the last third starved to death."

The raising of the standard of reaction was the signal for a resurgence of violence. In 1881, a tide of pogroms swept the Pale. In 1882, the May Laws were promulgated. Jews were expelled from numerous towns and villages, the Pale was sharply reduced in size, herding the entire Jewish population of Russia into closely hedged districts. Jews in educational institutions were limited to five per cent. in Moscow, three per cent. in St. Petersburg, and ten per cent. within the Pale. As a result, in 1900, there were more Russian Jewish students in attendance at universities outside of Russia than in Russia itself.

The great flight of East European Jews to America now began in earnest. Between 1881 and 1900, more than six hundred thousand Jews came from Russia and Roumania to the United States. Between 1903 and 1907 another five hundred thousand fugitives made the long trek. Within one generation whole towns were transplanted from the Polish Pale to New York's East Side. The Jewish population of the United States was doubled and redoubled, rising vertically from year to year. From 1880 to 1930, the number of American Jews jumped from four hundred thousand to four million.

The Russian Government at first made a feeble attempt to check the flight. Eventually, it became conscious of the stupidity of attempting to keep in Russia a class which it did not want. Ultimately, it encouraged emigration. Eagerly it anticipated the solution of the Jewish problem by migration.

With the turn of the century the Czars discovered a new reason for hatred of the Jew and a new mode of exploiting him. All the repression of liberalism by the government could not inhibit the growth of revolutionary movements in Russia. In these movements the great masses of Jews took slight active interest. But to Jewish intellectuals, those few individuals who had acquired some knowledge of the world and of the new spirit which infused it, republicanism, socialism and nihilism offered at once emancipation for the Jew and salvation for Russia. It was inevitable that Jews should play a prominent part in movements of protest and liberation.

The activities of younger Jews scarcely encouraged tolerance on the part of Russia's rulers. But now the government proceeded calculatingly with its anti-Semitic program. It sought to kill two birds with one stone. A carefully planned pogrom could be made to serve a dual purpose: to repress the Jews and to divert the attention of the Russian people from much agitated questions of reform and revolution. A massacre is, after all, a spectacular affair. Properly staged, it would be the equivalent of *panem et circenses* to millions asking for the right to live free lives. In 1903, the Russian régime used the Jew as a bloody red herring for the first time. The barbarity of the Kishinef Massacre was organized and unleashed by the police. The world protested; but the experiment had been a success. When, in 1905, the failure of Russia in its war with Japan precipitated a revolution, the device was used again. In 1911, it was tried once more, this time in a new form. The blood accusation was raised against the Jews in the notorious Mendel Beilis case. How long and how successfully the game might have continued can not now be determined. Nineteen hundred and fourteen found the Jews of Eastern Europe still a class of outcasts.

World War I exacted a terrible toll from the Jews. One thing even the Romanoffs had predicted: they had foreseen the fate of residents of the borderlands of Russia in case of war. That was part of their logic in the establishment of the Pale. From 1914 to 1917, the German, Austrian and Russian armies swept successively across the Jewish settlement, driving its residents back and forth. That neither side gave special consideration to Jews goes without saying. The Russian army especially was guilty of pillage, rape and pogrom. With the counter-revolutions against the Soviet Government came the white terror. In 1919, thirty thousand Jews were butchered under the Petlura régime in the Ukraine.

It is estimated that over a quarter of a million Jews were murdered in cold blood in various parts of Russia by anti-Communist forces. To the horror of violence was added the slow death from famine.

From all the suffering of Jews in Slavonic Europe, two diverse blessings emerged. Under the Bolshevik régime in Russia, anti-Semitism has been rigorously suppressed. For the first time in centuries, the Jew of Russia came to know the meaning of political, economic and cultural security. But even this advantage has its drawback. The Jewish religion, like all other religions, is in legal theory protected by the Soviet régime, though in actual practice it operates at a disadvantage and under disabilities, less so however than used to be the case. Perhaps the situation in this respect will go on improving. The Jewish minority culture, like others, is not only tolerated officially but encouraged, at least in those elements which pass Marxist muster, which excludes all religion and much else also. The Russian Jewish community, isolated from world Jewry ever since the Bolshevik revolution, was permitted for a time during World War II to resume its contacts with Jews abroad, but now seems to have been returned to its former seclusion. And Zionism in Russia, though it has always been sternly repressed, may be entering on a better day, now that Russia has declared itself in favor of a Jewish State in Palestine. All in all, both gains and losses have been entered onto the ledger of Jewish welfare in the Soviet Union, the former in the realm of the political, economic, and social, the latter in the domain of the spirit.

The second benefit that emerged from the First World War consisted in the formal confirmation in international law of Minority Rights. At the Versailles Conference or through the League of Nations there were written into the constitutions of newly established states guarantees for all minorities, Jews included, of full civic status, economic equality, and cultural and religious freedom. Unfortunately, these treaties were no sooner signed than they were evaded, surreptitiously at first and then in complete openness. In the end, the lot of the Jew in Poland, Roumania, Hungary, and the Baltic States turned out to be little better after World War I than it had been before. Pogroms and riots were frequent, the *numerus clausus* in educational institutions almost universal, anti-Jewish agitation widespread, and economic disability and boycott of the Jew the normal order of the day.

When, a century and a half after the French Revolution, Hitler turned East, the Jews he encountered and destroyed were in one fashion or another persons who had never known the fullness of freedom, for whom Emancipation was still a hope, not a reality.

CHAPTER IX

DISSOLUTION OF BALANCE

FOR a half-millennium the Jew, rejected by the world, had secluded himself within ghetto walls, unconcerned with what lay without. But the day came when the world would no longer be denied, when it insinuated itself into his retreat, upsetting his balanced life and disturbing his peace. It hinted beguilingly of freedom and emancipation, of a fuller and richer existence. It beckoned and the Jew crept forth. He tasted of this strange thing called liberty, found it sweet and wanted more. And so he abandoned his ghettos for the pursuit of it. He stripped off the segregation which had protected his group being. Only when it was too late did he discover that the world had not been sincere. It had been playing with him, it had never intended fully to keep its promises of liberation. But for all that the modern world refused to receive him, it took advantage of his defenselessness. It bent and twisted his personality, thumped, kneaded and shaped him. He emerged from the mills of emancipation a new creature, scarcely akin to what he had been. He became the Jew as the world knows him to-day.

The story of the Jew in the modern world is then the history of the dissolution of an ordered ghetto into chaos, and of a fixed individuality into flux. It is a record formless and inchoate, for it describes not the purposeful stability of a healthy organism but its degeneration and decay. When a social system like that of the ghetto is alive, all its powers are

167

concentrated upon intelligible, unifying objectives. It is then possible for the historian to describe its activities in terms of sweeping universality. Such was the character of our analysis of medieval survival. But when that organism disintegrates, conflicting energies play against each other in pointless confusion. No generalization possesses more than partial applicability. In this fact lies the root of the untidy incoherence of any account of the modern Jew and his group life. Unity has been displaced by mutually contradictory diversities. Henceforth every reference to the Jew will need to be taken with the traditional grain of salt, will demand the recognition that broad statements can involve only partial truth.

And it is a tale of pain, this process of the progressive emancipation of the Jew subsequent to the French Revolution. When an old world dies and a new world is not yet born, the soul of the individual is left homeless. It can no longer find rest in the order which is perishing. The new society in which it is to incarnate itself struggles toward birth but is not yet actualized. Such is the fate of all who are so unfortunate as to be born during an age of social transition. Such was the fate of the Jew during the nineteenth century when the ghetto at last collapsed, leaving him with a refuge neither in the old world nor in the new. The ghetto may have been chokingly confining, yet it was a dwelling-place for the soul. But now the ancient dwelling was no longer habitable, and the mansions of the world were still inhospitable. Torn by yearning for a peace that had vanished, without sure abode for his spirit, the modern Jew has moved restlessly from one to the other, finding surcease nowhere.

If the history of the Jew in the Middle Ages be an epic, the record of his modern life is a satirical comedy. For the essence of the epic is the heroic theme, and not a few Jews of late have acted unheroically. The act of renunciation may often be futile and unintelligent; it is always dignified. When the medieval Jew renounced the world, the light of martyrdom clothed him with something like majesty. The very gesture of self-sacrifice bred a tragic dignity that obscured his physical squalor. But the modern Jew is done with the renunciation of his fathers. From the very moment that he first tasted of liberty, he developed an insatiable appetite for it. The world, however, has been a grudging giver, it has liberated the Jew only bit by bit, it has always withheld more than it granted. As a result, the Jew has found himself a perpetual suppliant; he has been compelled to wheedle and flatter for additional favors; he must always beg for the portion of liberty which has been withheld. His posture is neither dignified nor graceful. An Achilles sulking in a tent is a fitting theme for a Homeric poet; an Achilles scrambling headlong after an ever elusive tortoise is a theme only for a comedian or a philosopher.

If the Jew was aware of the meanness of his pursuit, he placated his outraged self-respect by assuring himself that the end justified the means. If his emancipation entailed a loss of dignity, at least the game was worth the candle. But after he had played the game of self-humiliation long enough, he became oppressed with a sense of futility. This whole business of winning unreserved recognition from the world seemed discouragingly prolonged. It was like one of those nightmares in which one wanders through labyrinthine corridors hoping always to find a way out but never quite succeeding.

Did the Jew succeed in winning economic freedom, then

he could not vote. When he had the right of ballot, he might not hold office. Was he guaranteed the right to stand for election, he discovered that his Jewishness made a political career difficult even in most liberal lands. When education was theoretically open to all regardless of race, religion or color, the Jew still experienced some difficulty in gaining admission to universities. He was always conscious of the fact that regardless of his merits, it was almost impossible for him to move freely toward academic advancement. When these bars had been lowered, entrance into certain professions still remained a virtual impossibility. Even when all formal obstacles had been eliminated, there was still the wall of social exclusion. There were always clubs into which Jews were not elected, societies that were by policy entirely Christian in membership, drawing-rooms where no Jew had ever sat. At each stage the world has held something back, at each step it has insisted—thus far and no farther.

For a time each generation of Jews engaged in wishful thinking. It believed, because it was more pleasant to believe it, that the whole evil would disappear if only certain trivial factors in the situation were modified. Now, the Jew told himself, the fault lay with himself: he was too clannish, too stubbornly loyal to his identity; perhaps he was not sufficiently urbane, not adequately cultured, not completely Americanized, Anglicized or Teutonized. Or else he might pin his hopes on changes in the scene external to the Jew. He assured himself that he would be accepted when some reactionary government was liberalized. He argued that the root of his difficulties lay in specific economic evils. He looked, in other instances, to the spread of democracy. Above all, he tended to lay responsibility for his lot to ignorance. He felt assured that when popular education had been universalized, when every Gentile had been taught to read and write, to enjoy music, art and fine literature, that then anti-Semitism would disappear like some evil mist before the rising sun of a tolerant intelligence. Assiduously he went about confusing causes and effects, symptoms with the disease.

The Jew remade himself, he dissolved his clannish bonds, he stripped himself of distinguishing Jewish marks. He became urbane and polished; he eliminated all ghetto crudities and eccentricities. Then he waited confidently for the word of welcome. To his pained surprise the world seemed to approve of him no more in his transformation than it had before. Meanwhile, the reactionary government fell, the economic evils he blamed were mitigated, democracy became an ideal widely accepted, and literacy attained to a delightful universality; Gentiles heard good music with keen appreciation, they read literature of unimpeachable nobility. Still salvation refused to come, acceptance was not complete. The old flies in the ointment had been removed only to reveal the presence of others hitherto unsuspected.

And then came the disillusionment of the last generation. Minority rights in Eastern Europe turned out to be scraps of paper. The German people under the Hitlerite frenzy turned against the Jew. Despite a century of Jewish emancipation, despite the refinement of the German Jew, his assimilating tendencies, and his contributions to Teutonic culture, the security attained by one hundred years of struggle was blown sky-high. The unkindest cut of all, from the point of view of Jewish hopes, has been the betrayal by educated classes. That the ignorant masses should seek to submerge the Jew may be painful; it is at least thinkable. But that universities and professors should, for all their culture, lead in the hymns of hate is too dreadful by far. For these were the corner-stone of the edifice of Jewish hope. We shall consider later, in Chapter XIV, the causes of this modern tragedy and its impact on Jews, and Judaism. But one effect of it must be noted now. Haunting fears have been put into Jewish heads and hearts, the misgiving lest what happened in one place happen in others also, the awareness that if Jews could be exterminated in Europe they may well be in jeopardy everywhere.

The upshot of the whole process has been a progressive disappointment and disillusionment. No game is worth the candle if the game can never be won, or if the prize can be taken away in the very last inning. The Jew tends to feel resentfully that he has abandoned the dignity and serenity of the older way of life for mythical crocks of gold, located at the ever-receding feet of rainbows. Complementing the sense of futility goes a sense of disgust. The Jew to-day is likely to be ashamed of himself. The act of self-abasement is always painful. But when one has debased oneself in vain, the reaction tends to be nausea.

That out of the chaos, the pain, the ungraceful pursuit, the disillusionment, the Jew is now beginning to derive a new attitude of self-respect and a new philosophy for a tolerable existence in the modern scene we shall see later. Our immediate purpose is to set modern Jewish life in vivid opposition to the medieval. The elements of contrast between the two can be summarized in four antinomies and a conclusion.

1. On the one hand, the ordered homogeneity of a stable order; on the other, the formless, inchoate confusion of a society in disintegration.

2. A self-contained serenity as opposed to restless vacillation between two worlds.

3. The dignity of renunciation against the humiliation of persistent beggary.

4. An order rich in a satisfying culture and adequate ideology as contrasted with one impotent by lack of program and sicklied over by abstract alternatives of to be or not to be.

And the final crushing recognition that the tolerance of the world is an uncertain quantity, that final emancipation may never be conferred, that the Gentile is as likely as ever to suppress the Jew, that salvation must be won and can not be conferred.

The ghetto was gone, the life it sheltered went with it. Even before the process of emancipation was officially under way, the factors of medieval survival were beginning to lose their efficacy. Once the wild rush of liberating events was launched, degeneration proceeded with dizzy rapidity. A social organism which had lived for nigh on two thousand years, which had resisted violent attack and abuse, suddenly disintegrated. Age-old habits of life disappeared, hoary ideas and ideals dissolved, a whole society vanished in a puff of historic smoke.

That so solid a world should melt away so rapidly seems incredible. Not even the change in external circumstance quite accounts for it. The secret of the velocity of decay is to be discovered in the peculiar conditions of medieval Jewish stability. Equilibrium, whether physical or social, is an ambiguous word. It may denote merely inertia—the secure quiet of a book flat on a table. On the other hand, it may suggest the deceptive rest of a body in infinite motion. In that sense, the solar system is in a state of equilibrium. But the balance is unstable, it proceeds from the resolution of innumerable forces. Let one of these be withdrawn and the whole order collapses. The stability of the ghetto was that of a spinning top, it was the result of the interplay of social movements. It gave the illusion of firmness because the resolution of forces balanced exactly. Emancipation disturbed the stabilizing dynamism, the collapse of a society followed.

We have already had occasion to see that the factors of Jewish survival during the Middle Ages were fivefold. They were described as *the Factor of Preliminary Preparation, the Factor of External Pressure, the Ideological Factor, the Factor of Social Isolation* and *the Factor of a Compensating Culture.* It was the interplay of these elements which made possible the survival of the Jewish group and the maintenance of its unique culture. The events of the nineteenth century withdrew these sustaining forces one by one. Before each of them the hand of History wrote a minus sign. The mechanism of Jewish survival simply ran down like some slowly released spring. The top of medieval equilibrium reeled and fell.

The Absence of Preliminary Preparation

For the plunge from Palestine into homelessness, the Jew had been prepared. He had founded settlements throughout the world in which he could take refuge. He had evolved a scheme of living, a mesh of group habits to protect his values. The transition from the ghetto to the world came as a surprise attack in the night. The Jew had not expected his emancipation so immediately; it shocked him when it came; he did not know how to adapt himself to it when he had it. Besides, even the measure of adjustment which he attained was never final. He never knew when more liberty would be added, nor when accepted rights would be withdrawn. No person can make satisfactory adjustment to an environment that is constantly undergoing change.

It might have been expected that the favored few who had made contact with the world before the mass, who had attained a partial personal emancipation—that these would prepare the way, that by trial and error they would evolve an adaptation of traditional Judaism to its new habitat. Had that been done, the emancipating stroke might not have been a stunning blow.

But most of those Jews who first caught a glimpse of the possibilities of freedom were fascinated by the prospect. Their eyes were turned forward to the world, not backward to the ghetto dungeon. They were concerned primarily with greater freedom for themselves personally, broader opportunities for their children and ultimate liberation from restraint. Their hearts were set on individual salvation rather than on group survival. The exodus from the ghetto for them was very much like a jail-break. Their psychology naturally was one of every man for himself and the familiar fate to the hindmost.

Some few there were during the last century before the emancipation and during its earlier stages who recognized that the Jewish world was face to face with an emergency. These, as we shall see later, attempted to prepare against it, and once it had arrived, to guide the people through it. Their intentions were immaculately honest; they were, none the less, misguided. They took too literally the promise of freedom; they expected in too sanguine a mood its speedy fulfilment; they did not foresee the long slow struggle which ensued. Besides, their glimpse of the larger world blinded them to the unique virtues of their own tradition. As a result, most of the early efforts toward adjustment were made by individuals who had an accurate understanding of none of the factors of the case. We shall return to these individuals again to see exactly how they paved a pandemonium with their good intentions.

In consequence, before the whirlwind struck, no barometer had given clear warning. While the storm raged, no chart indicated directions, no compass pointed toward a port. The captains guessed, and guessed incorrectly. The beams groaned and strained, and the ship was dangerously water-logged before its crew had recovered sufficiently to survey the situation intelligently.

The Relaxation of External Pressure

The whole effect of the emancipation was to remove from the Jewish organism the confining weight of the world. In the medieval scheme the Jew was limited socially, ostracized legally and segregated economically. A line was drawn about him and every attempt to cross it was instantly detected and punished. In this way the Gentile helped the Jew to remain Jewish.

With the nineteenth century, all pressure was relaxed. The Jew might remain loyal to his past, but the Gentile world no longer insisted that he do so. He was now a free agent. The reaction to this new situation was immediate. Jews began to live where they chose, act as they pleased, and exhibit loyalty or indifference to their group as they willed. Just as the total effect of the world's pressure had been to drive Jews to cohesion in an almost mechanical fashion, so they reacted to the relaxation of the pressure in almost the same manner. Like a gas which has long been condensed under some weight, and which suddenly explodes, casting its molecules into space, so the old order blew up, strewing Jews in every conceivable direction.

The Negation of the Ideology

Sooner or later, it was inevitable that the Jew should awake to the fact of his intellectual medievalism. The awakening, unfortunately, was a rude one. For four centuries he had been cut off from the progress of general thought. During all that time he had cherished his own theology, philosophy and social theory. The walls of segregation sheltered him against the new winds of doctrine which blew through the world. Until the deluge of modernity, he continued his faith in a God who had personally elected him, who had destined Israel for a central position in the scheme of things. He believed implicitly in the promise of an other-worldly reward, and a this-worldly vindication. From these he derived a dignity and an assurance, a loyalty and a triumphant hope which made his persistence logical.

And then he walked abroad in the world and his eyes were opened. He became ashamed because of his ragged medievalism. He discovered that he was the Rip Van Winkle of Europe, still clothed in the tattered rags of a style of thought long obsolete. While he had slept, the world had been learning, and its lessons, when he studied them, shattered his old ideology for ever.

It must be said of the modern Jew that he was an apt student. In one generation he overtook the intellectual lead of Europe gained through five centuries. But in the course of this pursuit, he discarded one invaluable possession: his traditional theology, which was also his *raison d'être*. A blinding light streamed in on the Jew as breaches appeared in ghetto walls. He awoke suddenly to a Copernican astronomy and a Newtonian physics, to the skepticism, the materialism, the deism and the romantic German pantheism of the eighteenth and early nineteenth centuries. Each of these streams of thought beat against the bases of his weltanschauung. As he read the philosophy of his day, it converted his God from a vivid personality, such as might conceivably have chosen an Abraham, into a metaphysical abstraction, or, worse still, into pure nullity. It is no mere accident that Spinoza entertained a hearty contempt for the Jewish religion. Considered from the view-point of the Cartesian physics and psychology, it appeared to him as a vast hodge-podge of superstition.

The eighteenth century was essentially an age of rationalism. Its spirit infected the newly emancipated Jew. He began to discard all the paraphernalia of the past, all those unreasonable concepts which, for all their irrationality, still made survival possible and Jewish existence tolerable. He tended to drop the idea of a personal Messiah, of the final vindication of the Jewish cause, of a real reward in the next world. The study of comparative religion revealed the fact that he had no monopoly on claims to revelation. Indeed, the very concept of revelation became profoundly questionable. The pursuit of Biblical criticism shook his confidence in the divinity of his regimen of life. He applied his newly acquired acquaintance with the technique of research to his own history and discovered that the life of his group had been not that of a mystic agent of God, but simply that of a social organism struggling for existence. There was, he was driven to admit, no certainty of the eternal survival of the Jew—much less of any final vindication.

When a people has become habituated to a set of ideas over

a long period of time, these ideas come to possess an astonishing power of resistance. The ideology of the Jewish group was no exception. It resisted threatened death. Many a Jew threw overboard the whole complex of Jewish concepts. But most Jews clung to them tenaciously. Since they could no longer be maintained in their original form, they were allegorized, rationalized, so modified that they did not run counter to modern thought, reinterpreted in short to the point where it was possible to retain them without doing violence to the mind. From the point of view of the individual, this device was eminently successful. It enabled him to hold on to ancestral concepts. From the point of view of Jewish survival, the whole effort of reconciliation was futile. The old mental atmosphere had been dissipated. The Jew could no longer claim, save half-allegorically, election, divine guidance, personal immortality or an ultimate group victory. These positions were now either untenable altogether or radically doubtful. But these concepts had been the rationale of Jewish existence. With their dissolution, the Jew was no longer sure what his group was living for. As the old weltanschauung went fading into oblivion, the horrible possibility suggested itself that the whole of Jewish suffering might be a wanton, pointless, brutal jest.

Along with this dissipation of mental climate, went the disintegration of Jewish practise. For the theology and ideology had been not merely avenues of mental escape, not merely instruments for survival; they had been theories of sanction for a routinized living, props and shorings for form and ceremony. Once the modern world kicked these intellectual foundations out from under, the collapse of the superstructure was only a matter of time. Ancient group habits were now without a preservative rationale.

The Negation of Social Isolation

By virtue of the emancipation, the Jew lost his protective segregation. The world and he both canceled their tacit compact of no intercourse. By that act, the ghetto and its internal life signed their own death warrant. The bulwark of isolation had been demolished. No longer was the Jewish way of life protected against alien and disturbing influences, it was now out in the open, exposed to contagion. As soon as the Jew stepped out of the ghetto, he became aware of the contrast between his own habits and those of the Gentile. Life on the Judengasse had possessed its own excellences, but polished refinement of manner had not been one of these. Existence for the Jew had been too dour and grim to allow for concern with external graces. The elegance of Gentile life intrigued the newly emancipated Jew with its novelty. He found himself imitating the non-Jew before he was aware of the fact.

Even had the ways of the world been hideous compared to his own, the Jew would have adopted them. For these were the patterns of the master class and newly liberated slaves are especially prone to ape the standards of those who sit securely in the seats of power. Besides, with the emancipation, the Jew ceased to seek outlets for his ambition within the Jewish group. He now looked for his laurels in a larger arena. But if he was to be successful in a world predominantly Gentile, he must show that he could behave like a Gentile, otherwise, he would be denied even an initial hearing. Most of all, the Jew imitated Gentile conduct because he hoped thereby to attain fuller emancipation. At each stage in the liberating process, some restrictions still persisted. The Jew felt naturally that once he had shown to the world that he was no strange monster, that in Rome he could do exactly as the Romans did, the world in turn would recognize that the Jew was indistinguishable from the non-Jew and treat him accordingly.

The integrity of Jewish social pressure crumbled under the strain. So long as every Jew lived under the ever-watchful eyes of the group, divergence from traditional practise was impossible. But now the individual was no longer a mere cell within a larger body. He was a foot-loose person struggling to make his way in a new order. He was free to do as he pleased. His interests encouraged him to do as did the Gentiles.

The new economic order, too, made its contribution to the dissolution of ancestral forms. In the ghetto, business had been regulated into conformity with Jewish group practises. With the emancipation, the Jew ceased to concern himself with an economy which was all his own. He eagerly availed himself of the opportunity to participate in the larger affairs of a larger world. But the economy of which he became part was Gentile. It had no respect for Sabbath or Holy Day. For the first time in two millennia, the Jew was compelled to choose between ancestral sanctities and economic advantage. The efforts made by many Jews to preserve traditional forms, often at the cost of their financial interests, were laudable. In the long run, they were doomed to failure. The wheels of industry continued to revolve sacrilegiously, grinding to destruction rite and ritual.

Some Jews resisted desperately the encroachments of the new economy upon Jewish practise; the vast majority decided that the observances of their fathers were no longer practicable. They kept the Jew from his shops on Saturday; they broke into the normal business day with numberless irrelevant interruptions; they erected a barrier of diet between him and his recently acquired Christian associates. The Jew cast about for some logical reason to justify all this troublesome inconvenience. He found none. The old rationale was no longer satisfying. He yielded to the demands of his interests and compromised.

The process of attrition, so long inhibited, now began in earnest. As a result of free contact with Gentile society, from considerations of personal advantage, out of the failure to find justification for Jewish practise, the Jew began quietly, imperceptibly, to depart from the practises of his fathers. There was generally nothing precipitate about the sloughing of Jewish habits; the automatisms of conduct rarely break sharply; they are worn away only gradually. But once the first concessions are made, a landslide has begun.

With the passage of time, the individual Jew yielded more and more, conformed less and less. With each successive generation the process of riddance went on with accelerating momentum. Of all the lands of the world it has moved most rapidly in the United States. For here, to the normal conditions which of themselves tended to encourage divergence, one unusual circumstance was added—the disruptive effects of migration. Millions of Jews were lifted from their setting, from familiar scenes and places suggestive of tradition, and deposited in a new world.

But whether slow or rapid, the progressive sloughing off of old forms goes on apace. Many a Jew now alive refused in his youth to violate the Sabbath. In his old age he transgresses with an untroubled conscience. Within the span of one generation, many a home once filled with Jewish ritualist symbols has been entirely emptied of them.

Contemporary Jewish practise is a crazy-quilt, a mass of contradictions and conflicts. In part, this is due to the difference in the tempo of emancipation. The Jew from Poland, fresh from the ghetto, is neighbor to the Jew who for a century has been subjected to the disintegration of freedom. Medievalism intact walks side by side with a shattered modernity; the full tradition rubs shoulders with its broken remnants. Another part of the explanation lies within the individual. Some few Jews there are, even in free lands, who have made no concessions, who know that *facilis descensus Averni.* There are others who have yielded in some things and not in others. And there are those who, in more than a dietary sense, have gone "the whole hog," whose lives are distinguished by not a single traditional form or practise. Toward that end the whole group slips relentlessly.

To Israel Zangwill we are indebted for the most apt characterization of this non-conformist chaos, of this ceremonial "catch as catch can." He puts into the mouth of an Irish maid employed in a Jewish household, this sage observation: "To-night being yer Sabbath, you'll be blowing out yer bedroom candle, though ye won't light it; Mr. David'll light his and blow it out too; and the old misthress won't even touch the candlestick. There's three religions in this house, not wan."

The Negation of the Culture

In one other realm did the new order shake the old society. It destroyed the scheme of learning, the tradition of a sanctified scholarship. For untold centuries the Jew found in his study courage in suffering, escape from a threatened insanity and a compensation for his lot. He cherished it with the intensity with which a mind threatened by degeneration clings to elements of lucidity. He trusted in its value, he was assured that no system of thought was so accurate, no literature so valid, and no culture so elevating as his. Then Western knowledge unfolded its ample page, rich with the spoils of time. The intellectual pride of the Jew turned to confusion. He discovered that his philosophy was obsolete, his science hopelessly mistaken. He awoke to the fact that his culture had none of the music and art which made Gentile civilization graceful. The tradition had been satisfactory as long as it had existed in a vacuum of isolation. It seemed ludicrously inferior when subjected to invidious contrast.

Elemental intellectual honesty compelled the Jew to turn his efforts from his own outdated culture to the thought of the new world. It was pure perversity to continue to study the Talmud when Shakespeare, Goethe and Gibbon were available for the asking. Maimonides seemed hopelessly antiquated in comparison with Kant and Hegel; Judah Halevi was only an interesting archeological survival compared to Schiller or Lessing. As rapidly as the Jew made intellectual contact with Gentile civilization, so rapidly did he turn his attention to the thought life which was now opened to him. Blinded by a novel brilliance, he gave scant attention to the quiet light of his native culture. He assumed that its outmoded exterior reflected an essential irrelevance.

While, in great measure, the abandonment of the tradition was nobly motivated, it was not without selfish and unworthy objectives. Not all Jews changed their intellectual allegiance on ideal grounds. As soon as the Jew was in the mills of emancipation, he developed a distinct sense of inferiority. He was not the equal of the Gentile politically, socially or economically. He felt inferior intellectually as well. The same imitative impulse which led him to adopt non-Jewish folk-ways, drove him to acquire an alien culture in preference to his own. He knew that the former was modern and fashionable, that it was a prime means of advancement in the world. If he and his children were to make their way successfully, they must be learned in that learning of which the world approved.

This combination of motives, selfish and unselfish, meant the end of the system of Jewish education. In the first stages of the emancipation, the old pedagogy managed to hold its ground. Traditional studies were maintained. Individual students supplemented them by teaching themselves modern languages, the sciences and literature. Many a student spent long days in the Yeshivah over the Talmud, and then, in secret, during the night (for at first such alien studies were forbidden) prepared himself for admission into some university. As the emancipation advanced, progressive Jews founded schools built on Gentile models, offering full curricula in modern subjects but including also courses of a specifically Jewish character. Before long, Jewish children were attending public schools and spending some time in a Jewish school after regular hours. But as Jewish allegiance disintegrated, this second education came to be regarded as a hardship on both the child and the parent. Then the Sunday-school appeared. The typical Jewish child to-day is given Jewish instruction one morning a week for one and a half to two hours.

This progressive abandonment of traditional learning was naturally not simultaneous in all lands. It ran parallel to the irregular movement of emancipation; it has gone farthest in those countries which most quickly liberated their Jews. It is least advanced where the emancipation is not yet really under way. There are still Jews in Eastern Europe and Asia to-day whose entire intellectual life has been traditional, who are completely innocent of any knowledge of Western thought. There is an ever-growing number of Jews in the West and East alike who are abysmally ignorant of the tradition of their own people.

The emancipated Jew to-day is in matters of Jewish culture pathetically uninformed. He knows nothing of it. His children, if possible, will know less. His knowledge of Jewish history is negligible; his understanding of his own past distorted and unintelligent. He presents a strange paradox to the world, a man who knows all literature except his own, all philosophies but that of his people, who reads books in all the seventy tongues but who generally can not construe a word of Hebrew.

Such is the story of emancipation and of how it canceled one by one each factor of survival. That during the nineteenth century the whole Jewish people did not disappear is due in part to certain external conditions, to the fact that at no time was emancipation full and complete, to the fact that liberation was so retarded in some lands as to provide constant reserves of human material. But much more was it due to elements internal to the Jewish scene. Somewhere, within this strange people lay unsuspected powers of resistance which drove them toward life. As soon as the tide of degeneration set in the Jewish will-to-persist set in motion creative vitalizing cross-currents. The old factors of survival disappeared, new ones were evoked. Before these can be examined and evaluated, the record of disintegration must first be completed.

CHAPTER X

SUICIDE

THE death of the old order was more than a spontaneous disintegration; it was also an act of suicide. It must be said in all fairness that the Gentile did not do the whole job. Jews contributed actively to the degeneration of their own life, to the process of decay they themselves gave accelerating impulses. The emancipation could never have disrupted the Jewish scene so rapidly had it not received positive co-operation from within.

True, not all the participants on the inside had the same objective, not all plunged the knife into the decaying body for identical ends. There were some who struck because they felt that Judaism was dying in any event and that the sooner it perished the better for all concerned. Others were totally without interest in such general objectives. Their sole ambition was to make their way into a newly opening world. In their rush for liberation, they trampled on the prostrate society of their people carelessly. But most dangerous of all to the failing strength of Judaism were Jews with good intentions.

It was perfectly obvious that Israel's body politic demanded surgical treatment. It was overgrown with beliefs which were untenable in the new world. The ceremonial life of the ghetto had become encrusted with all sorts of bizarre customs, rites and superstitions which had lost all meaning and significance. The ghetto knew no modern language.

For literary purposes it used a frozen Hebrew; in daily conversation, the corrupt German dialect called Yiddish.
Above all, the Jew needed schooling in that intellectual life
which had been so long denied him. It was necessary that
he be awakened to the science, art, literature and philosophy
of the modern era. In so far as Jewish leaders of the eighteenth and nineteenth centuries set themselves to correct
these ills of the Jewish masses, they were engaged in a mission of mercy. Only through such measures could the Jew
be prepared for life in the modern world.

Unfortunately, the healers were ignorant both of the true
anatomy of the diseased organism, and of the circumstances
under which it had to make its recuperative convalescence.
As a result, they cut blindly, severing veins and arteries, and
excising vital organs.

"Chiropodists," said Heine, "have sought to cure the
body of Judaism of its fatal excrescences, and on account
of their unskillfulness and their cobweb bandages of
reason, Israel must be bled to death."

For all the divergence in intention, the activities of all
three groups—assimilators, fugitives and physicians—led to
an identical consequence, the speeding and precipitation of
the death of the old order, rather than to a wholesome read-
justment of it to its new circumstances.

Moses Mendelssohn was at once the first and the finest
representative of the school of misguided surgeons. In his
life he was ever a devoted Jew, a noble and kindly soul, an
honest if not an inspired thinker. He loved his people and
its tradition passionately, his major ambition was to serve
them. But for all his integrity of purpose, he made the

single most significant contribution to their dissolution. His story will bear brief retelling.

Moses Mendelssohn was born in 1729 at Dessau, the son of a poor scribe who earned a meager livelihood by writing scrolls of the Law. His early education was typical of the ghetto. He was thoroughly grounded in the Bible and Talmud. The sole divergence from the normal in his instruction lay in the fact that the rabbi of Dessau introduced him at an early age to the great philosophic classic of Moses Maimonides. At the age of fourteen he followed his teacher to Berlin to continue his studies. It is expressive of the political restrictions suffered by Jews that the young Moses had difficulty in gaining admission to Berlin, that for many years he lived there only as a protégé of a tolerated Jewish family, and that not until 1763, when Mendelssohn had won considerable repute as a writer and philosopher, was a royal grant issued confirming his right of residence.

The capital of Prussia was a different place from the small conservative ghetto in which Mendelssohn was born. Berlin at that time already had a considerable number of prosperous Jews. While its ghetto still conformed to the medieval pattern, there were already within it some individuals who had acquired some non-Jewish culture and many more who were beginning to introduce the customs and manners of the Gentile into their own homes. Thus it was possible for Mendelssohn to find among his fellow-Jews one qualified to teach him mathematics, another Latin, a third French and English.

By a fortunate chance, Mendelssohn won the warm friendship of Lessing, the most tolerant Christian of his day. The intimacy of the two was tremendously stimulating to the young Jewish student. Lessing's criticism perfected

Mendelssohn's German style, their collaboration in literary experiments started Mendelssohn on his career as an author appealing for audition to the non-Jewish world. In 1763 Mendelssohn created a minor sensation by submitting a successful prize essay in a contest sponsored by the Berlin Academy of Sciences. In retrospect, it is slightly amusing to consider that his contribution was preferred to one offered by Immanuel Kant.

With the place of Mendelssohn in German letters and philosophy we are not concerned. What is significant is his work in preparing the German ghetto for the emancipation and for the internal collapse which followed upon it. Between 1778 and 1783, he published a translation of the Pentateuch in classical German. This single work was fraught with tremendous consequences. In all the ghettos of Germany until this time Yiddish had been the vernacular. A barrier of language separated the Jewish masses from the Gentile world. The translation taught the Jew to speak German and prepared him for his impending liberation. The spirit in which Mendelssohn undertook this task can be seen from the following extract from a letter which he wrote describing his purpose:

> "I found after some investigation that the remainder of my energies would suffice to render a service to my children and perhaps to a considerable number of my people, if I provided them with a better translation and explanation of the Holy Scriptures than those hitherto available. This is the first step to civilization, from which my nation, alas, has held itself so aloof that one might almost despair of the possibility of improvement."

Note the phrase, "first step to civilization." That Mendelssohn, a Jewish scholar and loyalist, should be capable of uttering it is significant. It suggests that even he had so little appreciation of the Jewish heritage that he regarded it as no civilization at all. This chance phrase must not be pressed too far. It is not truly expressive of Mendelssohn's attitude. But it does show that he, too, had been infected by a sense of cultural inferiority. For all his steadfast love of Judaism there were moments when Mendelssohn must have felt that only the Gentile possessed a genuine and vital culture. From this attitude an interesting corollary could be deduced—that the only honest course open to Jews was to abandon Judaism and its poverty for the richness of Christian civilization. Though his successors deduced it promptly enough, Mendelssohn refused to draw this implication. To the end he insisted on his Jewishness. "Indeed, I do not see how those who were born in the House of Jacob can in any conscientious manner disencumber themselves of the Law."

Stubbornly, Mendelssohn remained observant of all Jewish forms in his personal life. The sum effect of his labors was, however, destructive of the very tradition to which he clung. The influence of the translation of the Pentateuch has already been indicated. In 1781 he helped to organize in Berlin a Jewish school where instruction was given not only in the Bible and Talmud, but also in technical sciences, in French and German.

Perhaps the most destructive aspect of Mendelssohn's thinking was his complete rationalism. One of the first books of non-Jewish philosophy which he read in his early youth was Locke's *Essay Concerning the Human Understanding*. The common-sense empiricism of that work, its insistence on reasonableness in all things, influenced him profoundly. Besides, rationalism was in the air during the

eighteenth century; it moved contagiously through all thinking. By its standards, no belief was valid if it was not susceptible of proof. The mysteries and dogmas of traditional
religions were pooh-poohed as so much superstition.
Mendelssohn himself was in full agreement with this position. "I recognize no eternal verities except those which
can not only be made comprehensible through the human
intellect, but can also be demonstrated and confirmed by
human forces."

As a result, he was quick to point out that Judaism had no
dogmas, no doctrines binding on the intellect, choking
thought within unreasonable confines. In a rationalist
world, this was a major virtue and Mendelssohn doubtless
felt that his assertion put Judaism in an enviable light.
From one point of view Mendelssohn was entirely correct.
There was in the Jewish tradition no authoritative statement
of doctrine. If that had been all he implied, the statement
would have embodied only an observation of a fact. But
the affirmation was not so innocent as it seemed. By implication, it denied the validity of all those traditional concepts
which could not be demonstrated by reason, but which none
the less had enabled the Jew to survive. The old weltanschauung of the Jew was done for in any event. Mendelssohn's blow merely added a slight impetus to its passing.

Judaism, from Mendelssohn's position, was less a religion
than a divine revelation. On the fact that God had commanded the Law, he rested the authority of Judaism. Why,
out of the total complex of traditional concepts, he should
have selected this one for preservation can not be determined. Certainly it was no more a reasonable article of
faith than many which he rejected by implication. The
probability is that Mendelssohn saw the consequences of his

rationalism. If he allowed it to continue unchecked it might leave the whole of Judaism without justification. He stopped short, hoping that by limiting to one of relative simplicity the hypotheses on which Judaism rested, he might still contrive to save it.

The attempt to ground all of Jewish existence on one article of belief was motivated then by the noblest intentions. It was nevertheless pathetically insufficient. Those who came after Mendelssohn challenged that concept as he had challenged others. In an age of skeptical rationalism revelation itself was a doctrine suspect, one easily attacked. Those who refused to stop short with Mendelssohn, who insisted on following the argument to its end, quickly exploded such an argument. The total effect of Mendelssohn's efforts was to undermine the foundations on which Judaism had once rested without creating a substitute theory to support the superstructure.

Perhaps it is not fair to blame Mendelssohn for the débâcle which followed his death. After all, he did not create the circumstances of his time, he was a product of them. Nothing he did, or left undone, could ultimately have affected the sweep of subsequent events. But débâcle is the only word which describes German Jewish life for the next half-century. Even the family of Moses Mendelssohn proved to be no exception. One by one his children or grandchildren drew the implications implicit in his position. When, in 1871, Alexander Mendelssohn, a grandson of Moses, died, the last Jewish descendent of Moses Mendelssohn had passed from the scene. The entire family had gone over, bag and baggage, to the world, deserting the cause for which the head of the family had labored with so much devotion and so little success.

The spirit of the whole Jewish scene during the early stages of emancipation reveals itself nowhere with such vividness as in the salons of Jewish social leaders. Jewesses of wealth and position strove to make their homes the rallying place for intellectuals, Jew and Gentile. In themselves, such social gatherings would have been harmless, had it not been for the attitude which motivated them. Literary lights were lionized, especially if they were not Jewish. With the arrival of the Christian guest, the salon attained its goal. Then the presiding hostess could assure herself that she had really freed herself from the stigma of her Jewishness, that Gentiles respected her sufficiently to treat her as an equal.

Henrietta Herz in many respects represented the whole class. Brilliant, beautiful and cultured, she was given an indulgently free hand by an equally cultured husband. In her Berlin home she gathered the leaders of German intellect. Among the habitués of her salon were numbered Jean Paul Richter, Schiller, Mirabeau, Alexander von Humbolt, and especially Schleiermacher. Like most members of her group, she ultimately made the leap of baptism.

Of like character was the salon of Rahel Levin. Her life repeats the story of her contemporaries, Dorothea Mendelssohn and Henrietta Herz. It contained the same assemblages of prominent and brilliant Gentiles, the same ultimate conversion and the typical marriage outside of the faith.

This reference to the social life of Jewesses may seem trivial and unimportant. And so it is. It describes the ambitions, the aspirations, of a group of women whose major purpose was to win the friendship of Gentiles of prominence. It is, at best, a story of social climbing, but it is revelatory of the type of thing which inspired Jews of position. It was also not without serious consequences.

For these women, by wealth, position and intellect, represented the upper level of Jewish society. Jews, like other
human beings, tend to imitate those above them. The example which the arbitress of fashion so carelessly set was
scarcely conducive to a healthy Jewish life. She was aped
until every Jewess who could afford it yearned for a salon of
her own. Little things often change great movements.
These women destroyed the integrity of whole Jewish communities. They set before the socially ambitious a new
standard. Social success came to be estimated in terms of
acceptance by Gentiles.

That an epidemic of baptism should have swept the sick
body of Jewry was inevitable. Whole communities were
dissolved in holy water. Within thirty years, half the Jews
of Berlin entered the church. The half-emancipated, fret-
ting under a freedom that was only partial, sought to liberate themselves. Those who desired unrestrained entrance
into a larger social life found a change of official religion
an easy escape. It seemed a slight price to pay for the privilege of complete liberty. Besides, only a Christian could hope
for a career in the professions. The young man or woman,
with all of life ahead of him, felt that his Judaism was, in
Heine's phrase, a misfortune. If fate had blundered by
making him a Jew, certainly it was the part of wisdom to
correct the blunder. It was left to Heine to crystallize the
spirit in which baptism was accepted: "The baptismal cer-
tificate," he remarks cynically, "is the admission ticket into
European civilization."

The motives of the flight to the church are revealed in the
fact that many a Jew who could not bring himself to take
the step had his children baptized. The feeling seems to have
been that the parent must not allow his honorable com-

punctions to hinder his child's future. This was the compromise adopted by the father of Benjamin Disraeli. This appears to be the spirit in which the father of Karl Marx became a Christian when his son was six years old.

Most of the fugitives suffered little from pangs of conscience. But those of finer sensibilities resented to the end the price of an admission ticket into world affairs.

> "From my way of thinking," Heine wrote to a friend, "you can well imagine that baptism is an indifferent affair. I do not regard it as important even symbolically, and I shall devote myself all the more to the emancipation of the unhappy members of our race. Still I hold it as a disgrace and a stain upon my honor that in order to obtain an office in Prussia—in beloved Prussia—I shall allow myself to be baptized."

The Jewish loyalist may take comfort in the fact that treason proved unprofitable, that the admission ticket was more often rejected than honored. He may console himself with the fact that Heine, shortly after his baptism, wrote regretfully:

> "I am hated by Jew and Christian alike. I regret very deeply that I had myself baptized. I do not see that I have been the better for it since. On the contrary, I have known nothing but misfortunes and mischances."

The desertion swept on apace, taking from Jewish ranks its finest spirits and best brains—its Felix Mendelssohns, its Henrietta Herzes, its Disraelis, Heines, Eduard Ganses, Karl Marxes and Ludwig Bornes. In the hour of sharp attack, the Jewish people was bereaved of its most promising children. It was deserted by those who, had they given their

devotion, might have converted the emancipation from a
rout to a successful passage.

By the middle of the nineteenth century the torrent of
conversion in Western Europe had dwindled to a trickle.
The most ambitious Jew tended to be convinced of the futility of baptism. But as the movement died in the West, it
began in the East. The tolerance of Alexander II raised
high hopes among the Russian Jews. The partial emancipation which he sponsored encouraged the Jew to hope for
more. It created conditions analogous to those which had
prevailed in Germany a half-century or so before. Similar
consequences resulted. That baptism in Russia never became a mass movement is due to conditions peculiar to the
Russian scene. In the first place, Jewish life was more vigorous in the East than in the West, it still followed the old
patterns, it still evoked a full loyalty. Again, the Russian
emancipation was short-lived and feeble, it was never allowed
a full opportunity to set its machinery in motion. But, most
of all, baptism had little to offer the Jew on the czarist scene.
The Jew there had no feeling that the culture of the Gentile
world was superior to his own. In any event, in a land
where all were slaves, there was little sense in exchanging
one bondage for another.

Baptism, none the less, was a fairly common expedient.
Daniel Chwolson, the Orientalist, is a case in point. Only
his conversion made possible his appointment to the chair
of Oriental Languages at the University of St. Petersburg.
That his apostacy meant little can be seen from the fact that
his life was devoted to a scholarly defense of his people
against anti-Semitic attacks.

Sometimes, among these converts, loyalties long forgotten
asserted themselves tragically in the face of a crisis. The

mystic bond of blood, lax for decades, suddenly grew tight
and led to some strange dénouement. Consider, for example, the case of an obscure apostate called Abraham
Zimmerman, and the fate which overtook him. Zimmerman was born into a family of wealthy Jewish pietists. In
his early youth he manifested unusual intellectual abilities.
Encouraged by his parents, he spent his childhood over the
Talmud, in which he acquired remarkable proficiency.
Were it not for a curious accident, he might have lived out
his entire life in the security of the Pale. When he was fourteen years of age, his father engaged a German-Jewish engi-
neer to build a mill. This Jew, entirely emancipated, was
attracted by the brilliant intellect of the young student. He
felt that it was being wasted in the sterility of an obsolete
literature. In personal conversation, he described to the
eager youth the glories of the outer world. Zimmerman's
whole-heartedness was gone; he was now torn between two
ambitions. Ultimately he fled his home and entered a
secondary Russian school. Long accustomed to intensive
study, he moved brilliantly from gymnasium to university
and thence into the school of law. Again he won scholastic
honors. Upon graduation, he was offered an instructorship
provided he would accept Christianity. For some time he
hesitated and then abruptly made the plunge.

For many years his career was full, useful and happy.
Slight cause was given to him to regret his decision. And
then the false dawn of Russian liberalism faded; Russia
reverted to its old anti-Semitism. Zimmerman began to
feel a coldness of manner in his colleagues. His lectures
were transferred to inconvenient hours. In vain he protested his Christianity; in vain he pointed to the regularity
of his attendance at church. Baptism or no baptism, he was

still a detested Jew. The fact that attendance at his courses
fell off was used as an excuse to dismiss him. For some
years he drifted from place to place, holding in succession
less and less important positions.

The end of his career was so melodramatic as to be scarcely
credible were it not sober fact. Zimmerman had reared
his two sons in full ignorance of their Jewish descent. One
night they returned home, stained with blood and laden
with booty. They had taken part in a pogrom. At the
sight of the blood of his fellows on the hands of his children,
Zimmerman's long dormant loyalties awoke. A storm
broke within him. The feeling came over him that this
was a just retribution for his treachery. On the next night,
dazed and half-crazed, he made his way into a Jewish
cemetery and there shot himself. This case of Zimmerman
may be spectacular, but it demonstrates that the act of conversion was not so easy as it might appear; that there were
times when an outraged loyalty rose to take silent revenge
upon the renegade; that the hands of a dead past were not
entirely impotent.

Thus did misguided surgery, self-seeking and conversion
drain the ebbing life of the old Judaism. But their disruptive influences were negligible compared to certain psychological attitudes which came to dominate the Jewish
mind. The first of these was a crushing sense of cultural
inferiority. As emancipation freed the Jew, he came to
assume as an unquestionable fact the superiority of Gentile
civilization to his own. This feeling we have already noted
in Mendelssohn. It infected most partly emancipated Jews.
It was taken for granted that everything Gentile was good;
everything Jewish, bad. Overwhelmed by the specious
superiority of the outer world, it seemed to many the part

of wisdom to adopt it *in toto*. The Jew developed culturally a bias against his own culture.

Side by side with the feeling that all excellences were Gentile, went a reasoning which drove the Jew further from himself. Why, the half-emancipated asked themselves, did the world refuse to complete the process of liberation; why would it not confer unreserved recognition? A plausible answer had it that the fault lay in the Jew himself. So long as he insisted on being a distinct personality, on clinging to his otherness, he had no right to expect full acceptance. The logic of the case seemed obviously to demand a deliberate remaking of the Jew into a Gentile. The more the Jew took on the manners, habits and ideas of the world, the more readily would he be treated as the equal of the non-Jew. The greater the emulation, the less the discrimination.

From these two attitudes, that of the superiority of Gentile culture, and that which saw escape in a conscious self-transformation of the Jew, several consequences followed. The first was the tendency to blind imitation to which we have referred again and again. Granted these two premises and emulation becomes automatically a positive ideal. Jews are by nature neither more nor less inclined toward aping than other people. But mimicry of the Gentile world under emancipation was almost a matter of principle.

The same logic, carried to its ultimate implications, formed the framework of the philosophy of total assimilation. If Judaism be not only an unworthy heritage but one that brings in its wake suffering for the Jew and discomfort for the Gentile, if the friction could be abated by the Jew going part way to the Gentile, there was no reason why he should not go the whole distance and lose himself entirely. Then, at last, the Jewish problem would be solved

both for the individual and society, for there would be no
more Jews.

The leaders of Jewish thought during the century following Mendelssohn were acutely aware of the genuine need for
introducing Western culture into the ghetto. It was in
recognition of a social necessity that Mendelssohn himself
had translated the Pentateuch into pure German and had
founded a school on modern principles. All the Jew could
call culturally his own was a civilization which had, from a
position of preeminence, fallen behind the march of the
world, and then stagnated. The Jewish people needed instruction. The *Haskalah,* or the Enlightenment, was a cultural movement which undertook to furnish it.

In so far as the Haskalah introduced Western thought into
the ghetto, in so far as it taught the Jew the language of
his land, the science, literature, art and philosophy of the
world, in exactly that degree it was a blessing of light amid
darkness. Unfortunately, however, the Enlightenment as a
whole was shot through both with the sense of cultural
inferiority and with the program of imitation. Had the
Maskilim, as the protagonists of the Haskalah were called,
had a profounder perception of the abiding values of the
tradition, had they undertaken to reconstruct and supple-
ment it from the general spiritual possessions of the world,
they would have spared the Jew a weary century in the
wilderness. With certain notable exceptions, however, they
were concerned less with the conveyance to the Jew of
the things he did not have than with the substitution of these
for the inheritance of Israel. Their manner was one of intolerance for the old Judaism; their attitude that of the missionary who contemptuously brings to benighted barbarians
a new gospel of salvation. As a result, in their very instruc-

tion, they robbed the Jew of his self-respect; they infected him with a sense of inferiority; they alienated him from his own heritage; they falsified the problem which faced the Jew under emancipation and they retarded a successful solution.

With Moses Mendelssohn the Haskalah may be said formally to have begun; his own work set the pattern for German Maskilim. The achievements of the Enlightenment in Germany were, however, largely inconsequential. They consisted in some original composition in Hebrew, much translation from other languages, and a constant effort to reform Jewish education so as to include secular subjects. In 1783 a group of Maskilim launched the first Hebrew periodical of a secular nature. Their use of the Hebrew language is interesting. In part, it sprang from a genuine love of the tongue of their forefathers, but much more from the fact that they had no alternative choice. Yiddish, which the masses spoke, they detested as tainted with the ghetto. German was still an unknown tongue to most Jews. Wherefore, they used Hebrew to convey non-Jewish culture to Jews.

By 1811 the Hebrew periodical was dead. So successfully had it won the Jew to the German civilization that there was no longer a body of German Jews interested in a Hebrew magazine. The pupils learned so rapidly that they outstripped their masters, that they were soon able to dispense with encouragement and guidance. When the German Maskilim began their work, the problem had been one of introducing Western thought to Jews. Twenty-eight years later, it had become questionable whether any Jews would be left.

Nevertheless, even from the strictly Jewish view-point,

the German Haskalah was not without some compensations. As it trickled into other hands, it stimulated a new productivity in Jewish scholarship. In Italy it helped mold Samuel David Luzzato into a scientific philologist and editor of medieval poetry. In Galicia it equipped Nachman Krochmal and Solomon Rapoport with the tools of scientific research which they used for an accurate reconstruction of Jewish history and literature. The loyalty of these men was too firm to be swerved from Jewish ends. But these were only accidental and unintentional by-products of the German Haskalah. The Maskilim had undertaken to modernize the Jew at any price. The price turned out to be Judaism.

Like the emancipation, the Haskalah penetrated into Eastern Europe tardily. There it found a scene of activity radically different from the German. Jewish life in Russia, for all its stagnation, was still sufficiently vital to resist destruction. The old régime was still powerful and still enlisted intense loyalties. The very Maskilim of Russia were of a different complexion. For all that many of them were blind to the virtues of traditional Judaism, for all that many sought to break its hold, there was in them no contempt for ancestral ways. Russian Maskilim were learned in Jewish lore, they were loyal to it, they were passionately devoted to the Jewish people as a people. Above all, they were relatively free both from a sense of inferiority and a desire to win Gentile approval. As a rule, they sought to educate the Jew for the Jew's sake, not so that he might be free to attempt to become something else.

As early as the first quarter of the nineteenth century, Isaac Baer Levinsohn timidly began in Russia to speak the language of the Haskalah. He objected to the concentration of Jews in commerce, to the typical life of the Jewish student

which was devoid of any concern for a future livelihood. He
advocated that Jews enter into agriculture and the handicrafts. Because Levinsohn was himself a pious Jew, because
his contentions were always supported with quotations from
the Bible and the Talmud, the orthodox took no offense.

Then the Haskalah began to speak more boldly. Moses
Leb Lilienblum attacked the stupidities of ghetto Judaism un-
sparingly. Judah Leb Gordon, the Hebrew poet laureate of
his day, took up the hammer. Savagely he criticized the
ideals of Jewish learning, the contempt in which the Pale
held manual labor, the inequities and injustices of traditional
Jewish law and ritual. In addition, countless volumes of
works in Hebrew and Yiddish appeared, works of poetry
and science, art and literature. Those which were original
literary creations were often stilted in style and puerile in
content. The translations were generally inexact and inadequate. But, in either case, the volumes were filled with
the modern spirit, with untraditional ideas that subtly
threatened the old order.

The Pale, however, for all its paralysis, was not impotent.
The supporters of the old order fought back against the
Haskalah. The Judaism of Eastern Europe still had the
power to coerce and to crush. In Germany, the Enlightenment had been a triumphant march. The Eastern Maskil
generally found life difficult. He, his books and his ideas
were excommunicated, ostracized and condemned. The
very possession of a modern Hebrew or Yiddish book, un-
sanctioned by rabbis, was *prima facie* evidence of heresy and
sympathy for those who troubled the age-old peace of Israel.

None the less, the Haskalah moved onward in Russia,
growing bolder as it went. Especially in the Yeshivah did
its ideas make their way. Despite a rigorous interdict on all

the works of the Maskilim, books were smuggled in and eagerly consumed. The young student secretly read science, literature and history until his faith was shaken. He heard of the world outside of the Pale where students did not always remain pointlessly students, where they became doctors, lawyers or professors. More and more did students desert the Talmud for the secular university, more and more did they diverge in conduct and thought from the accepted pattern. Indeed, even conversions were becoming common. By 1870 Russian Jewry was apparently on the same royal road to destruction which German Jewry had taken a half-century earlier. The vast majority of East European Jews were still unaffected. But there already existed a sufficiently large number of the discontented half-emancipated to threaten the traditional scheme with dissolution.

Then came the pogroms and repressive legislation of the 'eighties. The most enthusiastic Maskil stopped in his tracks to re-evaluate the scene. It became apparent at once that the Haskalah was not enough. All efforts to enlighten the Jewish masses to the end that they might take their place in Russian life had been rewarded with a demonstration of the fact that Russia disliked its Jews, traditional and enlightened alike. Obviously, the Haskalah offered no salvation if it could not improve the lot of the Jew. The Haskalah died an abrupt death, abandoned as pointless, unavailing.

Despite its sudden disappearance from the scene, it was not without permanent influences. It introduced thousands of East European Jews to Western thought, it had incidently created a new Hebrew literature. In its major purpose, it had failed. It had promised the Jew that if he modernized himself he would become a free member of the world's society. That promise it was unable to fulfil. In fact, the

Haskalah had aggravated the problem. It had made count-less Jews dissatisfied with the traditional way of life; it had coaxed and cajoled them out of it. And then, suddenly, it deserted them, leaving them members neither of the old order nor of the new.

CHAPTER XI

DUSK CHILDREN

"And each of us with the light of, the God in his heart
Went forth at dusk time to seek his star.
But the time was one of chaos and void, when the boundaries grew
confused
Between beginnings and ends, between annihilation and creation, be-
tween age and youth.
And we, the children of the dusk, aware or blind,
Bowed down in homage before two rival Gods."

CHAIM NACHMAN BIALIK

THERE is always a touch of melancholy about the passing of an age. Hopes and dreams, aspirations and fears, customs and institutions come to their end and all that remains of the pageantry is a fading memory. But to live through the death of an old order is to participate in its agonies. When a society is in the full bloom of health, the individual reflects its vitality. When it gasps for life and resists threatened death, something of its desperation infects each of its human components. That is why Sophocles is a poet of sanity and clarity, while Euripides is turgid; why Dante is serene in the inferno, while Shelley gropes even in the sunlight. For the last days of a passing world are murky and confused. The landmarks of centuries have been swept away, their verities become uncertain. And each soul must find its way along paths which it does not know, toward goals which it can not discern.

One last phase of the tale we have been unfolding is still to be recorded, the agony of the passage from one world to the other. For underneath the chaos of the ghetto in decay

207

and its civilization in transition, runs in somber undertone a refrain of restless pain. The Jew all through the emancipation was a man of sorrows, of split personality and divided loyalty. If he was normal, he loved the past of his people and was possessed of an instinctive allegiance to it. He surrendered it grudgingly and hankered after it when it was gone. Even though he might be conscious of its weaknesses and limitations, the realization that it was doomed cut him to the quick. But since he was human, he recognized that his selfish interests lay in another, unrealized realm. He was, therefore, tortured between two allegiances, that of the past of his people and that of his own personal future. Choice between the two was excruciatingly painful. Try as he might, he could not dodge an ultimate selection. That was a necessity imposed upon him as a "child of the dusk," born in that dark hour when the old sun faded and no new sun had as yet arisen in the sky.

Nor was the pain entirely one of sentiment. The transition affected each individual closely in his personal life. Aside from the great issue of ultimate allegiance, it forced upon him a multitude of minor decisions. He must determine how much of the tradition he would accept for himself, what part of it, what rites, ceremonies and attitudes of the older world he was still to hold as valid, and how much he was to concede to the world. And always he was haunted by the great question—Judaism, or the world? Even when the decision was made, the Jew had no surcease. If he elected the larger society, his conscience accused him of a lack of self-respect and of treason. If he clung to his loyalties, he reproached himself because of lost opportunities and futile self-sacrifice.

It would be possible to illustrate the painful vacillation

with literally hundreds of instances. It will be wiser and more completely revealing if our account describes the inner struggle of a few selected dusk children.

Heinrich Heine offers a vivid example of those who chose the world and who ate their mess of pottage regretfully ever after. He was born during the first and most favorable phase of the emancipation when the hopes of Jews were highest. The Jewish education he received as a child was negligible, and during his early manhood he was a habitué of the salons of Berlin. Despite these influences, he acquired mysteriously a positive Jewish consciousness and a respect for the culture of his people. When a group of young Jewish intellectuals organized the *Verein fur Kultur und Wissenschaft des Judentums,* an organization for the study of Jewish culture and for the encouragement of loyalty to it, Heine joined most enthusiastically. Despite all the initial zeal with which the society was founded, despite the fact that its members hoped that it would put a stop to the unseemly march to a hypocritical baptism, they, one by one, began to adopt the course they were resisting. In 1825, Eduard Gans, the first president of the society, discovering that an academic career was impossible for him so long as he remained a Jew, embraced Christianity. The example of Gans convinced Heine that only baptism would open the doors for him. In 1825, he also officially adopted Christianity.

How distasteful he found this step can be seen from his insistence that he had been "merely baptized, not converted." How deeply his conscience was troubled can be detected in his promise—obviously a salve for his self-respect—to do all he could for "the emancipation of the unhappy members of our race." He was convinced that as a result of conversion he was hated both by Christian and Jew, that he was at home nowhere. In an attempt to punish himself for his offense against his people, in an effort to expiate his treachery by self-mortification, he attended Temple in Hamburg so that he might writhe when the rabbi in his sermon castigated baptized Jews.

But if Heine detested himself and his fellow-fugitives for their cowardice, he despised the church all the more, because, knowing the motives for conversion, it still accepted Jews. No religious rite came in for so much scorn from him as did this one to which he had himself resorted.

"Do you believe," he wrote savagely, "that one's inner nature can be wholly changed through baptism? I don't believe it, and to me it is a melancholy as well as ridiculous sight when the old lice who date back to Egypt, to the Pharaonic plague, suddenly persuade themselves that they are fleas and begin to hop like Christians."

All through his subsequent career, Heine was driven by the sense of a wrong which he had done. Especially during his last years, when he lay on his "mattress grave" did he seek to placate his conscience, to atone for the sin of his youth. He, who was officially a Christian, wrote the *Romanzero* with its lovely picture of Judah Halevi, the *Prinzessin Sabbath* idealizing the poetic ceremonies of the Jewish home. The satirical strain in Heine was much too strong to allow for much sentimentalizing, but, so far as his natural irony permitted, he took a morbid delight in idealizing the Judaism which he had renounced. Despite his cosmopolitanism, there was one deep loyalty in his soul—a loyalty to his people, which, for all his savage asides, made his theme the glory of Israel.

No tribute to the Bible and the Jew can be more eloquent
than this:

"If I do not err, it was Mahomet who named the Jews
'The People of the Book,' a name which has remained
theirs to the present day on the earth, and which is
deeply characteristic. A book is their very fatherland,
their treasure, their governor, their bliss and their
bane . . . absorbed in the city of this book, they observed
little of the changes which went on about them in the
real world. Nations rose and perished; states bloomed
and disappeared; revolutions stormed forth out of the
soil; but they sat bowed down over their book and observed nothing of the wild tumult of the times which
passed over their heads."

In perverse chauvinism the renegade found release and a
sense that he was making restitution to his people.

"I see now that the Greeks were merely handsome
striplings. The Jews, however, have always been men,
strenuous and full of power, not only at that time, but
even at the present day, in spite of eighteen hundred years
of persecution and misery. I have since then learned
to value them better, and, if every kind of pride of
birth were not a foolish contradiction in a champion of
revolution and democratic principles, the writer of these
pages might be proud that his ancestors belonged to the
noble House of Israel, that he is a descendent of those
martyrs who have given to the world one God and a
moral law, and have fought and suffered in all the battle-
fields of thought."

The Jews, to Heine, were the "Swiss guard of Deism";
they "have had highly civilized hearts in an unbroken tradi-

tion for two thousand years." But even Heine was aware that most of this was an idealization. The Jew who had remained a Jew did not need to idealize his people. Only the Jew who had betrayed Judaism felt such a necessity; it was the only service which he, as a renegade, could render.

As much as Heine loved, abstractly, the Jewish people, Jewish culture and Jewish institutions, just so much he despised the living Jews of his day. Above all, he hated the sleek, contented Jewish bourgeoisie with their little imitations of the Gentiles and their petty attempts secretly to erase their Jewish traits. In part, his resentment sprang from a consciousness that he, for all his merits, was denied the ease which they enjoyed. But even more he disliked the Jewish middle class because their fawning and cringing, their self-degradation and imitation reminded him in another form of the same treason of soul of which he had been guilty. He who had sold his Jewish heritage objected because

"Jewish girls of wealth and fashion,
Future mothers of free burghers,
Culling all the latest knowledge
In the dearest Paris *pensions,*

"Know by heart the names of mummies,
All the stuffed Egyptian Pharaohs,
Merovingian shadow monarchs
Whose perukes were yet unpowdered,

"Also pig-tailed kings of China,
Porcelain-pagoda princes,
Pat from tongue it all comes tripping.
Clever girls! But oh, good heavens!

"Should you ask about the famous
Names that formed the golden triad

Of our Jewish constellation,
Our Arabic-Spanish singers,

"There three stars if you should ask of,
Our Jehudah ben Halevi,
Or our Solomon Gabirol,
Or our Moses ibn Ezra,

"Should you bring up names of that sort,
Then with large eyes will regard you
All the girls, the pretty darlings,
Dumb-struck, mud-stuck, disconcerted."
                        Translated by Israel Zangwill.*

The bitterness of Heine was, of course, largely a matter of temperament. It was accentuated by a blasted love-affair in his youth, by the ordeal of a dishonest baptism, by the failure of conversion to create a professional career, by poverty, ill-health and the mattress grave. But among the motifs which are interwoven into a pattern of satire that is often spiteful, must be enumerated the restlessness of an unhappy conscience, an oppressive sense of guilt, a feeling of betrayal against a people. This remorse never left Heine. Nor was his heart any the lighter because the baptism had been futile. When, at the end of his life, Heine remarked whimsically, *"Dieu me pardonnera, c'est son métier,"* it is not unlikely that the sin which he felt most needed pardon was that one committed against Israel.

The attempt to atone for a desertion of the Jewish people by an idealization of it was not confined to a Heine. It was manifested in thousands of instances of which Benjamin

---

* From the Introduction to *Selected Religious Poems of Solomon Ibn Gabirol,* Jewish Publication Society of America.

Disraeli is one. Nominally a Christian, he could still assert with a great show of pride, "one half the world worships a Jew and the other half a Jewess." But here the fundamental motive was different. Disraeli had little of Heine's feeling of outrage. Instead, he suffered subtly from a sense of social inferiority. Beyond all else, Disraeli idealized the old English aristocracy—the hunting, drinking, gaming squire. He envied the secure social position, the confidence of descent which the manor possessed.

Since Disraeli was a Jew by birth, all the conversions of the world could not make him into an authentic English aristocrat. The best he could ever achieve was to mingle socially with British nobility, to attract their attention and approval. The sense of social inferiority in Disraeli is a psychological trait which perhaps explains much of his personality. It accounts for his colorful clothes and flamboyant manner, adopted apparently in the spirit of making the "swells" sit up and take notice. The Jewish pride of Disraeli was a compensatory mechanism. By it, he endeavored to convince himself that he was not only the equal, but even the superior of the squire. His very conservatism sprang in part from this sense of Jewish inferiority. Only a Tory could have the approval of the aristocracy. In his love for the old English order, Disraeli defended it at every turn. He was a Conservative largely because, if he could not participate in the life of the idealized landed nobility, he could at least protect it.

But it was in the east of Europe that the divided soul appeared in its full suffering, that the choice between orders imposed the deepest agony. Here Jewish loyalties were still powerful, here the old régime still persisted intact, in sharp contrast to the world without. Here the passage from one to the other involved a profound emotional wrench. Every young Jew found himself confronted by a dilemma: should he choose the tradition and die wretchedly with it, or, despite affection and instinct, should he throw his lot in with the world and save himself by desertion?

Consider the pathetic existence of Mordecai Zev Feierburg, an obscure Hebrew author, who enriched the culture of his people with some few pages of poignantly tragic prose which everywhere reflect the bitterness of the choice. Feierburg was born in Eastern Europe in 1874, just when the Haskalah was beginning to shake the hypnotic hold of the tradition. His father, a *shochet,* or ritual slaughterer of cattle, was a man of stern unbending piety, who determined that his son must be a profound scholar in the sacred lore. His, then, was the sad blasted boyhood so typical of ghetto children. In his earliest childhood, he was hurried into the study of the Talmud.

Here is a fragment from a tale by Feierburg entitled *The Calf.* It will serve to give some insight into the youth of these dusk children, some hint of the playless, joyless boyhood of ghetto men.

"It was then summer time and I was not yet nine years old. . . . The sun sank low in order to look with its burning eyes into our dark schoolroom. As though to embarrass our teacher, it cast a derisive beam at his dirty fringed shawl; it tangled its rays with his pointed beard to annoy him, and poured its golden glow on to the mire and mud, on to the drainage ditch in the street. . . . And with its mighty magic it hinted to us smilingly, 'Foolish boys, why sit here shut in with the teacher?' Indeed, how dear and lovely was the sunlight which flickered and wavered in sweet kindliness through the window! How nice it was outside! What pleasant things were there! How lovely was the mist as it rose from the canal, how happy the boys who ran about there, who wrestled in the dust and made mudpies and dried them in the sun. But the teacher is hard and stern, he knows no relenting. He sits and teaches, he sits and reviews. Drops of sweat fall on to the page of the Talmud; my shirt is wet and sticks to my skin, my hands are heavy, my head aches, my voice is shrill. But the teacher reviews, teaches and reviews. . . ."

When Feierburg turned fifteen, he was sent to the Academy to continue his studies. There, at last, he found himself in a congenial atmosphere. The large study hall, filled with students, each intoning in a plaintive chant, captivated him; the pious intensity of Yeshivah learning appealed to his idealism. In his first sketch, entitled *Shadows,* written when he was but nineteen years old, he gives vivid insight into the fascination which the Academy and its books held for the sensitive spirit.

"And at night, when a vague something oppresses my heart and a hidden spell is woven about me, drawing me I know not where, when I feel that my soul hungers for something that the cupboard can not provide, when my eyes fill with tears—then I flee to the Academy and amid the numberless hosts of shadows I find peace, by the light of a flickering candle, in the sacred books.

"The books are holy—aye, and the cases are full of them. I know not how it is, and yet it is so, that there are moments when I do not see the books at all but rather a multitude of men, the procession of the centuries, men tall, proud and with shining faces. These men rise from the book shelves, standing partially veiled in the black shadows, and lo, from under their feet, flow streams of blood, while wails and lamentations rise to heaven. Before them a river of blood and tears—behind them more blood and tears.

"Here I am not alone. Here are many as blessed as I. How broad is my world in this place. Here I shall live and here I shall die. Here I shall suffer as did all these that rise from the ancient book chests. And here I shall hope as they hoped—in vain.

"My heart swells with pride and strength as I see that these countless lost ones still live. Aye, they live more really than those who built cities in the waste places, live in rotting chests amid leaves yellowed and stained.

"Happy art thou, Israel. When others embalmed the bodies of their heroes and mighty ones, thou didst embalm the souls of thy poor and afflicted. Wherefore the bodies have hardened to stone, but thy souls, Israel, live and move like shadows in broken chests and yellowing leaves."

But the life of scholarly devotion was not to continue undisturbed. The Haskalah had already penetrated into the Yeshivah, and Feierburg met students who had read illicit literature—books on science, philosophy and history. In secret, Feierburg himself pored over these works of the Enlightenment. They shattered his religious faith, they made him discontented with ghetto life, they filled him with dreams of the freer existence which lay without the Pale; in brief, they confronted him with the old alternatives and demanded a choice. In the tale from which we have just quoted, all of this is presented symbolically. As the student sits over his books, dreaming amid the shadows, the world obtrudes itself noisily.

A chance occasion takes him from his books into the town tavern. There he is momentarily tempted:

"The room was large and spacious, well ordered and tastefully arranged. . . . Many men sat about enjoying themselves and amusing themselves at dice.

"The bright light which reigned everywhere, the tumult, which struck my ears after my long experience with infinite darkness and deep silence, told me that I had entered upon another world of different men living another kind of life, and this life, how lovely and pleasant! Here there were no stains, not even a single shadow. Here everything shone and radiated. Here the sea of life flowed in great sweeps of noisy, turbulent waves. My whole soul pulsated with joy. . . .

"Ah, Life, Life. I, too, love life. . . ."

In the story, the student makes a quick and a heroic choice; he elects to die with the old order. His experience with the false glow of the tavern tells him that its attractions are meretricious.

"Again I am among the shadows, enveloped in darkness. My soul desires some outlet into a broader, larger world. Indeed, I love the shadows, but more than that, I love the sun. But it must be the sun which shines over and illuminates everything. . . . The sun of righteousness which will rise over all, small and great alike. When that sun appears, I will go forth from my academy, I shall flee from the shadows."

But in life, the decision was neither easy nor romantic. What was Feierburg to do? He could not stay at the Yeshivah if he no longer had faith in what he studied. There was no career awaiting him if he returned home, only, at the best, a starved livelihood in some ghetto shop. The old Judaism was dying away, of that he was convinced. He put later, into the mouth of one of his characters, an old pious Jew, this confession of despair:

"The Messiah has not come, all the ages have not brought him, and our generation has grown weary of waiting. The men of faith die away. . . . Now, I will tell you a deep secret though it may be hard to understand. It is *predestined* that parents send their children to Gentile schools; it is *fated* that the Maskilim read heretical books. The ancient holiness has left the world. . . . He who has eyes can see clearly that the earth has been emptied of all sanctity. Woe to us; woe to us."

Then he raised his voice in a lament:

"We have no hold on this world; we have no place in it. We are in exile, and the Divine Presence is in exile with us. . . ."

On the other hand, in the world without, there were unlimited possibilities—universities, professions, a life not stricken by poverty, perhaps wealth and fame. All that was needed was the determination to leave the Yeshivah of shadows for the university of light. It was all very simple, but it involved deserting a sinking ship, going over to the side of the enemies of Israel. There lay the rub. Feierburg could not bring himself to make the change. He left the Yeshivah, but it was for the Judaism that was dying.

From that time on his life was pure misery, both mentally and physically. The old problem of the choice would not down. To aggravate it, existence became intolerable for several reasons. His father soon discovered his son's unorthodox leanings, and his home became an inferno for young Feierburg. A petty business in which he had engaged failed.

A betrothal, on which his heart was set, fell through when his prospective father-in-law caught a rumor of his heresies. Then his health failed him completely. As he lay dying of tuberculosis, he wrote his *chef d' œuvre*, the masterful story, *Whither*, in which he epitomized all the pain and struggle of his spirit, into which he distilled the agony of soul of those who were called on to serve two rival gods, that of their ancestry and that of their own future.

"He looked at his father again and a story he had heard in his childhood, came to his mind suddenly. Once upon a time there was a mighty king who conquered many lands and seas and islands, and ruled from India to Ethiopia. And this king had an only son who was good and wise and strong in arms. And the prince grew up and fought in his father's wars, subduing many great nations. And on a day he came to the kingdom of India, and there he saw the king's daughter, and he wished to take her for his wife. But the king of India would not give her to him. So the prince called together his army and declared war upon him. And the war lasted many years; thousands of men were killed; myriads of men were wounded; widows and orphans and bereaved parents were many as the sands of the sea. . . . The last tower was captured. The prince and his host stood in the royal palace—and lo! the lovely princess lay dead on the ground before them. . . . The warriors returned home. The old king died. Generations came and went, and still the prince stands in the ruined palace and weeps for his beloved. . . . The city has become a heap of ruins, but the prince still lives and day and night he stands before the body of his love and cries bitterly.

"Alas, how dreadful it was, and yet how true! He saw his father and all the old men around him sitting like the prince and weeping for their beloved. . . . Generations came and went, nations came to birth and died, the face of land and sea changed, multitudes were born and died, fought and made peace, loved and hated, the wheel of life revolved with all its uproar—and in a desolate corner, through it all, stands the prince, deserted and forgotten. . . . What to him is time, what are generations and nations? He stands and weeps for his love!

"Alas, unhappy prince! . . . From the day he first knew his father, he saw that he lived in the far distance, among the ruins of Zion and the spirits of the dead, the spirits of his fathers! . . . All his talk, all his dreams, his hopes and aspirations, they were the ruins, the forgotten spirits; with them and in their midst, he passed his life, and with them and in their midst, he reared his son. . . .

" 'You tell me,' he said to his father, 'that in exile we are living upon what we produced before the destruction of the Temple. Say what you will. It seems to me as if the entire people of Israel has been sitting for two thousand years and weeping over graves.' "

Feierburg died shortly after he had finished *Whither* at the age of twenty-five. In volume, his works are not extensive. His collected prose writings embrace only one hundred and forty-six pages. Stylistically, they are by no means beyond criticism. In spirit they are often bombastic, melodramatic and sophomoric. Feierburg did not live long enough to write much; he was given no opportunity to evolve a finished style nor to outgrow adolescent traits. And yet, for all the meagerness of his work, he is infinitely significant in Jewish history and literature. He incarnates the chief problem of an age.

Santayana, in his *Poetry and Religion,* divides all poets into two classes. There are those who in their verse express only their own personal emotions, without reference either to a cosmic outlook or the genius of the age in which they

live. These he denominates the poets of barbarism, of ir-
responsible and capricious feelings. But there are some
poets whose poetry is more than individual, whose verse reflects the weltanschauung of a society, its universal values,
its general hopes, fears and aspirations. These, Santayana
calls the poets of civilization. In their songs an epoch finds
expression, the *Zeitgeist* takes on voice.

Chaim Nachman Bialik is a superb Hebrew poet; perhaps,
with the possible exception of Judah Halevi, the greatest since
the days of the Bible. His command of the Hebrew language
is broad and sure. His themes are adorned by a wealth of
striking simile and metaphor until they come to resemble
some richly embroidered tapestry. But the major importance of Bialik lies less in his poetic genius than in the fact
that he was the "Mouthpiece of the Folk," the spokesman of
Israel during its transition. He was himself one of the dusk
children and their most audible voice. How consciously he
felt the tragedy of his generation can be seen from the quotation which heads this chapter and which characterizes
superbly the confusion and vacillation of his contemporaries
and himself.

Like Feierburg, Bialik was born just as the old order began to crumble. His education was again typical of his day—
the same childless youth, the same premature aging by over-
study, the years in the Yeshivah, the same disruptive contact
with the Haskalah and the same awakening to grim alternatives. What makes Bialik unique is not his personal experience, but the fact that he caught its spirit and im-
mortalized it in his poems.

The old Judaism is present in his lines, the loveliness of
ancient folk-ways, the quaint legends and tales of the medieval Jewish mind. The dour aspects of the ghetto are there

as well. Like most Jews of the ghetto, Bialik knew the
meaning of abject poverty. That, too, finds expression in his
verse—expression for himself and for a whole people.
"Would ye know," Bialik says, "whence I inherited my
song?" To answer the question, he describes a typical Sabbath in his father's home—the Sabbath table without wine,
meat or white bread, the candlesticks in pawn, the flickering
light of candles that "make the walls to dance," the meal of
crusts of black bread and herring brine, the tear-filled eyes of
his mother, the beaten look on his father's face. And then,
Bialik continues, when all joined in a vain attempt to sing
happily the Sabbath hymns, when with empty stomachs
seven hungry children joined in the chorus, the cricket, "the
singer of poverty," raised his voice. That, says Bialik, is how
he acquired his song.

"And whence came my sigh, would ye know that?"

Then follows a description of the widowing of his mother,
of her struggle to rear her family, of how every penny she
earned was "cursed, wet with her blood and drenched with
her gall."

> "At dawn, at cock's crow she arose
> Silently busy with the work of her house.
> From my dark room from my crib
> Through the door, I saw her broken body. . . .
> A quiet whisper and dry sigh,
> Torn from her, came from the room beyond,
> 'Lord of the world, strengthen and support me!
> What is my strength, my life, I am only a woman!'
> And my heart tells me, and I know
> That the tears of her eyes dropped into the dough.

And when she divided the hot morning bread to
    her children
From the dough of her baking, the bread of her
    tears—
I swallowed it, and her sigh came into my bones."

Even as Bialik gave voice to the poverty of the ghetto, so
he expressed the spirit of its student life. The *Mathmid,* the
"Student," is the classic picture of all the panorama of the
Yeshivah—its students, their lives, their occupations, the
heroism of their devotion, and the futility of their self-
sacrifice.

No tribute to the Jewish school is as full, as moving as
this. No poet has ever recognized the vital influence of
learning in Jewish life as did Bialik in his *If Thy Soul Would
Know.*

"If thy soul would know the fountain
Whence thy martyred brethren drew
In days of evil such strength, courage of soul
To go rejoicing to meet death, to bare the neck
To each keen blade, to each swinging axe. . . .
If thy soul would know the bosom into which were
    poured
All the tears of thy people, its heart, its soul and bitter-
    ness;
The place where they flowed like water, where its sighs
    burst forth,
Sighs that shook the womb of Hell beneath,
Sighs that froze even Satan in horror,
A lament that shattered flint but not the hard heart
    of the enemy,
Which was stronger than flint, more cruel than
    Satan. . . .

Ah, my poor brother, if thou knowest not all this—
Then turn to the academy, the old and venerable.
In the long desolate winter nights,
In the burning flaming summer days,
At noon, dawn or deepest night—
And if God has preserved a tiny remnant—
Then perchance even to-day thine eyes may see
In the wealth of the shadows of its walls, in the dark,
In some lone corner or by the oven,
Scattered sheaves, a shadow of what once was,
Jews beshadowed, with wrinkled troubled faces,
Jews, the children of exile, who bear the weight of its
    yoke,
Who forget their toil in a withered page of the Talmud,
Who lose their poverty in fabled stories of old
And express their anxiety in hymns of psalms. . . .
(Alas, how trivial and sad this must seem
To a stranger who does not understand!)
Then thy heart will tell thee
That thy foot treadeth on the threshold of the house of
    our life
And thine eye beholdeth the treasury of our soul."

But if the old Judaism is present in the poetry of Bialik,
lovingly depicted, so also is the problem of the dusk children.
Bialik himself wrestled with the specter of allegiance. It
is because he vividly portrays his own vacillation that he is
an authentic spokesman for his age. In *On the Threshold
of the Academy,* Bialik laments the decay of the Jewish life
of his fathers, though he asserts confidently its abiding influence. For he recognized that the old order was doomed.
In a poem entitled *Alone,* Bialik depicts the lonesome desola-
tion of the Academy, now deserted by all except him, while
the Presence who haunts it pleads for his loyalty.

"All of them the wind swept away, the light dissipated,
A new song rang through the morning of their lives;
And I, a poor fledgling, have been forgotten
Under the wings of the Presence.

"Alone, alone am I left, and the Presence too
Tremblingly rests its broken wing on my head.
I know its heart, that it trembles for me,
Its son, its only one. . . .

"And when my heart yearns for the window, for light,
And when the space under its wing grows strait for me,
It bows its head to my shoulder, and a tear
Drops to my page of the Talmud.

"Quietly it weeps over me, leans upon me,
And as though sheltering me with its broken wing—
'All of them the wind swept away, the light dissipated
And I shall be left alone, alone . . . ' "

But the time came when Bialik grew weary of problems
and dilemmas, when he refused to allow his life always to
be sicklied over with tortured thoughts. After all, his few
days were passing, bringing to him none of the joys of
living.

"They say that there is youth in the world.
Where is mine?

"To one more secret will I confess
And my soul burns with its flame.
They say there is love in the world.
What is love?"

Again, Bialik is typical of his whole generation of dusk
children. For, after long wrestling with problems, a mood

of resentful lassitude passed over the group. Enough of
anxieties and cares. *Vivamus et amemus*. The mood, however, was of but short duration. The pogroms and
massacres, the cruelty of the Russian state, obtruded
problems once more. It was impossible to indulge in personal pleasure while a whole people suffered. Bialik returned from his retreat again to face the challenge of Jewish
identity. He returned now to castigate his fellow-Jews who,
blind to the great issue, refused to rise to its challenge.

Bialik is, then, the faithful spokesman of the generation
of dusk children. He is also more. He rose from doubt to
affirmation, he transcended vacillation in a positive philosophy of Jewish life. To follow him into his new phase
would be a fascinating adventure. Unfortunately, such an
excursion is irrelevant to the task before us—the description
of the pain attendant on the dissolution of the old Judaism.
But he who wishes to know what sensitive Jews felt in that
age when foundations were destroyed and pillars trembled,
should turn not to history with its formal externality, not to
the philosophers of the day with their abstractions, but to
the poets and story-tellers among the children of the dusk.
There he will find the distracted soul of the Jewish people in
all the blood, sweat and tears of its ordeal.

In its early days, Israel left a bondage for a freedom, and
a whole generation died in the desert. The dusk children
were the sacrifice indispensable to a later passage through
another wilderness.

CHAPTER XII

THE CHARACTER OF THE MODERN JEW

THE witches in *Macbeth* put the liver of a Jew into their boiling caldron. Modern society improved on Shakespeare; into its seething pot it plunged the entire Jewish personality. Freely it applied the corrosives of emancipation, the acids of rationalism, the solvents of social intercourse, and the spirits of modernity. In this elixir, the Jew has been cooked until his older personality has all but dissolved, until by a transformation almost magical, he has been totally remade. Thanks to a century and a half of this experience, a radical metamorphosis in character has taken place.

When one recalls the figure of the ghetto Jew in its pre-emancipation lineaments, one is tempted to postulate some magician's device, some sorcerer's charm to explain how, from what he once was, the Jew became what he is to-day. For only the strongest alchemies of destiny could so completely reconstruct the characteristics of a people.

At the beginning of this book, it was promised that an explanation of the character of the Jew would be forthcoming; that after certain unavoidable preliminaries, it would be told how the chemistry of history came to effect so tremendous a transfiguration. Now at last we are in a position to fulfil this promise, to account for the making of the modern Jew, for his "typical" traits. As a matter of fact, part of the story has already been told. Some peculiarities of personality have already been explained. Thus the long confinement of Jews within ghettos accounts for their tendency to live together even when they are free to live apart. It explains their business acumen and their intellectualism, their emotional loyalty to the group, their cohesion and unity in the face of the world, and their secretiveness and suspicion in the presence of the Gentile. Incidental to the description of the dissolution of the old order, an explanation was advanced of the divergent attitudes of Jews to their tradition. The contrast between the observant Jew and his entirely indifferent fellow was grounded in the irregular and uneven tempo of emancipation in different lands, and in the diverse reactions of individuals to it.

It remains only to complete the list, to catalogue the traits which are commonly observed among Jews and to trace them to their grounds in Jewish history. At first glance it may seem illogical to assert that the same history shall lead to such divergent consequences in personality as we shall record. Diverse individuals, however, react differently to a common experience. Jews have been no exception to this rule. To identical conditions they have responded each in his own peculiar fashion. That is why modern Jews, all products of the same circumstances, exhibit such variety of types. And yet, ultimately, each reaction, much as it may differ from others, is the result of identical causes.

It is easy to understand the Jewish religious skeptic. All groups have their share of doubters on issues divine. The tenor of contemporary thought is scarcely conducive to piety. Among Jewish intellectuals, doubt is both more general and more vehement. In no group is so large a proportion of the educated unchurched. Nor is the reason hard to find. Unlike Christian theology, Jewish religious speculation had no opportunity to make progressive adjustment to the development of the modern mind. The church, Protestant and Catholic, adapted itself successively to the Copernican revolution, the Newtonian picture of a world machine, and the Darwinian evolutionism. And yet, even Christianity has been deeply shaken. But, for the Jew, the inroad of scientific knowledge came as a surprise attack. The Jew, as he emerged from the German ghetto, was offered the whole content of modernity in one dose. When Western ideas reached the student in an East European Yeshivah, they included an astronomy, a history and a philosophy which challenged his entire outlook. The rabbis and teachers of Israel were equally unprepared for such an onslaught. They knew nothing of the character of the attack; they had evolved no defense against it. They took then the only course open to them. They attempted to suppress the destructive ideas, or else to deny their truth. Eventually, they abandoned the hopeless struggle and stood by impotent while the collapse continued.

As a result, Jews, as they came to know modern thought, tended to reject religion bag and baggage. In the rejection a note of bitterness can even now be perceived. Emancipated Jews of the first generation are likely to feel that they have been deliberately betrayed, that their rabbis for centuries have been misleading the people, that they have consciously taught a false doctrine. They are tempted to regard the totality of the Jewish religion as a superstition, once foisted upon an innocent people by a group of witch doctors, but fortunately exploded when the world turned on the light.

The bitterness of this anti-clericalism tends to disappear after the first generation of liberation. But while it endures it is astonishingly intense. Many a Jew now living can re-

call the time when he helped arrange a dance for the eve of
the Day of Atonement in the conscious desire to torment the
benighted faithful. This same mood cropped up a few years
back among Russian Jews. That the Gentile Communist
set his hand to destroy the Greek Orthodox Church is
understandable. The church in Russia served as a major
instrument for czarist exploitation of the masses. This
accusation can not honestly be leveled against the synagogue
or academy. And yet the *Yevseksia*, or Jewish Communist
group, was much more rabid than the Gentile. It persecuted
the Jewish religion vindictively as one who has been crippled
by the malpractise of a quack might seek revenge against
him.

Now, too, the Jewish assimilationist becomes comprehensible. Once the traditional atmosphere has been dissipated,
the Jew can no longer claim for his group election, divine
guidance or an ultimate victory. Such positions may have
been possible in the medieval scene, they are not on the
modern. But those concepts have historically formed the
rationale of Jewish existence. Once they are gone, the Jew
is no longer sure what he is living for. He is compelled to
cast about for a new apologia for Judaism, for a new logic
to justify it, and he fails to find one. In addition, escape
seems easy to-day. There are no ceremonial habits to be
torn away, no fixed wall of hostility to breach, nothing of a
leap from a well-known world to another totally unfamiliar.
In fact, assimilation demands almost no positive action. It
requires only that the individual stand aside and allow
events to take an unobstructed course. He need only permit
traditional customs to die in his home, his children to go
without a Jewish education. He is called upon only to
interpose no obstacles to intermarriage, and his Jewish iden-

tity will disappear. Struggle may be necessary if one wishes to live. Death requires only acquiescence.

The assimilationist, then, considers the pain and frustration which Jews suffer simply because they are Jews, the exclusions, the cultural and economic handicaps and, even in the twentieth century, the massacres and repressions. He weighs the troublesome irritation which society suffers from its Jews, from the presence of a divergent, protesting, unassimilating group. What point can there possibly be in maintaining consciously the whole surface of friction? What purpose will be served if the Jew is to continue to suffer? Obviously it is wiser that Israel lose itself, that the scrawled slate of prejudice be wiped clean.

Furthermore, the assimilationist has his positive and ideal reasons for his program. He points to the dream of an international cosmopolitanism, to the hope of a mankind which shall no longer be torn apart into conflicting groups. The extinction of the Jew then is more than the removal of a problem, it is a step forward toward Utopia.

Like most theories, this one has its limitations in practise. Escape turns out to be by no means as easy as might be expected. Emotional loyalties to the Jewish group often hang on stubbornly and continue for a long time to plague the fugitive. Nor is the world too cordial. It may impose no legal barriers, but it does not welcome even the de-Judaized Jew. Before assimilation can be successfully effected, a long process of painful approach must be completed. The assimilationist must suppress any instinctive sense of allegiance, he must consciously remove characteristics which are recognizably "Jewish," he must deliberately mold himself and his life on Gentile patterns. Above all, he must be prepared for rebuffs from the world. He must be ready to swallow humiliation and return for more.

The price is high, but the assimilationist feels that it is worth while. He consoles himself with the thought that, if he himself can not reach his goal, his children or grandchildren will, as a result of his efforts, be free from all taint. A few generations, a few intermarriages, and he will attain retroactive emancipation in his offspring.

But even the future is not secure for the assimilationist. He must gamble against a violent recrudescence of anti-Semitism such as the Christian Front in America or Hitlerism in Germany embodied. He is never certain but that his children may grow disgusted with the whole effort, or that some atavism may assert itself generations hence, some throw-back to old Jewish loyalties. Ridiculous as it may seem, he must even concern himself with biology. The assimilationist can be ruined by a trick of fate. Let his children be born with curly hair, swarthy complexions and aquiline noses—and the game is up.

Assimilationism is by no means as popular a doctrine as it was a half-century ago. Many Jews argue for it, but fifty years of experience have taught the Jew something about the perils of this speciously simple procedure. What the Jew refuses to see, the Nazi has hammered deep into his head. People of the assimilationist view-point still debate the question, but they generally make few active efforts to implement their position. They end up, not lost in the Gentile world, but in the company of other Jews who are of a like frame of mind.

No accusation is more commonly leveled against the Jew than that of crudity. It is widely asserted that Jews are noisy, dirty and vulgar, that they are naturally not "nice" people to be with. These charges are not made by Gentiles alone.

One often hears Jews indulging in the luxury of criticizing themselves in just this fashion.

For each of these impressions there is some valid basis in fact. The ghetto quarters of modern cities are not distinguished even for that measure of cleanliness which poverty allows, nor is the Jewish group free from boisterous individuals blessed with raucous voices and shrill laughs. To be sure, the most that can be said accurately is that *some* Jews are crude or vulgar, unclean or brash, or that the Jewish group suffers disproportionately from such failings. But if this be true, it is because history and circumstance have made it so.

The ghetto, it should be remembered, is for many Jews just one generation removed. The East European Jew especially, has just emerged from it. Its influences are still to be discerned in him. He is not overly clean because no medieval society, Jew or Gentile, was especially concerned with external cleanliness, because the abject poverty and persecution of the Pale made the amenities of life appear inconsequential in the presence of the struggle to live. No Gentile, if he could be transported to the streets of a city of the Middle Ages would expect to discover modern standards of hygiene. The Jew is a fragment of a fast fading medievalism injected into the modern world.

The very lands from which Jews come have their share in determining these distasteful characteristics. The Jew who has spent his early life in Poland, in Russia or Roumania, brings with him to a Western country not only the influences of the ghetto, but the influence of his native scene. He is generally as quiet, as restrained and as cleanly as the peoples among whom he was reared.

Last of all, it should be remembered that the Jew is the

product of a civilization other than that which bred the American or British Gentile. He is, to be sure, demonstrative and emotional; he does gesticulate more than the Anglo-Saxon; he does talk vehemently and laugh or cry readily. But the society from which he came did not disapprove of these traits. The American traveler who visits Italy is interested in the colorful demonstrativeness of the Italian on his native soil. He is not offended at the fact that Italians talk rapidly, use their hands sweepingly to illustrate their points, greet each other effusively and laugh whole-heartedly. On his return to America, he is likely to characterize the Italian as a quaint person, refreshingly unrestrained. But when he observes the same Italian exhibit the same colorful abandon on an American street, he takes offense, and with no show of logic, condemns all Latins as unrefined.

The analogy to the Jew is exact. In the ghetto, which also had its delicacies and proprieties, it was taken for granted that hands had their place in speech, that conversation was to be intense. Much of the supposed crudity of the Jew is due to just this fact, that one society considers gauche what another society regards as in perfectly good taste.

Closely related to the social crudities of the Jew is his aggressiveness. The Jew is an ambitious and self-assertive person. Many an American Gentile refuses to employ Jews for just this reason. The Jew is too buoyant to be confined to a minor position. It is said that, as soon as he is hired, he has already set his heart on being president of the firm, or that when he comes to know the business, he will refuse to remain a minor executive, that he will launch his own competitive business. That the charge is grossly exaggerated is perfectly apparent. Thousands of Jews remain put in minor offices. Indeed, it is an interesting contradiction in the American psychology that the ambition of the Jew should be felt as a failing. For, to the American mind, aggressiveness and the spirit of the go-getter are prime virtues. But this is not the only instance of a cast of mind which finds fault with the Jew for a trait which is approved when it appears in non-Jews.

The ambition and aggressiveness of the Jew, where they exist, are equally products of the Jewish past. The Jew has from necessity learned to be industrious and resourceful. He transmits his own earnestness by precept and example to his children. Especially when he is suddenly freed from inveterate restraints, does he assert himself. In the lands from which he came, he had no opportunities at all. In Western countries a dazzling prospect unfolds itself. It is natural that, like a starved man at a banquet board, he exhibit some measure of eagerness.

The ostentation of the Jew is also the result of a release. The plump Hebrew matron bedecked with diamonds and the elaborate home of the Jewish parvenu have long been the butts of satire, good-humored or malicious. But here again it should be remembered that the Jew has just stepped out of abject poverty, directly from the ghetto to freedom. Like all *nouveaux riches,* he is proud of his unwonted possessions. They dazzle him and he likes them to dazzle others. They are his insignia of success before his fellow-Jews, the only means he possesses by which to impress the Gentile of whose ill-concealed dislike he is acutely conscious.

All of these traits, vulgarity, crudity and ostentation, are largely confined to the first or second generation of emancipated Jews who still bear the impress of the old order. The Jew adapts himself quickly. With the passage of time he grows accustomed to his new liberties and opportunities.

to his possessions and privileges. He loses his aggressiveness and his ostentation, he gradually drops those traits of his life which clash with his environment. He takes on the *mores,* the amenities and the color of the general scene. This process of adaptation is clearly perceptible when one contrasts the first generation of German or Russian Jews in America with the second or third. Eventually the Jew becomes totally indistinguishable in external characteristics from his Gentile fellows.

But if the past of the Jew accounts for some of his obvious failings and weaknesses, it accounts also for his major virtues. The modern Jew who is still close to the medieval pattern inherits a complex of ethical values which is a direct result of centuries of purposeful indoctrination. Thus he is, generally speaking, a sober and a temperate person. His family life is likely to be strong and intense. The relationships between husband and wife, between children and parents, are close and affectionate. Jewish families tend to hold together against divorce and against natural disintegration. A fine spirit of mutual helpfulness dominates the typical Jewish home.

Jews as a class are charitable. They have been schooled in generosity for generations. They give liberally to help their less fortunate fellows, their social service is of high caliber and they can generally be expected to respond to an appeal to their philanthropic instincts. Many a Jew who has apparently lost all distinguishing Jewish traits still retains this one of a predilection for charity. Jews among themselves are severely critical of their own generosity. They feel, no matter how much money has been raised, that the sum should have been larger. They are likely to assert that their reputation for philanthropy has been grossly inflated.

Indeed, there is a common saying among Jews that there is only one thing about which two Jews will agree—and that is how much the third Jew should contribute. For all of this self-criticism there is much valid reason. But the fact that the extent of Jewish philanthropy has been exaggerated does not militate against its very real intensity.

The ancient rabbis of the Talmud asserted that the Jews were the "merciful sons of merciful fathers." Aside from his charities, the Jew who is still under the influence of the traditional way of life tends as a whole to be a kindly person. Jews commit a disproportionately small number of crimes of violence. They indulge rarely in the more cruel sports. They have a cultivated aversion to war. It is significant of the abiding influence of medieval Jewish ethics that only of late, under direst provocation, did Jews take to arms.

But of all the traits which the modern Jew has inherited from his past, the strongest is his intellectualism. In the course of our narrative, we have examined the mental life of the medieval Jew and the devotion with which it was pursued. We have observed its decline under the emancipation. We have watched the Jew turn from it as obsolete, and give himself to the culture of the modern world. But all that meant only that the Jewish intellect had been diverted. Modern life could change its direction; it could not dissipate its intensity developed over centuries. A love of books, a respect for scholarship have persisted among Jews—except that the books are different, the scholarship lies in other realms. The Talmudist now becomes a scientist or a man of letters, and to his new efforts he brings the same spirit of consecration with which once he approached the Hebrew tome. Even the emancipated Jew has spent his youth in a home where his father studied and where both his par-

ents impressed him with the importance of education. When
he left the ghetto, he carried with him a standard of values.
In the universities of Europe he took his learning seriously.
He bequeathed this same reverence for knowledge to his
children after him.

A story which has been told again and again on the American scene is the tale of the sacrifice which Jewish immigrants
have made for the education of their children. Innumerable Jewish parents have slaved in poverty so that their offspring might take full advantage of the schools of the land.
Had they remained in the Pale, these same parents would
doubtless have bent their energies to the end that their son
might become learned in the tradition. Once in a new
world, they recognized regretfully that Jewish scholarship
was obsolete and pointless. If it could not be Jewish erudition and Hebrew books, let it be at least some kind of learning and some kind of books. In a home where marks and
grades were a matter for family discussion, where the school
was of vital importance, it was natural that the child become a proficient student.

As a result of this inherited ideal, Jews have flocked to
universities, they have tended naturally to crowd the professions to the point of suffocation. With such an impulse
behind him, it was inevitable that the Jew become a brilliant figure in contemporary literature, science and art, that
he produce scholars, authors, professors and a large share
of the winners of the Nobel Prize.

From certain angles, this intellectual bias of the Jew has
been unfortunate. It has led to a peculiar lack of balance.
The Jewish group has to-day more of its youth in the professions than society can absorb. A secondary impulse has
contributed to this result. For, in the medieval ghetto,

where the handicrafts were impossible in any event, the glorification of the intellectual life went hand in hand with the deprecation of manual labor. This contempt for physical toil has been carried over to the modern scene. As a result, Jews to-day engage either in the professions or in business. They become laborers unwillingly, under the lash of necessity. But for all its perhaps unfortunate consequences, the intellectual tradition of the ghetto has made the Jewish group culturally creative far beyond its numbers. Without the medieval background of the modern Jew, the world might be without a Bergson, a Brandeis, a Freud, a Wassermann, an Einstein.

As the objectionable characteristics of the group tend to be erased by intimacy with a new environment, so also do traditional Jewish virtues. The longer the Jew lives in the world, the less he exhibits the vices or excellences of his background. His family life, subjected to the same influences as work upon the Gentile home, tends to lose its unusual unity, divorce becomes increasingly frequent, the abnormal affection of the clan is toned down to a normality. Charity ceases to be a major ideal, it receives a place more nearly akin to that which it holds in general society.

He drops even his intellectual intensity. To any close observer of the Jewish world, it is immediately apparent that each successive generation is less and less passionate about learning, that reverence for erudition fades away with time. Jews of the second generation tend generally to be less abnormal as students than those of the first. By the third or fourth generation after emancipation, the violent impulse toward books and toward the professions is largely dissipated. This, in brief, is the total effect of emancipation on Jewish character; it takes on completely the coloring of its environment, it acquires the virtues and vices of the background against which it moves.

This assimilation of the Jew to his scene is in part the natural movement of any creature toward a protective coloration. It is also the result of a servility of spirit. All through the process of emancipation, the Jew was compelled to plead for equality. He was placed in the false position of a beggar, he acquired unconsciously a beggar's psychology. He came to regard the Gentile as a somewhat superior being, possessed of desirable traits which he must acquire. Thus was born that sense of inferiority which drives so many Jews to imitate Gentiles blindly. The spirit of indiscriminating imitation has infected every phase of contemporary Jewish life. No names are so immaculately Anglo-Saxon as those with which Jewish parents afflict their offspring. It is almost a safe assumption that a Biblical given name belongs only to a Gentile. Jews find such names too revealingly Jewish. Gwendolyn and Guinevere, Montague and Pierpont seem more attractive to the newly emancipated than Sarah, Rachel, Moses or David. Indeed, the process of naming a child has come to involve a complicated literary exploit. By tradition, Jewish children are generally named after dead relatives, usually grandparents. But Jews three generations ago generally had Biblical or rabbinic first names. The parent is then confronted with a problem. He adopts some "American" name vaguely suggestive of the Hebrew original, or one that possesses one letter in common. Isaac becomes Irving or Isador, Aaron becomes Arthur. In this way, ancestral pieties are unviolated and the child spared a too, too Jewish name.

The half-emancipated Jew is likely to proceed systematically. He learns to eat foods he does not like, to engage in pastimes toward which he has no inclination—all because such is the fashion of the Gentile. He insists that his children shall be reared as little Hebrew versions of the Anglo-Saxon, that they be trained in the amenities and graces of the world even when these appear totally inconsequential. The very ritual of the synagogue is often appraised by the standards of the outer world. Many a modification of Temple ritual has been effected with an eye to the possibility of some stray Gentile visitor. Even the leaders of the Jewish world are never without the haunting thought, "What will the non-Jew say?"

The Jew is a subtle person and when he is accused of an indecent lack of self-respect, he has his answer ready. He points to the persistent hostility of the world and ascribes it to Jewish distinctiveness. Obviously, the less apparently the Jew is a Jew, the less the Gentile will find cause for criticism. By this logic, he rationalizes his program of imitation.

The Jewish social climber is the product of this same psychology. Cursed by a sense of inferiority, overwhelmed by a presumption of the superiority of non-Jewish society, the Jew determines to win acceptance from it. In many respects, the Jewish social climber suggests the assimilationist. Ultimately, a fundamental distinction divides the two. The conscious assimilationist is an idealist. He believes that the preservation of Jewish identity is hopeless and futile. He seeks therapy for himself and his family but also for the Jew and society generally. The social climber is interested only in admission into some club, recognition by the Gentile, a flattering, condescending pat on the head. He is without a redeeming feature. Gentile society rarely opens itself to him. It is, however, uniformly polite. It never tells the unwanted Jew the unpleasant truth. It even, on occasion, gives him grounds for hope. Never discouraged, yet never successful, he eats out his heart in impotent rage.

The whole history of the emancipation has been the record of a continuous frustration. Liberation has never been complete; it is socially imperfect now. Out of perpetual disappointment, many a Jew has turned to counsels of despair.

The rise of the Jewish radical reflects in part just such a device of desperation. The ghetto rebel is a familiar figure on the Jewish scene. The world still remembers the ancestry of Karl Marx, of Ferdinand LaSalle, the founder of German Social Democracy and known in his own day as "the terrible Jew," and of Trotsky. Even were it tempted to forget, it has heard too often the strident voice of the ghetto revolutionary from his soap-box. It believes that Jews are, as a rule, radicals and, as such, subversive of any order in which they live.

Whether the Jewish group has more than its share of social revolutionaries is a moot point. In any event, certain factors, medieval and modern, logically incline the Jew toward programs of fundamental correction in society. In the first place, he is heir to a great ethical tradition which persistently stresses the rights of man and the ideal of social justice. In the second, he is relatively a newcomer in Western society. He regards the world with a fresh objectivity, with a critical appraisal undimmed by habituation. Again, he has been persecuted so long that he is instinctively sympathetic to the exploited in any condition. His own pain is too vivid for him to be calloused to that of others. Besides, those who persecute him are generally those who exploit his Gentile fellows. In rebellion against them, he gives expression to a dual resentment. But, in large measure, the

Jewish radical is a direct result of the vagaries of emancipation. When the Jew has lost his old world, he turns to the new, only to be refused complete entrance. He tends to feel that Gentile society is allied against him. No wonder, then, that he is likely to rise in rebellion, that he makes common cause with those movements which promise to shatter the inhospitable order to bits and remold it nearer to his heart's desire. If the world insists on raising its afflicting hand against him, it must be expected that his fist will strike back against his oppressor.

It is then no accident that Jewry produced a crop of brilliant radicals in Germany during the early nineteenth century when emancipation moved slowly and falteringly. And the soap-box orator who comes from Russia and who preaches his gospel on ghetto street corners is readily intelligible. For, when emancipation died an early death at the hand of the Czars, the young Jew naturally threw in his lot with Russia's revolutionaries. If the old régime could be overturned, two birds would be killed with one stone. The masses would be freed and the Jews attain emancipation. Radical movements then had numerous adherents among the Jews of Eastern Europe. When these Jews came to America or England, they brought their political and social ideologies with them. Since the American scene also possesses its injustices, radicalism does not die away with undue rapidity. The fanatical revolutionary on the street corner is then the curious product of rabbinic ethics, of a late entrance into the world, of a natural sympathy with fellows in persecution. Above all, he is the result of a society which nags the Jew into rebellion against itself by refusing him full emancipation.

The further the ghetto recedes into the background, the

wider the liberty accorded to Jews, the more the Jew begins to have some stake in the *status quo,* the less radical he becomes. Thus, in Germany, Jews eventually became, generally speaking, a conservative or, at most, a liberal group. Radicalism was present among them but in no unusual degree. It disappeared together with the conditions that gave it birth. The same process has been duplicated among East European Jews in America. The revolutionary fervor persists until the Jew comes to recognize the extent of his liberties, until he makes a place for himself in the new world. With the passage of time, with each successive generation, radicalism slips toward liberalism and then again toward conservatism. Depending on one's economic and political philosophy, one will applaud or deplore the drift. It exists undeterred. It is one more instance of the tendency of the Jew to conform, to take on the color of his background.

And if, either by reason of temperament or of training, the Jew can not become an idealistic radical, he tends to be a cynic. What faith can be put in the professions of the Western world, when his own lot demonstrates their insincerity? From personal experience he knows that the ideal of human brotherhood is a dishonest myth, equality a Sunday-school aphorism, and the worship of democracy a lip service. He recognizes that those who speak most enthusiastically about such values are often most stubborn about applying them to him. He remembers that Christianity, for all its exaltation of love, has been historically an instrument of hate, that the most liberal may be illiberal in their Jewish attitudes. Acutely conscious of the failure in practise of human ideals, he is tempted to reject all idealism as a conventional lie of modern civilization. By background, the Jew is likely to be an idealist himself. The world often

embitters him. It has itself to thank for the mordancy of
the Heines and the Nordaus who expose its hypocrisies.

The same history which created social-climber, radical
and cynic has produced the Jewish chauvinist. Society
makes it perfectly clear that it does not genuinely want its
Jews. Disappointment, frustration and pride often lead the
Jew to contempt of the world. To compensate for the
stigma of inferiority which the Gentile insists on imposing
upon him, the Jew develops a fierce and explosive Jewishness. The foiled assimilationist is especially susceptible to
infection from this virulence. He has swallowed humiliation
and slight, only to find himself still an outcast. In resentment, he falls back upon his Jewish identity. If Gentiles
insist on regarding it as a badge of disgrace, he will insist
on flaunting it before them. If they will not have him because of what he is, he will revenge himself by being ab-
normally Jewish. The ancient rabbis of the Talmud sagely
remarked that, to the point which a penitent attains, the sin-
less never reach. This aphorism has received a strange, per-
verted illustration in modern Judaism. No Jew is so fanati-
cally self-conscious as the one who has failed in his efforts to
escape himself. In some persons, as in Theodor Herzl or
Ludwig Lewisohn, the reaction has led to positive and creative efforts. It is just as likely to lead to an empty chauvinism.
The answer to perpetual anti-Semitism becomes an unbalanced Jewishness. The old Biblical rebel cry is heard
again, "To your tents, O Israel." And less audibly, for even
the Jewish super-patriot fears Gentile censure, "A plague on
all your houses."

It is often glibly asserted that the Jew is a neurotic. Certainly his conduct impresses observers as unbalanced and
unstable. In an age when a psychological jargon is im-

mensely popular, the facile use of phrases about psychoses, complexes and maladjustments, appears satisfyingly scientific But if these mental abnormalities are epidemic among Jews, a partial explanation is to be found in recent history and contemporary conditions. The Jew stands to-day between two worlds. In one he can no longer live, the other will not admit him. He straddles two orders. One breaks under him whenever he rests his weight upon it, the other heaves in protest against him and seeks to shake him off. Only a people of acrobats could preserve a semblance of poise on a footing so unstable.

This entire chapter has been devoted to abnormalities and eccentricities of personality. It has been a record of the pathology of the Jewish psyche. Nothing has been said concerning that vast majority of Jews who are neither radicals nor social climbers, neither unrefined nor aggressive, who are simple, decent human beings, happily balanced despite the fact that they are Jews. The existence of such large numbers of the well-adjusted is a matter of common experience. Their character calls for no special explanation. Only strange, unique and divergent types demand interpretation.

And yet, from one point of view, the adjusted Jew must remain an exception. For balance is not inherent in the conditions of Jewish existence. There is a real presumption that the Jew will be a restless creature. Even if he has solved the problem of his own personality, he must of necessity still face another issue: Shall it be Judaism or the world and how much of each? As long as the individual wavers between these alternatives he can not be entirely normal. Only when he has decided his Jewish problem satisfactorily, can his own ego find a complete stability. If, then the Jewish eccentric is a persistent phenomenon, it is because he has not resolved the basic dilemma of his being. We have already indicated that the Jew tends toward normality and conformity the longer his emancipation endures, that he tends to take on, in habits, tastes, politics and manner, the color of his environment. But he can never become a fully balanced being until this issue is resolved, until he possesses an adequate philosophy for both realms in which he lives.

At the beginning of our discussion, we indicated the fact that Jewish survival and character were both the products of the same history. In the modern world a new and subtle relationship has asserted itself. The history which made the Jew has now set him at a parting of ways. He hesitates painfully and the spirit of uncertainty has infected his entire personality, rendering it incapable of serenity and equilibrium. When he has cast his lot with one course or the other, when he has successfully lost himself in assimilation or found himself in some adequate philosophy of Judaism, only then will he win an enduring and ultimate balance.

THE MODERN SCENE

CHAPTER XIII

FOREWORD TO THE MODERN SCENE

WHATEVER its meaning for the rest of mankind, for the Jews the Nazi episode was an experience of incalculable consequence. Nothing will ever again be for them what it once was in those dim days, so near yet so remote, before Hitler.

Therefore to the tale we have unfolded so far, which has related how the Jewish people managed to survive, how the Jewish personality came to be molded into its present-day shape, how Jewish life in its medieval setting achieved an equilibrium, and how that equilibrium was undone by the Emancipation, leaving Jews and Judaism at sixes and sevens —to this tale a postscript must now be appended, describing and accounting for this wildest and most tragic passage in all the fantastic history of the Jews, and evaluating its effects on them and their group destiny.

But while anti-Semitism, especially in its Hitlerite climax, has been the most spectacular and destructive incident in modern Jewish history, it is by no means its entirety, and perhaps in the long run not even its most important occurrence. Other developments of vast significance have been in process.

In the past half century, the Zionist program was conceived, launched and carried to its present pass. Already immeasurably creative in its impact on Jews and Judaism, Zionism, unless it suffers some catastrophic reverse, promises even greater things for the future. This too is a tremendously potent element in the future making of Jewish survival and character. As such it will require our attention.

At the same time, forces have arisen within the Jewries of the West, especially the American, which operate to repair the dislocations in the Jewish tradition effected by the Emancipation and to adapt Judaism to its new environment. Some of these forces are unconscious and without calculated design, being expressions of the instinctive pieties of individuals toward their people and ancestral heritage. Others are reasoned philosophies, devised to provide modern Jews with tenable theories and practicable procedures for their Jewishness. This turn of events too, since it is obviously relevant to the continued existence of the Jew and Judaism, needs to be considered by us.

Such are the three themes which await us: anti-Semitism; Zionism; Programs for Judaism. And with them one more also, perhaps the most fateful of all: the Jewish will to live, on which everything else may depend ultimately.

After all, if Israel, equipped with little more than determination, could effect the miracle which is Jewish Palestine, who dare say that, given like firmness, it cannot achieve religious and cultural rebirth in other lands as well?

Perhaps the truth rests with Herzl when he declared concerning another, far less likely prospect: "If you will it, it is no dream."

Chapter XIV

ANTI-SEMITISM

LIKE A constant in a mathematical formula, anti-Semitism is present in the new era as in the old, serving at one and the same time to preserve and corrode Jewish life.

It is a preservative in that it drives Jews back upon their Jewishness. This is a fact which Jewish loyalists are loath to admit, preferring to ascribe their continued existence to more positive motivations. Nevertheless, the entire problem would be transformed were this factor eliminated. If Israel still lives, it is largely because the world will not let it die.

The shield, however, has its other side. Anti-Semitism, which through the century has destroyed Jews in millions and Jewish communities by the hundreds, cannot be other than a threat, the greatest of all, to the physical survival of the Jewish group. What is more, while its impact on many Jews is to reawaken their Jewish loyalties, it operates for others to just the opposite effect. For, if there were no anti-Semitism, Jews would not be penalized as Jews; if they were not penalized, no eagerness to escape the Jewish identity would be engendered within them. Were it not for the prejudices they encounter, they would have no cause to elect assimilation, and at least one very sound reason to continue as Jews. After all, it is no slight thing to stand as legatee to a great patrimony of religious faith, ethical ideal, and cultural treasure. Only because its social cost runs so high does it occur to Jews to decline their inheritance. Whatever then anti-Semitism's contribution to Jewish life, its damage is greater. And Jewish survivalists are well advised when they say of it: "Neither thy honey nor thy sting."

If the survival of the Jew be one riddle of history, the hardihood of hatred for him must be another. For this, like the Jew himself, has outlived all vicissitudes of time. It has flourished among cultured and benighted peoples, in periods of prosperity and adversity. It has dogged the steps of the Jew like some shadow. It is almost as old as he is.

In large part, prejudice against the Jew is the direct result of indoctrination. Anti-Semitism is a time-honored component of Western culture, and the child who is reared to the latter is quite likely to acquire the former also, and to get the one where and as he gets the other—at his mother's knee, on the playground, from his teacher's desk, in the books and newspapers he reads, and in church.

Especially in the last, since of all the sources of anti-Semitic indoctrination, the Christian religion would seem to be the most potent. Certainly it is the oldest, the pulpit having for centuries taught worshipers to regard the Jew as the Christ-killer. This unhappy practice continues to the present, despite the doubts raised by Biblical criticism concerning the historicity of the crucifixion story, despite the further fact that the Jews who supposedly executed Jesus are dead in any case almost two thousand years. Of these considerations the child in his Sunday-School class, the

uncritical communicant in his pew, is unaware. What he
retains is an anger against the Jews he knows. So, at the
touch of a religion dedicated to love, he has been tainted
with a hate.

From this distressing practice, there are among the Christian clergy these days dissenters, and in increasing numbers.
But the exceptions, bright and reassuring as they may be,
are not yet so numerous as to nullify the rule.

Once the damage has been done it may be irreparable. A
chance remark by a Sunday-School teacher, a random passage in a sermon, and a prejudice may have been inculcated
which neither years, subsequent education, nor the most
eloquent exhortation can eradicate. The child, having grown
into an adult, may forget the experience which made him
an anti-Semite in embryo; he may break with the church
which afforded it to him, or even with all religion. His bias
may nonetheless outlive its causes. Such is Christendom's
sin, committed sometimes in full consciousness, more often
in carelessness, against the Jew and itself, the grievous guilt
of which will remain until Christian teaching and preaching
purge themselves of utterances contrary to their ideals.

Economics, along with religion, has a role in the creation
of anti-Semitism. In a competitive society, the hand of each
man is against his brother, every advance on the part of one
individual being achieved only at the expense of another.
The Gentile, struggling for a livelihood, takes the competition, even the greater success, of a fellow-Gentile with as
much grace as he can muster. But when his competitor is a
Jew, he grows resentful. This, he feels, is a competition to
which he should not be subjected.

From this elemental struggle for bread much of the impulse to anti-Semitism stems. The shopkeeper sees in his Jewish competitor an avoidable handicap. The unemployed Christian regards enviously the job filled by a Jew. History has fashioned the Jew into a shrewd merchant and trader; it has forced on him a skill in making his way, circumstances which serve only to fan the fury.

All through the centuries, economics has done this devil's work. Many a theological disputation with Jews in the Middle Ages, many a pogrom, all ostensibly to the greater glory of God and the Church, masked the most mercenary of purposes. Today too, the position of the Jew is rendered unstable by economic distress. Had Poland and Roumania been prosperous lands in the interval between the two world wars, they might not have been such pestholes of bias. Germany itself would have told a different story had its economic life not collapsed during the twenties.

What may become of anti-Semitism in a non-competitive order is a fascinating theme for speculation, one furthermore on which some evidence is already available in the Soviet Union. There, along with the differences effected by another economic structure, have gone determined efforts on the part of the Communist regime to educate anti-Jewish prejudice away, and to stamp it out where it persists. That considerable success has attended this attempt seems clear in the fact that Russia, once the most anti-Semitic land in Europe, is now among the least. But the record has its debit side. Signs persist of a smouldering under the surface. Anti-Jewish incidents, not so frequent as to be alarming, but not so uncommon as to be reassuring, never cease to be reported. During the Second World War, moreover, some of the Soviet minority nationalities turned on the Jews in their midst. All in all, it is too early for the testimony to be either complete or decisive.

A third root of anti-Semitism is human psychology. Thus, it is part of man's animal heritage to suspect the unknown, to fear what he suspects, and to hate what he fears. The Jew being in some degree an unknown, of different background and modes of living, the Gentile is tempted to suspect, fear, and hate him.

The unusual not only frightens, it irritates. For the familiar men have their habitual reactions. But for the exceptional they are not prepared, and must improvise special responses. They must stop and think. Objecting to the necessity of thought, always an effortful, painful activity, they carry over their resentment to whoever or whatever has forced it on them. To be specific, it is quite likely that a Gentile may dislike the Jews, among other things, because the attitudes, standards, and habits to which he is accustomed, which serve him well enough when he is dealing with his fellows, break down when he faces them. Uncertain of how to proceed with them, confused, compelled to reflection, he prefers to get along without them and the discomforts they occasion.

Implicated in group prejudice is still another psychological tendency, that scapegoatism whereby men and societies are forever prone to blame others for their own mistakes and misfortunes. For this role of standing as whipping-boy for mankind's sins, errors, disappointments, the Jew is ideally suited. He is conspicuous and influential enough to give some show of plausibility to any charges directed against him, but not strong enough to be able to set up effective resistance.

Under the insight furnished by dynamic psychology, a further cause of anti-Semitism has been suggested. Prejudice against the Jew, it has been proposed, may have another of its roots in a suppressed hostility on the part of Christians against the Christian morality which inhibits the satisfaction of their desires and impulses, a restraint from which they would be free were it not for Jesus, the Apostles, and the Prophets before them, all of them Jews. If this analysis be correct, then, as Mr. Maurice Samuel has contended, the anti-Semite would hate Jews not, as he claims, because they killed his God, but because they gave and imposed Him upon them.

Finally, anti-Semitism is in no slight measure the result of the fact that it is so useful, that it lends itself so readily to exploitation by unscrupulous persons. How many are the political and economic uses to which prejudice against the Jews can be, and has been put! It has been used to divert public attention from crimes, scandals, and mass discontent, as by the Russian Czarist regime. It has been heaped up as a steppingstone to power, after the precedent set by Hitler and copied by his many imitators. It has been exported to disrupt entire nations, to sow discord in their populations and so soften them up for conquest, a device brilliantly exploited by Goebbels against the Western democracies. Finally, as Carey McWilliams has demonstrated, it has been utilized as "a mask for privilege," economic, social, political, caste. Little wonder if, after so much cultivation, there is so much of the poisonous weed around.

These then are the four basic causes of anti-Semitism: indoctrination, in the first instance on the part of the Christian Church, but also on the part of Western culture in general; economics; psychological predispositions; and deliberate manipulation.

Compared to causes of such magnitude and power, the

peculiarities of individual Jews are of slight moment. To be sure, such qualities offer the anti-Semite his easiest rationalizations. He is able to point to exhibitions of aggressiveness or clannishness, ostentation or radicalism as justifications for his stand. But these are not his "real" reasons. Therefore, if one fails him, he will dig up another. And if he can find none, he will not hate any the less.

Is there a single charge leveled against the Jews and argued as an excuse for the assault upon them which has not been exploded time and again? That they are all radicals; that they are international bankers; that they have conspired to dominate the world; that they hold themselves aloof from it; that they are intolerably ill-mannered; that they are too smooth; that they are no people at all; that they are the race described by German ethnic pseudo-science, a race too dreadful to be permitted relations with the rest of mankind. Each of these absurdities has been refuted time and again. The prejudice persists. And that for a good and sufficient reason, because its sources lie elsewhere and deeper than these rationalizations.

Now we can understand what would otherwise be an incredibility, the difference between medieval and modern anti-Semitism. The anti-Semite of the Middle Ages objected to Jewish individuality and distinctiveness. He protested against the Jews that they would not become Christians like himself. The modern anti-Semite argues just the opposite case, that the Jews are assimilating themselves to him, that they threaten to become as Gentile as he. The mechanics of the shift are transparent. When Jews stood apart from non-Jewish society, that served as the excuse. But more recently, once they began to take the Gentile complaint at its face value and discard their isolation, that fact was made to do service. And as for the contradiction, what is logical consistency before a blind, fierce antipathy?

It was in Germany that this new anti-Semitism found its climactic expression. There, on foundations laid by others, the Frenchman de Gobineau, the renegade Englishman Houston Chamberlain, Germans raised that house of cards which is racialism: the bizarre fiction, demolished times beyond counting but ever resurgent, of ethnic superiorities and inferiorities.

The argument is a simple one: that as there are breeds among animals, differing from one another in physical and mental characteristics, so there are breeds of human beings; that of these breeds the Caucasians are the elite; that of these in turn the Nordic Aryans constitute the highest stratum; that by virtue of their heredity Jews are corrupt in body, mind, and spirit; that this is an inexpiable curse about which nothing can be done, since it is inborn in them; that the Nordic peoples are left therefore with no other course except to quarantine or destroy the Jews, thus protecting themselves against contamination.

This racialist reasoning has been refuted so often that there is no need for another rebuttal. Suffice it to say, the whole case is riddled with holes. The very existence of definite ethnic groups, such as the Nordic, Aryan, and Semitic, is questionable. No confirmation whatsoever has yet been found for the notion of the superiority or inferiority of one race over another. Nor has any correlation been established between external physical characteristics and internal aptitudes and attitudes. It is all nonsense but it worked, sufficing to sweep Hitler to power.

To be sure, anti-Semitism did not achieve all this alone and unaided. Many forces collaborated with it, among them the evil genius of demonic men; and, even more basic, the derangement of a very deranged society. For, like the leaders whom it followed with such wild enthusiasm, the German people itself was sick unto death, sick with the chronic diseases of militarism, authoritarianism, and national inferiority; sick from defeat in the First World War, the Versailles Treaty, reparations, inflation, and the depression. But if anti-Semitism was only one of the drives which eventuated in the Nazi nightmare, it was one of the most powerful in the complex.

And it remains the one element in his program in which Hitler achieved all but total success. The dreams of world conquest, a thousand-year Reich, a German people battening on the slave labor of the rest of mankind, German cities beautified with the plunder of nations—all these have vanished in bloody rubble. But the extirpation of European Jewry—in that Hitler almost had his way, and, in fact, has it still.

First, step by step, he destroyed Germany's Jews. By the Nuremberg Laws of September 1935, he stripped them of all political rights and immunities, denied them virtually any opportunity to earn a livelihood, and made them the butts of a regimen of systematic humiliation. By the time of the outbreak of the Second World War in 1939, three-fifths of Germany's half-million Jews had taken refuge in flight. Tens of thousands of others had been done to death in concentration camps. After the incorporation of Austria into the greater Reich in 1938, the same story was repeated in a new setting. In less than a decade, great, ancient centers of Jewish life and learning, all their institutions and cultural treasures, had been largely erased.

During the Second World War, what little remained of German and Austrian Jewry was obliterated, and the holocaust spread to all the lands of German occupation. Between October 1941, when the Nazi regime set itself to the mass extermination of the Jews, until its capitulation, some five to six million Jews were done to death with a brutality and ingenuity such as had never been exhibited before in all the long, blood-stained career of the human species. Those who survived were left sick, broken, rootless, orphaned, widowed, bereaved, and very generally without a rag or roof to call their own.

Not that the Jews were alone in the crucible. All of Europe was there with them. But no other people endured losses and underwent torment equal to theirs. And the lot of no other people was so little alleviated by victory.

More than two years after the cessation of hostilities a quarter of a million Jews still rotted in internment camps in Central and Western Europe and Cyprus. Many, perhaps most of the rest, were dependent for life and livelihood on the contributions of governments and of Jewries abroad. And of the property of which they had been robbed little had been restored to them, and that little with utmost reluctance.

Most tragic of all, Hitler's anti-Semitism outlived him. Hatred for the Jew has continued as fierce in Germany as ever. Thanks to Nazi propaganda and the dislocation of the war years, the native anti-Semitism of the other lands of Central and Western Europe has been sharpened to new acuteness. The disease is not only worse where it was long endemic; it has infected other areas hitherto free of it, most notably England. In America the fever chart of anti-Jewish prejudice has risen and fallen along with alternations of prosperity and depression, the waxing and waning of political self-confidence, the ebb and flow of German propaganda. According to most observers, the problem has been less acute in the United States during the immediate post-war years than had been feared. But it was certainly more urgent than some generations earlier, and there was none to venture confident predictions as to the future.

Nor is a resurrected anti-Semitism the sole aftereffect of the Nazi madness. A vast problem of relief confronts mankind in general and the world's Jews in particular, a problem which will persist for as long as any one can see into the future. What lingers on of Jewry in Central and Western Europe is shattered and largely hopeless, seeing no reasonable expectation of ever re-winning, in its present setting, what it has lost of resources, security, acceptance, and dignity. Desperate as was its situation under the Nazis, it is scarcely less desperate under liberation.

Which means that a titanic obligation by way of support, rehabilitation, and resettlement, let alone political sponsorship, has descended on those Jewish communities which have been spared the devastations of war and persecution. For many a long year, American Jewry, for example, will be drained of funds and manpower, diverted from domestic concerns and needs, involved to the neck in the solution of problems not immediately its own, because there is no one else to stand as stay and defender for the wrecked Jewries abroad. But all this is energy which the American Jewish community could well expend on itself. It may well spell the difference between ultimate Jewish survival in the New

World and complete oblivion. This too is a Hitlerian legacy of evil.

Finally, the Jewish communities wiped out in Europe are just those which, Palestine aside, were the most intense in Jewish loyalty, best endowed in Jewish learning, most devoted as to practice, and most promising in creativity. World Israel, in brief, has in a few short years lost not only over one-third of its total members but these, Jewishly speaking and on the whole, the best third. To retrieve such a loss will take no mean doing.

Has nothing good come out of all this evil, whether for America, mankind, or Israel? Some things, but these pitiably few, small and unsure against the dead certainty of the havoc. But some things nevertheless.

Thus, a beginning has been made, timid and precarious but still a beginning, toward world organization, and therefore a start, no matter how minute, toward hope.

Dedication to the democratic process and spirit would seem to have been strengthened in America as a result of the Nazi challenge. Americans have learned by tragic example how precious is the patrimony of liberty, how easily it can be dissipated, how grim are the alternatives to it. They understand better the nature and tactic of freedom's enemies.

Concern over civil liberties would appear to have become more widely diffused and earnest among the American people than ever before.

The recognition is broader than once it was that anti-Semitism is a threat not only to Jews but to all Americans and the American way of life. As a result, there is larger participation by Gentiles, as individuals and through organizations, in the struggle against prejudice, and in the effort to evolve educational techniques for neutralizing it. The government too has begun to take a hand in the problem. Through anti-discriminatory measures like the Ives-Quinn Law, enacted by New York State, through the proposed civil liberties legislation of the federal government, through the cumulative decisions of the courts, American society is taking measures for the entrenchment of its way of life to the benefit of all its citizens, Jews among others.

If neither international peace, the democratic system, nor the position of American Jewry is as secure as might be desired, it must be said that there are some grounds for hope in connection with each. This morsel at least of good has come out of the avalanche of evil.

So much for the objective effects of the Nazi eruption. Now what are its subjective consequences? How do Jews feel these days as a result of the experiences of hostility which have befallen them or, before their eyes, engulfed their brethren?

It should be observed of the Jews, first of all, that no sweeping generalizations can be made about them. It is of the nature of men they are different from one another, which means among other things that they can be counted on to respond diversely to any given set of facts. Being human and subject to the rules of human nature, Jews have reacted to the events of recent years not uniformly but in every fashion that can be conceived. Yet, they do exhibit tendencies, sometimes prevailing tendencies. Among these the following loom clearest and largest:

The Jews now feel altogether secure nowhere. If, after a century of equality, the Jews of Germany could be subjected to medieval barbarism and destroyed, if the Jews of Europe could be all but exterminated, if anti-Semitism could rear its head in England, then anything is possible.

Again, Jews have been shaken in their historic faith in man's decency. It must be remembered that it was not the Germans alone who perpetrated crimes against the Jews but all their collaborators, among both allied and enemy populations, and that even among those who resisted the Germans, there were not wanting some who both fought the Nazis and killed Jews. Almost as disquieting was the cool, studied indifference to the fate of Jews on the part of most of civilized mankind. Most shocking of all were the hollow pretenses of those who professed sympathy for the Jews of Europe but did nothing specific or practical to help them: the British who for disreputable reasons of their own kept the doors of Palestine shut, though death was the sure consequence for those they debarred from their promised haven; the Russians who, all through the dreadful years between Hitler's rise to power and his attack on the Soviet Union, found no room anywhere in all their vast territories for persecuted Jews from outside their borders; and the American government which, for all its pretensions of humanitarianism, could devise nothing better on behalf of the trapped Jews of Europe than such futile and unproductive conferences as the one held in Bermuda in the spring of 1943.

Still again, there has been an abatement, for most Jews, in the faith which they once held in the moral efficacy of education. There was a time when they told themselves optimistically that anti-Semitism was possible only among the uncultured and untutored. They believed that there was a strange power in books and ideas which transmuted character; that by virtue of association with literature and science a man was alchemistically rendered humane. In this assumption they were not alone. The world shared it with them. The events of the last decade have shattered this naivete. Jews now know that professors can be anti-Semites as envenomed as peasants and day laborers. They recognize that one may learn and learn, and still be a villain.

Side by side with this disappointment in education has gone a disillusionment with Christianity and the Christian Church. The Jew waited, he expected that Christendom would raise a voice of protest in his behalf in the name of its Master. It was not forthcoming. Or, if utterances were made, they were directed primarily to the preservation of the status and rights of either the Lutheran or the Catholic Church, and only incidentally to the protection of Jews. To this indictment there are exceptions, glorious exceptions ever to be treasured in the hearts not of Jews alone but of all men of good will. But the exceptions were fewer than was to be hoped, and not so numerous as to break the sad rule.

Nor has the Jew had much cause for satisfaction in the performance of liberals. Of these many expressed vigorously their revulsion against the savagery of anti-Semitism, and backed their convictions with their very lives. But in the main, the deportment of liberals, academicians, journalists, artists, or scientists, left much to be desired. And in many a Jew the melancholy conclusion has crystallized that liberalism is at best a timid sort of thing, a broken reed when tempests blow and one must lean on it.

One other fond hope of the Jew has been shattered in the upheaval of recent years: the assumption that if he proved himself a useful citizen of the society in which he lived, he would be treated decently by it. Persistently he told himself that by his fruits he would be known, that with his contributions to culture he would conquer the last citadels of suspicion and ostracism. That expectation has been largely dissipated. What German Jews contributed to Germany, Polish Jews to Poland, Jews generally to the civilization of the lands in which they lived, availed them little, if at all.

From all the foregoing one very general consequence emerges: almost without exception Jews these days, even those who never felt it before, have come alive to the fact that they are Jews. There were many who had forgotten, many in whom the awareness was only half awake. All that is of the past. Every Jew knows now that he is what he is.

For some few Jews, who were assimilationists to begin with, this has meant an accentuation of their assimilationist resolve. If they wished to cry quits with Jewishness at a time when both the world and they were relatively unaware of it, how much the more now, when sensibility to it is so excruciatingly heightened.

Nor are they deterred by the fact that dissociation from the Jewish group has become infinitely more difficult than it used to be. Every would-be escapist knows that whatever the case with Jews in the mass, there is always a chance, no matter how slender, for an individual. Besides, an objective need not be easy of attainment or attainable at all to be yearned after. To the contrary, its very inaccessibility may cause it to be sought after the more ardently. Accordingly, the Jew who refuses to remain a Jew in any case is not reconciled to his lot by the fact that he cannot under any circumstance evade it. He is merely the more embittered against it, and the more fiercely determined to throw it off.

As a result, some American Jews are trying all over again

the desperate devices invented and applied a century and more ago by their German brothers with high hopes and final frustration: studied isolation from Jewish associations; intermarriages inspired not by love but tactic; conversion to any and all the Christian sects; and beyond all else a consuming anti-Zionism, since Zionism is a classic expression of the survivalist spirit and poses boldly and permanently before the world, in the form of the State of Israel, that Jewishness from which the de-Judaizer seeks so ardently to be emancipated.

So with a handful of American Jews. Most, however, have responded to their sharpened sense of group identity otherwise and more positively.

As never before, they feel themselves bound up, whether for weal or woe, with the fate of their fellows. Ranks have closed; the sense of solidarity runs high.

A new militancy has come over the thinking and conduct of Jews as to anti-Semitism. Emboldened by American traditions of self-reliance, even more by the contrast between those who went passively to their death in Nazi gas chambers and those who died on the barricades, but most of all by the heroism of Palestinian Jewry, Jewish Americans quite commonly have come to the conclusion that the Jew-baiter is often a coward and always a bully, that nothing is to be lost and all is to be gained by standing up to him. This is the mood of individual Jews, it is the mood increasingly of Jewish civic defense agencies. There are, of course, ever so many Jews who still cling to the counsels of timidity and subservience. They are overwhelmingly outnumbered by the mass who have resolved, quietly but with determination, not to "take it lying down."

Among the most drastic changes wrought in American Jewry by World War II is the triumph of the Zionist idea. A generation ago, Zionists were a minority, largely concentrated in the latest Jewish immigration, and firmly opposed by the more Americanized elements in the community. Today, as public opinion polls have established, over eighty per cent of American Jews are Zionists and pro-Zionists; only ten per cent anti-Zionists; while another ten per cent remain undecided. A great battle for the minds and hearts of American Jews has been fought and won, in part on the open field of conflicting propagandas, but even more by events in Europe and Palestine.

Finally, out of the maelstrom of recent years most American Jews have emerged with the conviction that there is no escape from, or sloughing of, the Jewish identity; that assimilation in the sense of total oblivion in the Gentile world is an impossibility for all or almost all Jews. The test case, as we have already noted, was Germany. In that land, as in no other country in the world, Jews had taken on the color of their environment. The typical German Jew was for all practical intents and purposes simply German. He spoke, lived, acted, and thought in Teutonic patterns. For over a century he was busy with the enterprise of assimilation. Until the rise of Hitler he had congratulated himself that he was carrying it off successfully.

Then the whole endeavor went up in smoke. The anti-Semite disdained to inquire whether a Jew desired or refused to remain a Jew. Enough for him that he was a Jew. What is more, the assimilated German Jew, quite apparently, suffered more keenly than his loyalist fellow. For when the latter was persecuted he could tell himself that he was suffer-

ing for something significant. The former found himself
abused for being what he did not wish but could not cease
to be.

The failure of the advanced and systematic assimilation of
the German Jew has been a stunning blow to assimilationism
everywhere. It offers a demonstration, not complete but
quite convincing, that complete absorption by the world is
extremely difficult, perhaps impossible, in our time. A few
individuals may achieve it; the bulk of Jews must remain
Jews, if for no other reason than that the Gentiles will not
allow anything else.

Centuries ago, the prophet Ezekiel uttered a grim prophecy
in the name of the God of Israel. The Jew of the twentieth
century has experienced its fulfilment. "And that which
cometh into your mind shall never come to pass; in that ye
say: 'We shall be as the nations'. . . . As I live, saith the
Lord God, surely with a mighty hand and outstretched arm,
and with fury outpoured, will I rule over you."

CHAPTER XV

PALESTINE AGAIN

FROM one point of view, Zionism is as old as the Diaspora. At no time during the two thousand years of dispersion did the Jew forget the land of his fathers. In Scripture he read ancient prophecies of a return, in worship he prayed for their fulfilment. Next to the Day of Atonement, the most solemn fast in his ritual year was the ninth day of the month of *Ab,* commemorating the destruction of Jerusalem. In the Messianic vision of history's end, it was conceived that when the Deliverer came at last, he would reassemble the scattered remnants of Israel in Palestine. The oath, then, of the fathers was binding on the children: "If I forget thee, O Jerusalem, may my right hand forget its cunning."

For all the yearning of the medieval Jew for Zion, for all his mystic attachment to it, he did nothing to realize his desire. Redemption, he felt, was of the Lord alone. When He, in His inscrutable wisdom, was ready to inaugurate the return, it would come. Until then human devices were of little avail. As a result, the Jew for centuries was passive, praying and fasting on behalf of his hope, but for the rest waiting with such patience as he could muster for its realization.

Thus, despite all parallels between the age-old aspiration and modern Zionism, they are separated by the vast gulf which divides acquiescence from activity. The contrast between the two is poignantly caught in a short story in Hebrew, entitled *Tikkun Hazoth* or *Midnight Worship*. In this tale, the patriarch of a Jewish family arises at midnight, in accordance with an ancient practise. He seats himself on the floor of his room, dons sackcloth, puts ashes on his head and bewails the loss of his people's land, seeking so, by penitence and prayer, to regain it and its vanished glory. While he is thus engaged, his son enters the house, returning from a Zionist meeting. Father and son consider each other; the son smiling cynically at the futility of the old man's worship, the father shrugging off the pointlessness of human effort apart from God. Both have their hearts set on the same end. But they are as many centuries apart as the medieval and the modern mind.

Only once in Jewish history did the loyalty of Jews to Zion waver. During the first century of Emancipation in Western Europe, many of them renounced Palestine. The promise of liberation made them feel that their people needed no other home than the countries in which they lived. As one Jew put it during the first flush of freedom, "No man will take it amiss if the Jew finds his Messiah in this, that good princes have placed him on a level of equality with their other citizens, and graciously allowed him to hope that with complete fulfilment of the duties of the citizen, he would achieve all rights of citizenship."

In the face of such optimistic expectations, Palestine naturally came to appear irrelevant. If everything was eventually to favor the Jew where he was, there was no point in his looking elsewhere. Besides, interest in another land might be taken as an aspersion on the integrity of his newly acquired citizenship. The sooner he forgot his antiquated hope, the more readily he would be accepted in the country of his residence. The very theory of Reform Judaism, as we shall have occasion to note, encouraged the discarding of the dream of the restoration. For, if Judaism be a religion and the Jew a missionary of a faith, a return to an ancestral land, worse than unnecessary, would be undesirable. It would frustrate the very purpose of Jewish existence.

And then, after the middle of the nineteenth century, the Emancipation began to show signs of faltering, inconspicuous signs but significant to the discerning. The liberty it had bestowed on the Jews remained ever incomplete. Always some few reservations survived, if not legal then social. And, disappointing the widespread expectation of its disappearance, anti-Semitism gave disconcerting evidences of hardihood. The farsighted were filled with forebodings.

Their misgivings received confirmation toward the end of the century. The outcropping of anti-Semitism of those days appears trivial in retrospect; some relatively modest pogroms in Russia, the election of an anti-Semite as mayor of Vienna, the almost well-mannered, academic Jew-baiting of German universities, and the Dreyfus affair in France—all of these evoking world-wide protest. But they loomed large in their time, and they awakened in the minds of Jews who might otherwise never have thought of it, the question of their security and future in Europe.

Modern Zionism, then, is in part the expression of a disillusionment with the Emancipation. It bespeaks also the concern of Jewish loyalists over their ancestral culture. It was apparent that the Jewish tradition was disintegrating in modern Europe. The notion then arose of finding some place in the world where it might be the dominant, not the subordinate culture, in the hope that under these especially auspicious conditions it might spring to new life.

The first important and coherent statement of the Zionist position came, strangely enough, from a socialist, a collaborator of Karl Marx. As early as 1862, Moses Hess in his *Rome and Jerusalem* pointed to Palestine as a solution both for the problems raised by the Emancipation and for the salvaging of Jewish culture. The time was not yet ripe for such a program and Hess's book met a cold reception. Those Jews who deigned to notice it condemned it as "reactionary romanticism."

But the Jewish situation called so loudly for some such program that the idea asserted itself repeatedly during succeeding decades. It appeared in variant forms, in the *Am Olam, The Eternal People* of Perez Smolenskin; in the *Auto-Emancipation,* of Leo Pinsker. In each of these, the Emancipation was pronounced a failure, the status of the Jew an impossible compromise, and a vigorous assertion of Jewish nationalism eventuating in the resettlement of Israel in some land of its own an inescapable necessity. Among these forerunners of Zionism there was no unanimity on Palestine as the site for the national renaissance. Pinsker, for example, was open-minded on the matter. But on the necessity of a Jewish homeland there was universal agreement.

The thought was rapidly translated into action. By the eighties, the first practical attempts were under way. Nothing more clearly reveals the headstrong idealism of these visionaries than the stories of the early colonies in Palestine. Jews who knew nothing of agriculture betook themselves to an unknown land. There they learned, by privation and suffering, how to make a neglected soil yield a livelihood.

Malaria, overwork, and hardship took their toll of lives. Still the pioneers held on, affording one of the most vivid demonstrations in all history of the power of idealism. Nonetheless, the movement remained a minor eddy in Jewish and world affairs, the passion of a zealous but obscure coterie.

And then, suddenly, the genius of one convert won for the cause the international attention it merited. Theodor Herzl, founder of "political" Zionism, was the last person from whom to expect Jewish leadership. A Viennese journalist and a playwright, cosmopolitan in tastes and interests, he was for most of his short life a disinterested Jew. But he covered the Dreyfus trial as a reporter. And he could not fail to recognize that not Dreyfus the individual or the soldier had been pilloried, but Dreyfus the Jew; that the entire episode was a conspiracy on the part of French officialdom and the reactionary forces allied with it "to convict one Jew, and in him, all Jews," and through them in turn to discredit democratic liberalism. The problem of Jewish existence forced itself upon Herzl.

Der Judenstaat, the manifesto which resulted, was no novel revelation. It contained little with which Zionists were not already familiar. One early adherent of the cause, when urged to circulate it among his friends, responded, "I see no need for circulating this pamphlet. Its argumentation and theoretical portion will give nothing new to the Russian reader who is familiar with the pamphlets of Pinsker and Lilienblum; and when it deals with realities it is superficially written."

But if *Der Judenstaat* revealed no startling discoveries, it gave to Zionism a West-European vocabulary and a leader of the first magnitude. Herzl suffered, to be sure, from sharp limitations. When he wrote his brochure, he was virtually unaware of the progress toward Zionist ends which had already been made. He did not perceive that implicated in the problem was not only a social maladjustment but a cultural-spiritual issue as well. The very existence of modern Hebrew literature came to him as a surprise. In addition, he seems to have been aware of few of the grave obstacles in his way. It appears not to have occurred to him that Palestine, if that was to be the Jewish homeland, could not begin to accommodate all the world's Jews. He overlooked almost completely the possible opposition of the Arabs. He negotiated with governments as though he were in all actuality the authorized representative of a unanimous people, rather than the head of a struggling, upstart, splinter movement. At a time when funds were lacking for even the barest administrative expenses, he dared to conceive plans for vast projects.

Nor was he at the beginning genuinely committed to Palestine as the site of Jewish national reconstruction. In *Der Judenstaat* he referred to the Argentine as a likely alternative. Subsequently he considered the Sinai Peninsula and Uganda. Only a Jew ignorant of the pieties of his people could have wavered as did he. But he made up for his faltering on this one point with the utmost constancy on the large, major objective.

Once he threw himself into the cause, he gave himself to it completely, devoting the last eight years of his life to its advancement. His program was huge and ambitious. He labored to win from the governments of the world a charter for Jewish settlement in Palestine, refusing to be content with such "back-door" colonization as had gone on heretofore. He sought to enlist Jews of wealth and influence to the movement. He convened the First World Zionist Congress in 1897 which evolved the classic "Basle Platform," calling for the creation of a publicly recognized, legally secured home for the Jewish people in Palestine.

Much of his effort came to naught. Kings and cabinet ministers were impressed by his compelling earnestness, but no charters resulted. Jewish philanthropists dismissed him as unsound. When he summoned the First Zionist Congress to Munich, a city destined in twenty-five years to become the spawning ground of Nazism, its Jewish community protested for fear that its German patriotism be impugned. Aside from a few westernized Jewish intellectuals, he found following and encouragement only among the Ghetto masses of Eastern Europe. Burned out by unceasing struggle, broken by constant disappointment, he died at the age of forty-four.

Three things he bequeathed to his people: his personality, gracious, ardent, magnetic, dedicated, the personality of a prophetic leader; a full and rounded program with the Basle formula at its core; and a world-wide, democratically organized Zionist movement.

"The direction of Jewish affairs," he pointed out in summoning the First Zionist Congress, "must not be left to the will of individuals, no matter how well intentioned they may be. A forum must be created before which each one may be made to account for what he does or fails to do in Jewry."

In antithesis to Herzl stands his opponent, Asher Ginsberg, or, as he is commonly known from his pen-name, Ahad Ha-Am. The two men were worlds apart in spirit and background. Herzl, a citzen of the world, had little understanding, to begin with, of the Jewish tradition; Ahad Ha-Am was all his life a student of it, devoted and critical at the same time. One projected grandiose schemes of political action, the other argued in lucid and careful Hebrew prose the cultural necessity of Zionism. One came to the movement in reaction against anti-Semitism, the other in affirmation of Judaism.

Ahad Ha-Am looked to Zionism to preserve the Jewish heritage from extinction. In this, as he saw it, the essential Jewish problem consisted: that the Jews were everywhere a minority group and Judaism with increasing universality a second culture. But no culture can long endure, let alone be creative, under the domination of an alien universe of discourse. Therefore Judaism must find a home for itself where it might live freely, spontaneously, productively. Zionism, from this viewpoint, is concerned not with politics nor anti-Semitism nor settling all the Jews in Palestine. It requires only that a sufficiently large community be established there to sustain an autonomous Hebrew culture. As Ahad Ha-Am put it, "What we lack above all is a fixed spot to serve as a national spiritual center, a safe retreat, not for Jews, but for Judaism, for the spirit of our people."

Zionist philosophy today represents in the main a fusion of these two currents of thought. Organization, policy, financing, colonization, international recognition—all these stem from Herzl. But much of the ideology and most of the Hebraic renaissance, both in Palestine and elsewhere, are of the school of Ahad Ha-Am.

Born in 1897, Zionism developed slowly for its first twenty years, giving slight indications of its latent power. Then came the Balfour Declaration in 1917 and the establishment in 1922 of the League of Nations Mandate, wherein first

Great Britain and then the peoples of the world declared their sympathy with a Jewish National Home in Palestine. Thereafter the hidden power of the idea was released in a mighty upsurge of activity.

The. Jewish population of Palestine, seventy thousand at the end of the First World War, multiplied tenfold in one succeeding generation, and would have increased ever so much more had not Great Britain, in contravention of the Mandate, restricted immigration severely. As potential future immigrants, stand the quarter of a million Jewish DPs uprooted by World War II, who overwhelmingly have set their hearts on Palestine; the additional hundreds of thousands of Jews, not in internment camps and technically not displaced, but insecure or unhappy in post-Hitler Europe; a large part of the Jews of Moslem lands; and scattered Jewish individuals and groups in the Western world. All in all, a Jewish population in Palestine of two millions within another generation is not unlikely.

Jewish agricultural achievements in Palestine make a latter-day epic. The Zionist settlers have established hundreds of farm communities, converting the marshes of the Valley of Jezreel, the desert wastes of the Negev, the rocky hills of Galilee into fertility. Where necessity required, they leached the salt out of the ground, as near the Dead Sea, or pulverized rocks to create a soil. The intelligence and energy they have displayed, and even more their passionate devotion to the land have won for them praise from friend and foe alike. Among others, Walter Clay Lowdermilk has characterized the Jewish job of agricultural reclamation as the most remarkable anywhere in modern times.

Jews have built towns too, new cities in empty wastes,

modern suburbs about old cities sunk in filth and sloth. They have erected factories and established industries. Where once Palestine imported all its finished goods, it is now the most active center of manufacture in the Near East. All of which stood the Allied cause in good stead during the Second World War, when Jewish Palestine provided the British Army not only with thousands of men but with food and industrial supplies as well.

Side by side with this physical expansion has gone a renaissance of Hebrew culture. Palestine Jewry has been spiritually creative as no diaspora community in the last two thousand years. It has revived, rejuvenated, and modernized the moribund Hebrew language. It has evoked a vigorous new literature. An authentic folk music has come into being and with it the dance, the arts, and the handcrafts. A school system has been established, reaching from the nursery level to a climax in a great university. The long frozen folkways of Israel have been thawed into fluidity and renewed growth. In sum Zionism has made possible the rebirth of Jewish culture in one land and thereby its stimulation everywhere.

Intense idealism infused the Zionist movement from its inception. Nothing of what has been wrought achieved itself. Everything required courage, devotion, self-sacrifice. Young men and women by the hundreds abandoned universities, professional careers, comfortable existences in Europe or America for the hardships and dangers of pioneering in Palestine. Only by the generous expenditure on their part of sweat, blood, and life itself were desolate places, physical and spiritual, made fruitful. Nor was this extraordinary zeal limited to the earlier settlers who came of their own free will. The later immigrants also, to whom Palestine was a refuge from persecution, a deliverance from death, have quite understandably proved equally ardent concerning it. As a result, no community in the world discloses a deeper or more general spirit of group consecration.

Out of all this has come the new Jew, self-reliant and imperturbable, such a breed for courage and competence as Israel has not produced since the destruction of the Second Jewish Commonwealth; a generation of farmers tilling their own soil, mechanics working in factories they themselves have built; kinsfolk in temper to the American frontiersman with whose situation their own displays a remarkable affinity.

The mettle of these new Jews has been tried time and again, and not once been found wanting. They served in great numbers and with distinction in the British Army during the Second World War. They volunteered freely to be parachuted into Nazi-controlled territories to gather information for Allied intelligence and to rescue their fellow Jews from gas chambers and crematoria. Under the noses of the Gestapo they built an underground railway; under the noses of the British they kept it functioning when, the war over, Great Britain repudiated its pledges as to Jewish immigration. They stood up bravely to repeated Arab attacks. All this makes a tale of heroism destined to be oft told in generations yet to come, an episode of which not only Israel but all mankind may rightly be proud.

One other vision has motivated the Zionist movement from the beginning to the present: the determination on the part of its leaders and workers that the Jewish homeland should embody the best in Jewish and human idealism. Thus the Jewish National Fund, influenced both by Mosaic Law and Henry George, is committed to a policy of land purchase whereunder the soil remains the property of the entire Jewish people, never to be bartered or withheld from use, but to be leased out for self-labor only.

The same idealistic bend reveals itself in the Zionist attitude toward labor generally. Centuries of exclusion from agriculture and the handcrafts had forced Jews into trade and the professions. In the course of time they made a virtue of necessity. This abuse the early settlers in Palestine pledged themselves to correct, most conspicuously among them one Aaron David Gordon. Eager that the vices of the Ghetto be not imported into Palestine, where life was starting afresh, he insisted that Jews must do the work of the body as well as of the mind. Of physical labor Gordon made almost a religious cult, glorifying it not only as a prerequisite to the establishment of the homeland and a refutation of the libel of Jewish parasitism, but as a cure for sick souls and the only sound base for cultural renaissance.

Jewish Palestine, furthermore, is rich in economic democracy: cooperatives of all sorts, a highly developed labor organization, and, most significant of all, adventures in collective living, industries and farm communities in which all the instruments of production are the property of the group, each member contributing his labor and receiving in turn whatever he requires and the collective can afford. Experiments on this order are nothing new in history. But those now under way in Palestine have achieved such unprecedented success that they may well be establishing patterns in social living for the entire world.

Such have been the superb accomplishments of the Jews in Palestine. They are overshadowed by grave perils behind which stretches a long sequence of events.

As early as 1917, when the Balfour Declaration was issued, there was already opposition, both Arab and British, to the Zionist program and Britain's endorsement of it. Neither was total. The Emir Feisal, then the recognized spokesman of the Arab peoples, formally assented to Jewish aspirations in Palestine. And the British government at that time, though elements within it were bitterly opposed to Zionism, nevertheless, as its actions demonstrated, was preponderantly sympathetic. Each of the adverse forces has grown with time and circumstance, interplaying, corroborating, feeding on each other.

Arab opposition is not difficult to understand. It does *not* derive from any hurt, economic, social, or cultural, which the Jews have inflicted on the Arab community, the truth being that the Arabs have derived great benefits from Jewish enterprise. Arab numbers in Palestine have multiplied, Arab wealth has increased, the Arab standard of living elevated above that of any other neighboring countries. Similarly, there is no substance to the contention that Zionism has created a landless Arab peasantry. This charge, like the others, was once widely aired. One hears it no more. Too many impartial commissions have found it groundless.

The actual impulse behind Arab opposition is first and foremost a rising, inherently legitimate, Arab nationalism. Supporting this is a whole complex of other motivations: the objections of Arab aristocrats to the introduction into Palestine of democracy and its works; the inevitable disquiet on the part of any population over the entrance into its midst of masses of strangers, attended by alien ways of life; systematic agitation against Zionism conducted covertly by the British in varying degrees at all times, and openly by the Italians

and Nazis; British policy in Palestine which, whether consciously or unconsciously pursued, encouraged Arab intransigence; the support and agitation of the Arab league; finally,
the vacillations of the leading powers of the world, as exhibited in the reversal of position by the United States of America on the issue of Partition.

There were then, and have always been, some respect-
worthy elements to the Arab case. The Jewish side of the
dispute is warranted not because there is no other, but because
as between wrongs it works the lesser, and as between justices
it achieves the greater. Let the Arab argument prevail, and
a portion of the Palestinian Arabs will achieve a political
independence otherwise denied them. But that, while desirable and legitimate, is all that there is to the Arab plea.
Against that set the following: that the Arab world has vast
areas in which to realize itself politically, the Jews only Palestine; the problems of Jewish homelessness, insoluble otherwise; Judaism's need for a spiritual center for its rebirth,
perhaps even for its survival; the role of Jewish Palestine as
an outpost of democracy and modernity in the medievalism
of the Near East; the possibilities by way of spiritual creativity in Jews resident in their own land. Is it not apparent,
when the two arguments are contrasted, that not only is the
lesser injustice with Zionism but the greater promise of good
also?

Like Arab opposition, the British is a composite of many
ingredients. From the very beginning there were some Englishmen who, whether out of lack of affection for Jews, or
deficient understanding of their purposes, or simply out of
the conviction that Zionism was not to the best interest of the
Empire, arrayed themselves against the Balfour Declaration

and Mandate. Such persons unhappily were concentrated in the Colonial Office, which supervised the administration of Palestine, and among the officials assigned to do the on-the-spot governing of the country. Of these many cherished a different prospect for the Middle East, one to which a Jewish homeland would be an impediment: a League of Arab states, ostensibly independent, actually a screen for British control and a bulwark against Soviet expansionism. Concern for Arab oil, whether as a source of profit or a strategic necessity, made another factor. So too, among other things, did the disquiet of conservative British administrators of Palestine, recruited largely from backward colonies, over the political liberalism and economic radicalism of the Jews. Finally, prior to 1939, a conflict with Nazi Germany impended, an added spur toward British appeasement of the Arabs.

Out of all these considerations, Great Britain was seduced, first, into denying to the Jews the government aid in colonization which was their due, then into setting up obstacles in their way, next to the toleration and incitement of Arab violence, finally to a conscienceless shutting-off of Jewish immigration and land purchase, as proclaimed in the White Paper of 1939, and this in the hour of direst need for Europe's Jews.

Even so, when war came, the Jews of Palestine rallied to the Allied cause. Thirty-odd thousand of them enlisted in the British forces. Jewish Palestine, as we have already noted, made substantial contributions by way of resources, material, and repair services, to British armaments in the Eastern Mediterranean. This, the Jews knew, was their fight, no less theirs because of their disappointment with the British. Nor did they doubt that once Hitler had been defeated, once

Britain had ceased to be driven by fear and imperialist anxieties, it would abandon its policy in Palestine for something more equitable.

Then the war ended. A Labor government pledged to the abrogation of the White Paper came to office. The old betrayal went on as before, aggravated by new outrages. The former Mufti of Jerusalem, a criminal participant in the massacre of Jews both in Palestine and Europe, an arch enemy of democracy, was allowed to "escape" from "custody." Despite the intolerable lot of Jews in DP camps, Foreign Secretary Ernest Bevin refused to relax the iniquitous restrictions on immigration. Neither faith nor hope, it was now unmistakably clear, could be reposed in Britain.

Aliyah beth, "illegal" immigration, was one inevitable Jewish response. Measures for self-defense against the British and the Arabs was another. A third was that ugly phenomenon, born of despair and bitterness, repudiated by all responsible Zionist bodies: the terrorism of dissident groups.

Events spiraled downward. The Jews pressed underground immigration and self-defense. The British attempted coercion. Move and counter-move, violence and reprisal followed one another, winding up with the establishment of internment camps in Cyprus for Jewish "illegals."

Jewish opposition and the world's protest proving too much for the British, Foreign Secretary Ernest Bevin sought to inveigle American support for his course through the establishment of an Anglo-American investigatory commission, confident that such a commission, composed half of Britishers, could report only in favor of his policy. To his chagrin, the commission, after a careful study in Europe and Palestine, emerged with unanimous recommendations in favor of large-scale Jewish immigration into Palestine, the lifting of restrictions on land-purchase by the Jews, and international control of the country preparatory to the ultimate establishment of a bi-national state. At which Mr. Bevin, though he had promised to implement any unanimous recommendations of the commission, maneuvered the scrapping of its report.

The problem growing more troublesome from day to day, the British in the end were compelled to turn it over to the United Nations. In the spring of 1947, an extraordinary session of the General Assembly considered the issue; during the ensuing summer a U.N. Special Commission on Palestine studied it; on August 31, two reports were returned, one a minority pro-Arab verdict, the other a majority recommendation for the partition of Palestine into two independent states, Arab and Jewish, with economic union between them and an international trusteeship over the Jerusalem-Bethlehem area. On November 29, 1948, the General Assembly, after long and thorough debate, adopted the majority report by a vote in excess of the necessary two-thirds. At the same time it delegated implementation to a five-man Palestine commission and enforcement to the Security Council.

The Arabs had all along threatened violence. Had Britain or the United States or the Security Council made it clear in any fashion that they stood firmly by the decision and required good conduct from the Arabs, there would have been little trouble. But the British, to whom Partition was most unwelcome, busied themselves at once in undermining it. The American government, dominated by pro-Arab groups in the State and Defense departments, wavered and then abandoned it. And the Security Council, rendered impotent by American vacillation, failed to protest even verbally against Arab attacks on Jews, the invasion of Palestine by armies from the states of the Arab League, British support, open and surreptitious, of the Arab cause, and the United States embargo against the sale of American arms in the Middle East, which was, in effect, an embargo against the Jews only.

Deserted by the world, left to its own resources, Jewish Palestine never faltered. It fought off Arab attacks, which came in the main not from Palestinian Arabs, most of whom had no quarrel with the Jews, but from outside the country. Through Haganah, it consolidated militarily the Jewish position everywhere in the territory delimited as Jewish by the United Nations. It braced itself against future eventualities.

On May 14, 1948, the day on which Great Britain laid down its Mandate over Palestine, the Jewish Republic of Israel came into being and was promptly recognized by the United States of America.

At that time the situation was—as it will remain for many years—unclear and fraught with peril. Given enough Arab pressure, the continuance of United Nations' impotence and American evasiveness, given in consequence the ultimate military exhaustion of Jewish Palestine, and the final outcome may be the ghettoization, if not the destruction, of Jewish Palestine. Even the inception of a Third World War.

But other happier eventualities are not only conceivable but likely: the consolidation of the State of Israel, a solution of the problem of Jewish homelessness, the rebirth of Jewish culture, and the assurance that in that land at least, the place of their original creation, the Jewish people and the Jewish heritage shall survive.

But though the Jews in Palestine, Cyprus, Europe and the Middle East have much, perhaps everything, at stake on the outcome in Palestine, the American Jews are also deeply involved with it. In their case nothing less than the determination of their spiritual destiny may hang in the balance. For the impact of Zionism on them, already deep beyond all description, will be even greater in the future, to the good should events in Palestine be favorable, for evil should they prove adverse.

Let us consider some of the further-reaching influences of Zionism and Jewish Palestine on American Jewry. These, though overwhelmingly beneficial in the main, have not been universally so. No revolutionary improvement is ever effected without some undesirable consequences. Of such there would seem to be three of moment.

The first is an intensifying of resentment and intransigence in the more determined of Jewish assimilationists—a quite understandable reaction, since to Jews of this stripe Jewish Palestine appears, as it is in actuality, infinitely survivalistic in its effect, and their hearts are set on the end of Jewishness. What is more, it has enlarged to the dimensions of an entire nation the name, Jew, while they hope beyond all else that that word may be forgotten by the world so that it may in turn cease to be remembered of them. Little wonder then that in some die-hard anti-Zionists a bitterness has been engendered that will stop at little in its resistance to Zionism and tends to overflow that one issue into an exacerbated hostility to Jewish life in all its manifestations.

Again, in some Jews, the prospect of a Jewish State has stirred anxieties lest their own security be impaired thereby, lest, for example, they in America be held responsible for the

conduct of other Jews in Palestine, or lest, now that the
Jewish people has a homeland of its own, the anti-Semite
bid them be gone to it. Such forebodings are neither justified
nor dignified. No fair-minded person holds anyone account-
able for the acts of anyone else. The anti-Semite has never
in the past been deterred from trying to get rid of Jews by
the humanitarian consideration that they had no place to go.
To the contrary, it already appears that enhanced, rather
than lowered, Jewish prestige everywhere will be the final
upshot of the founding by Jews of an independent commonwealth of their own. In any case, remote, implausible calcu-
lations of this sort are altogether outweighed by very real
and immediate considerations, such as the plight of displaced
Jews and the requirements of the Jewish tradition. To suppress the latter out of concern for the former would be con-
siderably less than altruistic or heroic. Yet, unwarranted,
selfish, and cowardly as they may be, misgivings concerning
the Zionist program weigh on not a few American Jews,
constituting an inhibiting, even a paralyzing influence on
their Jewish expression.

Most important of all, the establishment of the State of Israel
has raised to fever pitch the issue of dual loyalties, the question
of the effect of Jewish Palestine on the American Jew and
the integrity of his American patriotism. Must it not be, it
is asked, that because of the free Israel, the Jew is torn in
sentiment and political allegiance between it and America?

This query has been raised more often out of fear or for
the polemical interests of anti-Zionism than because it is real
and poses a genuine dilemma. It is also put more often by
Jews than by non-Jews. Gentiles, since they are not personally implicated in the problem, since furthermore they are

free from Jewish insecurities and timidities, are quite generally capable of an objectivity and directness on Zionist matters beyond the capacity of Jews, especially frightened Jews. Wherefore, it does not occur to them to imagine that anything which happens anywhere abroad can possibly mar the political oneness of Americans with America. Besides, too many ties, cultural, religious, and sentimental, unite too many diverse groups in this country with the lands, traditions, and churches of the Old World for the Jews in their Zionism to be taken as anything other than one more instance of a common and acceptable phenomenon.

The question, however, has been posed. No matter then how artificial and unreal it may be, it requires an answer. Nor need that answer be improvised at this late date. Zionist theory has long been challenged on this score; its response is by now well worked through and authoritative. Almost from the very beginning, teachers of Zionism have insisted that Jews outside of Palestine would remain citizens of their respective lands and politically nothing else. The American Jew, accordingly, owes one and only one civic allegiance, to America. Were war to break out between the State of Israel and this country, he would be duty-bound to throw in his lot unswervingly with the United States, even though that meant bearing arms against his Jewish brethren. Which indeed would be no novelty, Jews having fought against one another in every war in modern times. On this truth there is, and can be, only one reservation: an issue of conscience, such a hesitation as arises when an individual believes all wars or some particular war to be morally wrong. But that issue of conscience has no special relevance to American Jews or to Jewish Palestine. It applies equally to all Americans and to any or all wars. In sum, the State of Israel leaves intact the integrity of the American Jew, just as the independence of Eire made no essential difference in the relation of Irish Americans to the United States.

But this is far from being the whole story. A free Jewish Palestine not only takes nothing from American Jews *qua* Americans, it enriches them as Jews and therefore as citizens. It offers them a solution to the headache and heartache of Jewish homelessness, otherwise irremediable—an impasse, furthermore, which must be broken promptly and thoroughly before it drains American Judaism of that margin of resource and joy which may make the difference between life and death. Next, Zionist effort and hope have supplied many American Jews with an activity which is useful and creative. Jewish loyalists have had their self-esteem raised by Jewish achievement in Palestine, by the courage with which Palestinian Jewry has met the perils in its way. Finally and most consequential of all, they have been culturally enriched and strengthened by the creativity of Jewish Palestine. They have been stimulated to the study of the reborn Hebrew tongue. They are now endowed with the literature created in that language and, in response to it, in other languages. The music and art of Palestine have penetrated into their lives, evoking aesthetic expression from them also. New folkways, expressive of Jewish religious, ethical, and cultural values, have bubbled out of the great fountain of Palestinian spirituality and now refresh the Jewish soul everywhere. The renaissance of Hebraism of one land has led to a corresponding renaissance throughout the world.

And more, transparently, is yet to come. It is this which justifies the risks of the Zionist enterprise. There are risks, and mighty ones, implicit in it. Should it fail, there will ensue not only the loss of all the promised gains, social, psychological, cultural, and religious, but also great, absolute and perhaps irremediable losses: the suffocating of world Jewry's most promising community, a blow to Jewish morale greater than all conjecture, a diminution of the Jewish prospect for creative living not only in Palestine but everywhere.

The risks are there, but they are "calculated." For the probabilities favor a successful outcome. And with that go all the high expectations we have just outlined for Jewry in Palestine, Europe, and the Middle East, for Judaism everywhere.

And one more hope also: that of Jewish Palestine as a bridge between the Occident and the Orient, between the old and the new, between the long experiences of the Jewish past, so heavy in tragic heroism, and the needs of mankind today. This is the dream that out of Zion rebuilt the Law will go forth, and the word of God from Jerusalem.

In ancient Greek mythology there is to be found the story of the giant Antaeus, who, every time he struck foot upon Mother Earth, was filled with tenfold strength. Israel seems to have some such half-mystical relation to Palestine. It struck once of old, and it created the Bible. It put its foot down again, and it released from itself Christianity and Mohammedanism. Simultaneously it created the reserve on which it has lived until the present. The foot of the giant has struck again. Already a new vigor can be discerned through the entire body. Nobody knows but that, when the foot is firmly planted for the third time, Judaism will be reborn once more to deliver a message of the spirit to all mankind.

CHAPTER XVI

PROGRAMS

So MUCH for the Jews. Now what of Judaism, their religion and the culture? What changes have been worked on it by the convulsions, external and internal, of most recent decades?

The disintegrative tendencies set in motion by the Emancipation have never ceased. Ignorance, indifference, escapism, the sense of inferiority continue to slay their thousands Jewishly. In consequence of their belated entrance into the modern, secularized world, irreligion among Jews is still disproportionately widespread. Observance, where it has not collapsed altogether, has not yet recovered from its dislocations. And the ideological vacuum, the void left by the evaporation of the ancestral rationale, has not been altogether filled to the present.

The old enemies within, in sum, remain at work, as corrosive as ever, more so in certain respects. For, like most life processes, de-Judaization gains momentum with time, being the less easily retrievable the longer it has endured. What is more, the Jewish sins of the fathers almost invariably are visited on the children. What his parents have not taught him, the son is quite likely not to know. What they have not observed, he will not so much as consider as ritually possible for himself.

To the cumulative depredations of time other adverse influences must be added: the great losses in recent years in Jewish numbers and leaders, the destruction of key Jewish communities; weariness and pessimism as to the Jewish prospect, plus all the other sequels to the two world wars and the Nazi interlude, as disheartening and debilitating to Jews as to others.

But if Judaism is undeniably worse off in certain regards, it is much better off in others. If indifference has grown apace in some Jews, interest in Judaism and a resolve as to its survival have been reborn or intensified in many more. And the period of blind groping seems to be nearing its end. The ideological problem is beginning to work itself out, if not in one universally accepted solution, then in a variety of answers, all aimed at and helping to effect the enhancement of Jewish life in the future.

This ideological problem consists ultimately in three rudimentary but far from simple questions: What is Judaism? What reason is there for its continuance? What needs to be done to insure that continuance in as meaningful a form as possible?

These issues are not new. They were evoked by the Emancipation, even by the first intimations that an Emancipation was at hand. Which means that they have been under Jewish consideration for nigh on to two centuries. Indeed, it would be no great exaggeration to say that, at least as to its more thoughtful and articulate elements, the entire Jewish community has been one vast debating society all through this period on just these themes. Now, at long last, out of the welter of controversy, various theories have emerged.

That these theories are theories should not lead us to take them lightly. In the first place, no theory is ever just a theory. Somewhere in every theory there is a program, and in the case of each of these theories of Judaism, an explicit program. Again, these theories are indispensable to Jewish survival. For, without them, the whole Jewish enterprise would be left in the intolerable position of being without a rationale. On this score again Israel is unique. Other peoples live without the need of justifying their existence. Only the Jews have to prove to themselves and others that they have the right to be. Not that such proofs, no matter how convincing, can of and by themselves cause Judaism to be. The point is that while ideologies cannot preserve Jewish life, it cannot be maintained without them. So it comes to pass that this business of theories ranks with anti-Semitism and Zionism as a controlling factor in determining the Jewish future.

The first attempt at a modern philosophy for Judaism, adequate .to the conditions imposed by the Emancipation, was Reform.* This began simply and modestly as an effort to adapt Jewish observances and doctrines to their new setting. As the Jew emerged from the Ghetto, he found much in his old ways that cried for correction. The ancient ritual had become encrusted with ceremonies which had lost their meaning. Conduct in the synagogue was informal to the point of indecorousness. Worship was unintelligible to many because of the exclusive use of Hebrew. In addition, there was much in the Jewish outlook which the Jew, once he became familiar with modern thought, could not accept. The nineteenth century was dominated by rationalism. In such an age, belief in Paradise and Hell, angels and demons,

---

* Reform theory and program underwent radical revision in 1937. Our discussion, therefore, in the next few pages treats of Reform as it once was universally, as it still is in some circles which have refused to follow the new ideology, but not as it is either preponderantly or officially any longer. Newer Reform will be presented subsequently.

a bodily resurrection and a personal Messiah seemed indefensible.

In 1801, when the Emancipation was still very new, the earliest corrective measures were launched. Israel Jacobsohn, financial agent to Jerome Bonaparte and head of the Jewish community in Westphalia, inaugurated reforms in the synagogue. He ordained order and decorum, abolished the chant with which the service was intoned, introduced prayers and sermons in German. From the church he borrowed hymns and the rite of Confirmation. In 1817, he started a similar movement in Berlin. A year later a Reform congregation was established in Hamburg.

Together with changes in observance went some modifications in the traditional faith. Thus, the statement of policy, issued on the establishment of the Hamburg Temple, included a formal renunciation of the belief in a Messiah. Once a beginning had been made all concepts and doctrines were reexamined and, if found wanting, abandoned or revised.

The conservative elements in German Jewry resisted as best they could; the times and prevailing temper were with the innovators. Rationalism was the spirit of the day. Slight patience was being shown to the unintelligible, whether in dogma or observance, whether in Judaism or Christianity. A newly awakened aesthetic sensitivity among Jews played its part too. The synagogue, when contrasted with the church, seemed bare, unadorned, unlovely; and now the first time in centuries its worshippers were in a position to draw comparisons. Other factors, less praiseworthy, were involved also: the sense of inferiority which plagued the newly emancipated Jew; his temptation to imitate the non-Jew in

all things; his desire to demonstrate that he too was capable
of the excellences displayed by the Christian. Ashamed of
his Judaism, he dreaded lest Christians visit the synagogue
and find it bizarre or mean. Therefore he retained in it only
such practices as an outsider was likely to understand and
approve. Much was discarded that was fine and poetic;
much that was trivial, borrowed.

But Reform could not long be confined to externalities.
It was compelled to face a complicated problem which
touched Judaism in its very essence. In the ghetto the Jew
had been a Jew purely and simply. He was a member of no
state, a participant in no society except his own. But now
that he had been declared a citizen of the land in which he
lived, he was bewildered as to his exact status. In what sense
was he a Jew, in what a citizen of his country?

This riddle he solved by redefining the nature of Jewish
identity. He observed that Germany had its Protestants and
Catholics, both equally German in nationality, culture and
social affiliation, differing from one another only in religion.
Whereupon he inferred that he too was a German in nationality, culture, and social affiliation, and that his Judaism, like
the Christian's Christianity, was entirely a matter of creed
and church.

This formula, which reduced Judaism to a denomination,
was seized on by the early reformers, partly because it was
simple and superficially convincing, but also because it was
something they wanted to believe. It enabled them to draw
gratifying analogies between Judaism and Christianity. By
reducing the extent and watering down the content of their
Jewishness it made it less conspicuous in their eyes and, they
hoped, in the sight of the Gentiles. At the same time it re-

duced sharply the budget of Jewish differences and obliga-
tions. All in all, it allowed them to identify themselves with
every aspect of the larger world except religion, and so to
take full advantage of the Emancipation.

Whatever their motives, their position, once formulated,
remained the official philosophy of Reform until very recent
years. In the Old World, where the tradition was deeply
rooted, the ideology made but limited progress. But in the
United States, a new land where the future loomed larger
than the past, where Jews were immigrants and, by that fact
alone, already somewhat removed from the ways of their
fathers, Reform, during the latter nineteenth century, won a
sweeping victory. In 1885, its American leaders declared, in
an official pronouncement: "We consider ourselves no longer
a nation but a religious community. . . . We recognize in
Judaism a progressive religion."

Having arrived at their definition of Judaism as a sect, the
theorizers of Reform were then compelled to go further. For
they were immediately confronted with the question: Why
Judaism rather than some other religion? The difficulties of
Jewish existence were so manifest that loyalty required justification. Besides, other denominations were quite similar to
Judaism in theology and morality. Was it not then the part
of wisdom as well as expediency for the Jew to give up his
separatism and join some communion akin to his own?
Reform, however, insisted on the preservation of the Jewish
group and faith, advancing by way of justification the doctrine of the "mission of Israel."

"We look upon the destruction of the second Jewish Commonwealth," said a group of American Reform leaders in
1869, "as a result of the divine purpose revealed to Abraham

which, as has become ever clearer in the course of the world's history, consists in the dispersion of the Jews to all parts of the earth, for the realization of their high priestly mission, to lead the nations to the true knowledge and worship of God."

This is the theory at which Reform arrived and on which it took its stand until 1937. It was not a tenable theory. In the first place, by its definition of Judaism as a religious sect, it falsified history. Judaism, to be sure, had always included a religion among its elements, as the chief among them, but it has never been what the Reformers sought to make it out, a religion only.

Again, if Judaism were what Reform theory said—a body of beliefs concerning God, the soul and morality, housed in a people and their synagogue—then no agnostic or atheist could possibly be a Jew. As soon as a Jew lost his faith, his Jewish identity ought to come to an end. And yet countless Jews who are not religious in any fashion consider themselves Jews, are claimed by the Jewish group and identified by the world as Jews. It is then a flat contradiction of experience to equate Jewishness with the acceptance of a theology. Finally, Judaism has never possessed an official creed, a circumstance which put Reform in the embarrassing position of declaring Judaism to be a religious faith but of being unable to state what that faith might consist in.

The major inadequacy of Reform, however, was not its lack of logical consistency. Many a system has been shot through with contradictions and, despite them, served useful purposes. It was the practical consequences of Reform, in its original version, which disqualified it as a program for Jewish survival.

For, once the nineteenth century metaphysicians of Jewish

life arrived at their ideology, they proceeded to make
Judaism conform to it, eliminating all its aspects which did
not fit into the Procrustean bed. If, they insisted, Judaism be
a church, then rites, customs, laws, and ceremonies possessed
only the secondary value of serving as symbols for doctrinal
affirmations. Every ritual practice which did not contribute
to this end was adjudged pointless. By the logic of this position, a large part of Jewish observance came to be discarded.
By 1844 in Germany, by 1895 in America, the authority of
the Talmud had been officially renounced. By the same line
of argument, the Hebrew language was remanded to the
background. For, once Judaism was conceived entirely in
creedal terms, any tongue could convey its message. Palestine too and the hope of a Jewish restoration obviously had
no place in such a system. The Jew could affirm his religious
attitudes in any free land. Nay, more, the doctrine of the
mission demanded that the Jews, being a college of preachers,
remain forever dispersed. And of the historic Jewish culture
all was jettisoned that was not found to be clearly theological
in import.

So Judaism was made into a pallid religiosity, a Unitarian-
ism slightly tinged with Hebraism; divested of the tradition;
stripped of most of its rich poetry of observance; denuded of
the Hebrew language, of which it retained only a few phrases
by way of sentimental tribute to the past; deprived of the
dream of a homeland in Palestine.

This negativism in early Reform must not be permitted to
obscure the positive, creative role which it fulfilled. It had
the courage to undertake the adaptation of the historic to
modern life, so blazing a trail for other contemporary ideologies and programs. It may well have saved Judaism in the

West. For, had there been no such movement, countless Jews, in rebellion against the tradition, would have been irretrievably lost.

Original Reform then, for all its deficiencies, made a substantial contribution to Jewish survival. Nevertheless, it was so inadequate on both logical and programmatic grounds, that a recasting of its ideology, whether sooner or later, was inevitable. Agitation to this end began early in the present century, mainly among younger adherents of Reform and, of these, especially on the part of those touched by Zionist thought. No more at first than lone voices, the advocates of revision gained in number and strength until, in 1937, they achieved the reformulation of the classic principles of Reform as enunciated some fifty years before.

Under the new ideology, Judaism, defined no longer in purely theological terms, is characterized as the "historical religious experience of the Jewish people," a formula which, by the adjective "historical" and the reference to the Jewish people, indicates that Jewishness is more than religion alone. The change in definition, furthermore, is freighted with implications for action, many of which are now being drawn. There has been a return, not total but still appreciable, to traditional ceremonies, to the Hebrew language, and a rapprochement with Zionism so general that well over two-thirds of the Reform rabbinate, once the focal center of anti-Zionism, are now thoroughly committed to the building of a Jewish homeland in Palestine. Reform having been itself reformed drastically, its future influence in American Jewish life waits to be determined.

The second of the latter-day ideologies expresses Jewish traditionalism in shocked reaction to the first. From the very beginning of Reform, many Jews objected to its tampering with the Jewish heritage, which they held to be of divine origin. Nor could they see any other outcome from making adaptations of Judaism to its environment than ultimate assimilation. Better, both ideally and practically, to refuse all traffic with compromise. With this conclusion, the Orthodox Jew came into being.

The orthodoxy of the Orthodox Jew is not the undeliberate conformity of his medieval forefathers. It is conscious and effortful. It takes its stand on one large, immovable first premise: that Judaism is a revelation of God. It contends further that if it is to survive, it dare not depart from that premise. No other course is right for the Jew or can conceivably be successful except that, like his ancestors, he shall confess the inspiration of the Torah, the election of Israel, reward in the next world for the individual and the vindication in this world for his people. Once this act, this leap of faith has been made, traditional doctrine and observance are justified throughout; the process of attrition and compromise is nipped in the bud; the Jewish scheme of life is preserved in its pristine integrity.

To thousands of modern Jews this is the sole acceptable solution for the internal Jewish problem. Their position is simple. At a definite moment in history, they maintain, God revealed His will to Israel. This revelation is contained in Scripture and the tradition. Since Judaism is the manifestation of an Omniscient God, it is not only sacred throughout but immutable also. For, what human argument can disprove what He declared, and what event warrant a breach in His ordinance?

From one point of view, Orthodoxy is the most comfortable of all Jewish philosophies. Given its fundamental assumption, all issues are resolved. But from another angle, there is no attitude in Jewish life which demands greater sacrifice. Personal convenience, economic interest, social advantage must all be subordinated to the way of the Law. Nor can there be any adjusting of it to circumstance. As it has always been, so it must remain ever.

But the gravest apprehension concerning Orthodoxy, even for those who are capable of its central act of faith, concerns its long-range staying power. Can a theory persevere which clashes, or seems to clash, with the findings of science and the modern temper? Can a regimen endure, no matter with what devotion it is cherished, which will not change with a changing world? Must not such a program be limited to a small group whose numbers will inevitably diminish as individuals fall away because of collisions, whether in thought or practice, between life and the tradition? The Orthodox Jew maintains stoutly that neither evil need come to pass. Whether he is correct only time can demonstrate.

Somewhere between these two ideologies lies a third, the Conservative, representing a reaction against the parties of the Left and Right alike. To this movement have rallied those religious Jews who, on the one hand, can no longer remain Orthodox nor, on the other, identify themselves with Reform. Dissenters against both extremes, they have banded together under the banner of "historic Judaism," that is, a Judaism which is historic in that it is richly traditional, but historic also in that it changes with time. Unfortunately, the adherents of this position have never achieved an official formulation of it nor any substantial clarification of either its premises or conclusions. They have been content, for the most part, with a purely pragmatic •approach of striking a "happy medium" between the old and the new. About such a technique there is a kind of commonsensicality which has enabled it to function to the present with some measure of success. But whether this state of affairs can long continue is profoundly questionable. For want of an ideology, minds are left uninstructed, hands undirected, the adaptation of the tradition to modernity unrealized and the diverse elements in the movement, since there is no agreement on what unites them, in constant peril of falling apart. Predictions are always hazardous. But it appears safe to assert that either Conservatism will acquire a philosophy or suffer the fate of all causes which are more explicit in their negations than affirmations.

Most recently still another, highly promising theory for Jewish life has been framed, true to the Jewish past and yet equal to the exigencies of the present. Professor Mordecai M. Kaplan has evolved a philosophy and program for Judaism which are closely reasoned, realistic, comprehensive, and creative.

Reconstructionism, as this system is called, stands on two postulates. The first is that even were assimilation readily possible, which it is not, Judaism possesses sufficient inherent value to justify its preservation. For all that much of the tradition is obsolete and untenable, its essential worth remains unimpaired. What is required is not wholesale rejection but re-evaluation and re-interpretation, that is to say, discriminating selection, adaptation, and innovation.

The second assumption concerns the necessity of thinking the Jewish problem through afresh, from the very beginning. The first requisite for a constructive philosophy is a clear definition of terms. This, Conservatism has been too timid to venture officially. Orthodoxy has its rationale, but one which can be maintained only by a heroic, anti-rationalistic act of faith. The ideology of original Reform is impossible by reason of its inconsistencies in theory and failures in practice. As for Reform in its revised version, that did not come into being until some years after Dr. Kaplan had published the outlines of his system. It has been more influenced by, than it influenced, him.

From these two premises, the Reconstructionist philosophy proceeds to examine Judaism objectively. How, it asks, shall one define it? The only terms adequate to describe it are *civilization* or *culture*. Judaism then comes to be understood as the evolving or dynamic culture or civilization of the Jewish people. Like any other culture or civilization, it is an organic complex of literature, language, cosmic outlook, folkways, group hopes, ethical values, and aesthetic judgments. Like any other culture or civilization, it is forever growing and regenerating itself. In this living whole, religion is the prime motif and the most ideal expression, but by no means the entirety.

This definition differs sharply from those of Orthodoxy and Reform. The former insists that Judaism is throughout a divine revelation and hence fixed and immutable. This new viewpoint maintains that, like all human institutions, the Jewish civilization ever evolves, ever remakes itself, that having always been subject to change, it must continue to adapt itself to its environment. Against Reform, on the other side, Reconstructionism contends that the attempt to reduce Judaism to religion entails the substitution of one of its aspects for the whole. It means the discarding of those many elements, from peoplehood to folk-art, which are not inherently religious in significance.

Nor should the distinctions drawn by Reconstructionism be taken, even for a moment, for mere logic chopping. As Plato demonstrated centuries ago, definitions are matters of vital concern, since from them flow streams of consequences, intellectual and pragmatic. Because Orthodoxy defines Judaism as a divine revelation it is compelled to insist on its unchangeability. Because the early Reformer denominated it a religion, he was driven to divest it of some of its most essential components.

The author of this new definition did not stop with nomenclature. From it he drew huge practical implications. If Judaism be a civilization, Dr. Kaplan argued, the Hebrew language and literature possess more than a half-sentimental, half-archeological value. They are as much part of its very essence as English and Shakespeare of the Anglo-Saxon tradition. If Judaism be a culture, then customs, ceremonies, and folkways are no longer irrelevant. Every society expresses itself in forms mirroring its spirit. Those of the Jewish group may require correction, modification, supplementing. They cannot be dispensed with if the organism is to be healthy. And, if Judaism be a civilization, it needs some one place where it can be at home, incarnated in a society of its own. This philosophy then follows Ahad Ha-Am in discerning in the Palestinian homeland both a necessity and an opportunity, a necessity by way of spiritual self-preservation, an opportunity in the direction of self-fulfilment.

To the old fear of divided loyalties which plagued the founders of Reform, Reconstructionism makes simple answer. It points out that each Jew is, in fact, the heir to two cultures:

that of his land and that of his ancestry. It insists that he must go on being just that. His only political allegiance will be to the country of his citizenship; his only religious affiliation will be with the faith of his father. But culturally he will inherit and be rooted on both sides. Nor will he be a jot the less patriotic or valuable to his political community because of his second endowment. To the contrary, he can, if he is alert, make himself the medium of an intellectual leavening. To the soul of his country he can bring the fructifying stimulation of another system of living.

In the light of this reasoning, assimilation, worse than impossible, is sinful. It means the jettisoning of a patrimony which has its contribution to make to the richness in spirit of the individual Jew, who will, if he follows the assimilationist way, be poorer than he need be. It entails the abandonment of a people in the hour of its need. Judaism and Jews today are locked in a last-ditch struggle for survival. Both are the weaker for each desertion. Last of all, implicit in de-Judaization is vandalism against the best interests of mankind. The world will be impoverished if the Jewish tradition vanishes, for, in that event, there will have been eliminated from the spectrum of the human spirit a unique and irreplaceable color which has lent so much, and has so much more to lend, to the beauty of the whole.

Such are the leading current ideologies of Judaism. There are others also, nonreligious and secular in temper and intent, being the theories and programs of such Jews as love Jewishness and are devoted to its preservation, but are either incapable of theological affirmation or disinclined to set it up as essential to Jewish group life. These philosophies, culturalism in both its Yiddishist and Hebraist versions, and nationalism, Zionist and Diaspora, will not now detain us. In America at least they are off-the-beaten-path movements. A description of them is available elsewhere.*

What then emerges from our description of the impact of contemporary events on the inner reaches of Judaism? This much: that if the Jewish people and its heritage have sustained grievous losses, they have also, in certain respects, most conspicuously in theory and program, made substantial gains. The disruptive influences continue at work, but constructive forces struggle against them, and with ever mounting capability and adequacy.

Thanks to the heightening of Jewish loyalties and interests, effected by anti-Semitism, thanks to the stimulation of Jewish Palestine, thanks to the emergence of acceptable theories and prospectuses for Jewish living, hopeful signs for the future can be discerned.

More American Jews today are more inquisitive about their group heritage and more concerned with its advancement than at any time since American Jewry came into being. The educational lag is being overtaken. Jewish pedagogy has ceased to be a matter of old-world teachers imparting unsystematic and irrelevant instruction to children to whom they are aliens. It has become instead the lifework of a corps of highly trained, dedicated modern men and women administering curricula especially devised for Americans, children, and, of late, increasing numbers of adults also.

An upsurge of Jewish expression is in process. A generation ago the most earnest Jew was liable to discouragement

* See Chapters X and XI in the author's *A Partisan Guide To The Jewish Problem.*

because of the meagerness of contemporary cultural materials. More recently, however, books and periodicals of Jewish relevance, in English, Hebrew, and Yiddish, old texts in
translations and new ones, have multiplied mightily. In the
arts, the Jewish spirit is beginning to find itself. And Western Jewries everywhere are now the beneficiaries of the
extraordinary spiritual fertility of the Jewish homeland. The
day is past when a Jew had to go unnurtured as a Jew for
want of aesthetic and intellectual provender. Many reasons
may remain for un-Jewishness; the cultural poverty of modern Judaism is rapidly ceasing to be one.

Religious belief too gives evidence of revival. The special
disabilities visited by history on the synagogue have largely
disappeared. Jews have got over the shock of their first
collision with modernity; they have as individuals and in
groups made their various adjustments to it, and for very
many Jews the return to the Jewish identity has induced a
return to Jewish faith also.

Developments in the realm of observance parallel those in
the domain of doctrine. Against the downward spiral of disintegration, forces of reintegration are asserting themselves.
The long retreat is coming to a halt, a counter-offensive on
behalf of ancestral practices is opening. Among the Orthodox, this has taken the form of a vigorous drive in favor of
the total tradition. Conservative and Reform Jews, who stand
not on the full traditional regimen but on adaptations of it,
are pressing the cause of modified observance with considerable ardor, seeking to recapture valuable traditional forms,
abandoned or unnecessarily compromised during the past
century, and to create new ritual patterns which shall round
out and complete the old. Most surprising of all are the

intimations of a change of heart concerning ceremonials on the part of many Jewish secularists. Nonreligionist as ever, they have come to discern in the usages of the group an opportunity for the assertion of the Jewish identity, disciplines whereby the loyalties of the heart may be reinforced by the actions of the hand, an aesthetic experience, an additional avenue for the transmission of values.

Lest too optimistic a construction be put on all this, let it be said at once that American Jewry remains very far from being generally observant of ancestral practices, no matter in what guise. And it is not impossible, too, that the flood which has swept multitudes from their moorings has gone too far to be reversed. But if so, it will not be for want of effort on the part of many ardent, thoughtful individuals and groups.

Finally, the American-Jewish community has with each day become better equipped for survival. Thanks to its favored position among Jewries, it has been able to bring to itself scholars of distinction and libraries from older lands. It has established a system of institutions of the widest variety, all dedicated to the propagation of some aspect or other of Judaism. Its physical apparatus for spiritual existence is, if not complete, well advanced. This too is no slight gain. If it does not by itself guarantee victory, it helps mightily toward it.

All in all, it can rightfully be asserted of the Jews in America and of their spiritual heritage, as they face the future, what an ancient prophet said long ago concerning Jewry in his time, not the most confident of predictions perhaps but not the most disheartening either:

"There is hope for thy latter end."

Chapter XVII

EPILOGUE

This book violates the Aristotelian canons of dramatic unity. It has a beginning and a middle, but no end. It closes not with any confident prediction as to the future but with a weighing of possibilities. It winds up with a question mark instead of ·a period.

Nor is any other conclusion possible.

In the first place, many factors are involved in the determination of what will yet happen to the Jews and Judaism. Some of these are external to the Jewish group and but little subject to control by it: issues such as the ultimate success or failure of attempts at world organization; the advance or retreat of the democratic spirit and process; gains or losses in economic stability; the waxing or waning of anti-Semitism; the expansion or contraction, the consolidation or destruction of the Jewish homeland in Palestine. Others, again, are internal to the Jewish group: the nature and character of its leadership; the adequacy of its educational procedures; the development of religious and cultural interests and institutions; and many more on this order. All the commanding influences are intricate, precariously balanced, unforseeable. Given so numerous and such complex forces at work, given a Jewish scene which is

> a darkling plain
> Swept with confused alarms of struggle and flight,
> Where ignorant armies clash by night

given such a present, who dare venture predictions?

But there is an even deeper reason why we must renounce prophecy and content ourselves with appraisals of fact and expressions of hope. That lies in the nature of one determinant of the Jewish future, the last and most decisive of all: the Jewish will to live. If this exists, and with sufficient vigor, almost no obstacles are insurmountable; if it fails, every problem becomes insoluble.

Now will in man is not an absolute; it is far from being altogether self-determining. Circumstances affect it. It can be worn away and strengthened, discouraged and fired, roused to life, brought down to passivity. In all of these, the judgment of the intellect, the verdict of experience play large roles. In the end, however, there would seem to be something self-generating about the will, a core of energy independent of externalities, an intentness which will sometimes, against all logic, cause it to assert itself in the teeth of adverse conditions, or contrariwise to capitulate, when all is favorable.

That is why the evolving of tenable theories and stimulating programs for Jewish life, why every creative, meaning-giving, happiness-lending encounter with Judaism and the Jewish group is so crucially important. For by each experience will is affected, and by all of them affected profoundly.

Yet ultimately, when everything has been done to bolster the will from the outside, there remains an irreducible core of the spontaneous. Therefore human behavior is never completely predictable, and of the Jews no assurances can be given, no matter how much is foretold of their circumstance in time to come, how they will respond to it.

The ultimate determination of the Jewish future rests with

the Jewish heart. It is the individual Jew who will decide
the final outcome, who, by what he elects, is deciding it every
moment. If he chooses life for his group and tradition, it will
live in despite of all disabilities; if death, it will perish in
despite of all advantages.

And how can I, an author, say now concerning you, my
Jewish reader, what verdict you are pronouncing, let alone
will utter in time to come?

It is all as in the haunting tale by Feierburg, wherein a
mother is described as spinning out to her child this parable:

"One morning the rabbi said to his pupil, 'My son, thou
hast been destined to be a great teacher in Israel. I can no
more be thine instructor. Here is a letter, go with it to
Amsterdam. There thou wilt study in the great Yeshivah.
Only remember well thy martyred father, remember me, and
remember the God of Israel, the One God. Know well, my
son, that Satan lies in wait to ensnare thy soul. Much have I
and your father fought against him on thy behalf. Now God
has commanded that thou leave me to stand temptation
alone. Here is my amulet. My staff, too, I give thee. And
it shall come to pass wherever thou liest down to sleep, thou
shalt describe a circle about thyself with my staff, and not
leave it till dawn. This amulet, too, thou shalt hold in thine
hand until thou awakest. Behold, I have warned thee. Be
strong and of good courage.'

"And the rabbi fell on the lad's neck and wept, and the
boy wept also. . . . And the lad took his pack on his shoulder and went forth. . . . The way was long. He must
traverse cities and towns, forests and rivers, to come to the
great Yeshivah in Amsterdam. It was his duty to go, wherefore he went. . . . Then his path passed through a deep

forest. On both sides towered tall trees. And the road stretched endlessly before him. The forest was deep, infinitely deep. The sun sank in the west, and the boy's feet grew weary. He paused to recite the afternoon prayers. Darkness covered the earth. He recited his evening prayers. . . . He drew the circle about himself; he took the amulet in his hand, placed his pack as a pillow—and fell asleep. His eyelids had scarcely closed when a sound startled him. He opened his eyes and beheld a pack of wolves moving through the forest toward him. The eyes of the wolves gleamed like fire, their mouths and large sharp fangs filled him with dread. The pack came nearer and nearer. It came to the very edge of the circle. The wolves sought to enter the circle, but could not. They pushed against it violently. They leaped and raved in anger. They could not enter. The pack turned and fled. And lo, a wild boar came toward him. It, too, came to the circle and stopped short, unable to go further and enter. . . . The boar disappeared.

"And then from the woods was heard music of surpassing beauty. The melody was wafted on the wings of the gentle breeze which stirred softly through the trees. . . . The lad's soul yearned for the musicians. . . . He wished to leave the circle. He hesitated, his heart melted from the intensity of his desire. His hands trembled so that the amulet slipped from them and fell to the ground. Almost by compulsion, he left the circle. The wind carried him off, far off toward the musicians. He crossed seas and rivers, fields and forests, cities and villages. And the musicians played before him— just a few paces before him, but he was unable to overtake them.

"Suddenly, he saw the town of his birth and the palace of

its Magic Prince. He stood before its open door. Then a mighty hand pulled him violently backward. A great struggle began. One power drew him into the palace, to the Magic Prince, and another pulled him back.

" 'I am thy father—thou art my son. Dost thou not recognize me?' called unto him a vision like unto the vision of his martyred, long dead father, which he had seen in dreams. 'I am thy father, and thou art my son. Thou art a Jew. Do not enter. . . . Go not after the music. The melody belongs to an alien god. My son, go to Amsterdam and study Torah. Harken not to the melody. Here is my amulet which thou didst lose in the forest. . . . Return, my son, return. . . ."

It requires no profound insight to see in this fable a metaphor for all of Jewish life. In the dim dawn of history, Israel set forth on a pilgrimage to the Great Academy. So long as it remained within the circle of its own existence and clung to its mystic amulet, neither the wolves of hate nor the boar of malice could touch it. But the Jew heard the music of the Magic Prince which is the world. He dropped his amulet and left his circle. He stands now on the threshold of the palace of Gentile society. Like the boy in the story, he hesitates. A martyred past calls him back to his pilgrimage, the riches and magnificence of the larger, freer world draw him on to enter. In only one detail does Feierburg's story call for correction. The door to the world which, in his day, stood wide open, is now shut. Even the Jew who wishes to enter, beats against it in vain.

In the Hebrew tale of Feierburg, the child to whom the fable is told, turns to his mother and asks: "Mother, what's the end of the story?" To which the mother replies: "The story is still a long one. Tomorrow I shall tell you the rest."

And so it must be. For the child who asks the question and the lad who wavers at the threshold are, in essence, one and the same. How then can the mother answer for him, when in the end he, and only he, can make answer for himself?

When, therefore, the Jewish reader asks for predictions as to the Jewish future, I can only return his inquiry to him, bidding him respond for himself. And if he press me and insist on knowing what form his own response will take, I can answer merely:

"I am no prophet, neither am I a prophet's son."